Contents

Accessing the Web Resource

A web resource is included with your purchase of a new print or e-book edition of *Studying Dance*. The *Studying Dance* web resource offers glossary terms and review questions from the book in Word format, dynamic extended learning activities not found in the book, and a list of links to websites you might find useful or interesting for further learning. All you need to do is register with the Human Kinetics website to access the online content.

Follow these steps to access the web resource:

1. Visit www.HumanKinetics.com/ StudyingDance.

2. Click the first edition link next to the corresponding first edition book cover.

3. Click the Sign In link on the left or top of the page. If you do not have an account with Human Kinetics, you will be prompted to create one.

4. After you register, if the online product does not appear in the Ancillary Items box on the left of the page, click the Enter Pass Code option in that box. Enter the following pass code exactly as it is printed here, including capitalization and all hyphens: **SCHUPP-AR798-WR**

5. Click the Submit button to unlock your online product.

6. After you have entered your pass code the first time, you will never have to enter it again to access this online product. Once unlocked, a link to your product will permanently appear in the menu on the left. All you need to do to access your online content on subsequent visits is sign in to **www.HumanKinetics.com/ StudyingDance** and follow the link!

Click the **Need Help?** *button on the book's website if you need assistance along the way.*

···PART one···

Your Dance Education Journey

Preface

Dance is a multifaceted art form. It has a rich history that exists across cultures and serves various purposes. Dance exists beyond the stage and studio, and it is always advancing. Just as dance is always changing, your approach to learning dance is also evolving. This book addresses new ways for you to investigate and understand dance. Many students new to dance on campus might initially prefer to "just dance," but the more you embrace the academic pursuit of dance, the more likely you are to succeed.

Dance is present in many parts of society. For some, dance is a recreational activity or social opportunity to meet new people. Others think of dance as a sport in which dancers compete for top awards. Still others participate in dance to get in shape or to express themselves. Few people comprehend the value of studying all aspects of dance. If you fully explore the historical, physical, artistic, intellectual, cultural, and educational components of the art of dance, it becomes a tremendous vehicle for understanding yourself and the world around you.

When I began studying dance in college, I was surprised by how different learning dance on campus was from learning dance at my local dance studio. At my studio, I trained with the same group of people for about 10 years, and I was considered to be one of the top dancers. I was familiar with my teachers' expectations, the dance styles, how classes were structured, and how dances were made and performed. In college, I was introduced to new ideas about dance, new teaching methods, and new courses. I suddenly realized that dance was no longer a recreational activity—it was my career. To succeed in college and beyond, I needed to find new ways to study and define dance. Like my college self, many students are confused by the types of dance and teaching methods present on campus. They are also struck by the differences of studying dance recreationally and academically. This book will help you expand your thinking about dance, which will lead you to success on campus and beyond.

This book is for young adults who are beginning to pursue dance academically. Most of you have dance backgrounds, ranging from intense technical training to informal dance experiences that have prepared you well to dive more deeply into dance. Your previous experiences formed the foundation of your dance education, and you are now ready to build on that knowledge. Studying dance on campus is not a new journey; it is a continuation of the journey you began when you started to dance. The joy and enthusiasm that you feel for dance can serve as motivation to learn more about the technical, creative, historical, and theoretical aspects of dance. Reading this book will help you develop an awareness of the expectations of studying dance as an academic discipline as well as strategies for academic success. This book will also present to you a survey of the larger field of dance.

The title of this book is *Studying Dance: A Guide for Campus and Beyond*. *Campus* refers to the time you will spend formally studying dance; *and Beyond* refers to the application of your studies, to your continued growth in dance, and to your cultivating a lifetime in dance. This book will help orient you to dance as an academic discipline, broaden your understanding of dance, establish solid approaches to studying dance, and connect dance on campus to your previous training and future dance interests. You will see the value dance can have to you and society through engaging with dance as an academic discipline.

Many books about dance do one or more of these things: discuss various creative approaches to making dance, provide details about the anatomy and physiology of movement, analyze various philosophical trends in dance, and discuss the historical or cultural impact of a specific dance genre. These types of books are invaluable for learning about specific areas of dance. However, this book is about you and your continued success in studying dance on campus and beyond. It demystifies dance on campus, empowering you to be proactive in your dance education. *Studying Dance: A Guide for Campus and Beyond* teaches you the breadth of dance as a discipline; the expectations of studying dance on campus; and the ways that your past training, current education, and future goals are intertwined.

Part I helps connect your past dance journey to your current pursuits and academic campus. Chapter 1 asks you to reflect on your dance training and how it relates to other interests, your community, and your current definition of dance. Chapter 2 teaches you how your specific dance program relates to general trends among campus dance programs. Chapter 3 covers how to approach dance as an academic discipline; the types of courses you will encounter; the importance of staying open minded, yet focused; and the need for academic and creative rigor. Chapter 4 addresses strategies for student success. It includes suggestions for effective learning and time management, critically engaging with material, the differences between learning in high school and learning in college, and creating a balanced life. The chapters in part I help you to assess your current understanding of dance so that you have a solid foundation to build on while studying dance on campus.

Part II introduces the various areas of dance and dance careers that exist. Chapter 5 introduces dance and artistry. It provides an overview of specific dance genres, examines various roles in dance and artistry, and addresses the many artistic purposes of dance. The links between dance and culture are examined in chapter 6. You will learn who gets to dance, where and when dance happens, and how dance reflects cultural values. Chapter 7 discusses the educational components of dance, where dance learning takes place, and what can be gained alongside physical coordination by learning dance. New, nontraditional practices and areas, such as dance and media, and dance and social justice, are covered in chapter 8. Chapter 9 provides an opportunity to think about dance as a reflective practice and as a means to engage with the world.

Part III moves from the larger dance world back to dance on campus, and it outlines general curricular themes and expectations. Technique and movement course expectations are covered in chapter 10, which introduces the types of technique and movement courses you may take, the approaches used in these courses, and the role of feedback. Chapter 11 discusses creative, compositional, and performance course expectations. The purposes and approaches of these courses are explained, and the importance of the creative process, making work, and performing work is explored. Chapter 12 details expectations in contextual courses such as dance history, kinesiology,

rhythmic awareness, and others, demonstrating how these classes are an important part of a complete dance education. Finally, the importance of personalizing your campus dance education, including individualized instructional opportunities, peer collaborations, and gaining practical skills, are outlined in chapter 13.

Part IV helps you visualize and plan your dance life beyond campus. Chapter 14 gives information about meeting the demands of a career in dance and how to start preparing for life after graduation. It discusses nutrition, cross-training, budgeting, and other life-balancing skills that are essential to your success in dance. Chapter 15 prompts you to consider how your previous dance experiences relate to your current dance studies and future goals, and to imagine the range of possibilities for yourself in dance so that you can create clear goals for studying dance on campus and succeeding as a young professional.

Each chapter includes a digestible amount of information and requires you to reflect on your dance learning, opinions about dance, and definitions of dance. Reflective prompts, opportunities to learn more about your dance interests, and review questions are included in each chapter. Additionally, a web resource is included with this book. There you will find learning activities, glossary lists, and web links. These tools personalize your journey through the book. Although you may read this book with a class or group of friends, you have many opportunities to relate this book back to your interests and experiences.

After reading this book you will be prepared to engage with dance on campus and beyond. The academic pursuit of dance does not mean that the physical expertise you bring to campus is not valued; rather, such expertise is deepened and built on in ways that allow you to experience dance in new and exciting ways.

Introduction to Your Dance Studies

LEARNING OUTCOMES

After reading this chapter, you will be able to do the following:

- Identify your current dance interests.
- Compare the various ways that dance is part of your life.
- Interpret various dance influences.
- Evaluate why you have selected to study dance on campus.
- Begin to formulate your dance aspirations.

Dance is an exciting way to engage with the world. As a dancer, you are eager to share your art form with the rest of the world through multiple ways such as performing, choreographing, teaching, interacting with your community, and writing about dance. The students in the photograph are performing a site-specific improvisation. Through this improvisation, students are interacting with their campus community, thinking about dance in unexpected ways, and challenging themselves as dancers. They are using their current understanding of dance to navigate the performance space, make new movement discoveries, and make creative choices while dancing.

Chapter 1 helps you assess your current understanding of dance. As you prepare to start the collegiate portion of your **dance education**—the learning experiences that educate you physically, intellectually, and artistically about dance as an art form—you must recognize where you are in your dance training, what you value about dance, and your future interests. In this chapter, you will begin to consider your dance influences, the ways that dance is part of your life and community, and why you have opted to pursue an academic study of dance. After completing this chapter, you will have a clear understanding of your current dance knowledge and be prepared to successfully build on that foundation.

Becoming a college dance student is similar to performing a site-specific improvisation. Just as the students in the photograph are doing something familiar in an unfamiliar place in new and exciting ways, your experience of studying dance on campus requires you to build on your dance knowledge in a new setting through innovative means. You will still be dancing, but you will face new challenges. It is important that you view your time studying dance on campus as an opportunity to expand your current **dance understanding,** which refers to a dancer's personal knowledge and practice of dance as an art form. It can include taking dance classes, teaching dance, performing, choreographing, or writing about dance as well as the knowledge gained through these activities. Your study of dance on campus is an opportunity to expand your current dance understanding.

ASSESSING YOUR CURRENT DANCE UNDERSTANDING

Before you start the collegiate portion of your dance education, it is helpful to assess your current interests and passions in dance. Where you dance, your reasons for dancing, and your personal dance style and preferences all contribute to your present dance understanding. Evaluating your current dance understanding helps establish a clear foundation that you can build on, not only in your first year of college but throughout your entire time on campus. Additionally, outlining your dance interests helps you to see how your interests, understanding, and awareness change over time as you learn more about dance.

Dance Locations

As the photograph at the start of this chapter illustrates, dance can take place anywhere. If you look around, you will notice that dance and movement occur everywhere. From the student on the bus bopping her head in time with the music on her MP3 player, to people dancing at parties or clubs, to concert dance performances, to ritualistic dances, people are moving and dancing everywhere. It is easy to think that dancing is appropriate only in certain settings, but we all come to dance in different ways. Some students start dancing in a formal setting, such as a local dance studio or conservatory. High school dance programs offer a gateway to dance for many students. Still others learn to dance in community centers or informally from their families and peers.

Reasons for Dancing

You have probably decided to study dance on campus because you love to dance, and you cannot imagine pursuing anything else. But, what specifically excites you about dance? Some people are drawn to dance because it values the intelligence of the moving body. Others dance because they can express ideas and emotions that cannot be stated in words. Frequently people dance because they like to perform and share their ideas through movement. Dance can be a way to engage with the world around you, to connect to different cultures or communities, and to learn about yourself. Many dance professionals are drawn to dance because they feel there is always more to learn about dance and through dance—and that challenge is exciting.

Your Dance Style

Many dancers have one or two dance genres that best suit them. **Dance genre** refers to a specific type of dance with its own history and ways of moving. Your time studying dance on campus allows you to intensely study your preferred dance genres and to learn new ones. For some dancers, the lineage of classical or contemporary ballet is vastly appealing. The ongoing experimentation in contemporary modern

• • • Dance can be a way to engage with the world around you, to connect to different cultures and communities, and to learn about yourself.

dance excites many dancers to keep trying new things. Musical theater dance genres, such as tap and jazz, are valued by many because of their use in entertainment and commercial venues. Urban dance forms, such as breaking, popping, locking, house, and waacking, provide an opportunity for dancers to connect with a larger community while also highlighting their individuality. Other dancers study diverse dance genres from around the globe as a means to learn about different cultures. Identifying the dance genres you currently practice can create pathways to studying new dance genres and new ways of moving.

Your Dance Performance Preferences

Dancers are usually drawn to certain movement qualities in different dance genres. For example, many modern dancers enjoy the sensation of connecting to gravity while moving, while dancers drawn to popping savor the isolated nature of each movement in a popping phrase, and other dancers are excited by the polyrhythmic nature of West African dance genres. All people have their own personal ways of walking,

standing, and moving, but dancers are much more aware of what makes their movement unique. Identifying your unique movement tendencies and preferences can assist you in learning new dance genres and movement forms and in deciding which dance genres you might study on campus. A ballet dancer who can clearly identify and embody lines in a ballet class can use that awareness to find shapes while studying yoga. A tap dancer's rhythmic awareness can assist in learning the complex rhythms of Flamenco or Bollywood dance.

As a student new to studying dance on campus, it is beneficial to outline your own movement tendencies and preferences so that you can identify skills you have as a dancer that might be helpful when studying new dance genres. Discovering your current ways of moving can also provide information about how to expand your current dance understanding. For example, students who prefer moving with a high level of energy would benefit from studying subtle movement forms so that their dynamic range increases. Dancers drawn to moving in a sustained and lyrical way could increase their musicality by studying dance genres that are percussive. Dance genres that take place primarily at a lower level in the space and require a lot of momentum would positively challenge dancers who are drawn to focusing on shape and lines in higher levels of space. Your time studying dance on campus is a tremendous opportunity to strengthen your individual movement preferences while also developing a more comprehensive embodiment of dance movement.

Your Choreographic Inspirations

Just as dancers have their favorite dance genres and preferred ways of moving, most dancers have specific ways of making dances. Some choreographers find their inspiration in music. Others get ideas for dances through reading about various topics and looking for connections to movement. Many dances have stemmed from the desire to tell a personal story, and many dances have developed simply from the desire to dance. After choreographers gather their ideas and inspirations, they work to create and compose movement into a dance. Some choreographers pre-plan everything on paper, others experiment in the studio with improvisation, and some create questions for their dancers to answer through movement. The dance movement used in the piece can range from something unique to the choreographer to codified movements from a given dance genre.

The approaches to choreography are vast. Recognizing your current approach to making dances helps identify strategies you use to find ideas, gather movement, and shape your ideas. It is important to recognize where your ideas for dance making come from, your performance inspirations, and how you make dances. Identifying these strategies will allow you to feel more comfortable expanding your choreographic skill set while studying dance on campus.

Your dance education up to this point led you to pursue dance on campus. Your previous dance education has given you many beneficial skills to build on, so it is important to identify the skills and knowledge that you already possess as a dance student. Doing so helps you link your previous dance understanding with your current academic pursuit of dance. It helps reaffirm your individual passions in dance so that you can clarify your unique dance interests while also gaining a larger awareness of dance.

STUDYING DANCE ON CAMPUS

Studying dance on campus not only grants numerous opportunities to become a better dancer; it lets you learn more about yourself, others, and the world around you. As your dance education continues in an academic setting, you will gain a more complete and holistic comprehension of dance. Your knowledge of dance will expand beyond your personal physical practice to include creative and contextual understandings of dance. Additionally, through applying new information, you will learn many important life skills such as leadership, creative problem solving, self-responsibility, and the ability to relate to others, to name a few. Essentially, through studying dance on campus, you can intensely study something that you are passionate about in a way that provides a broad awareness of dance as an art form, while also learning about yourself and the world around you.

Engaging WITH Dance

Alyssa Gersony (Arizona State University)

As a first-year dance student, I was an 18-year-old who chose to move over 2,000 miles across the country to study dance in a university. In high school I danced no less than 15 hours per week in private dance studios around Philadelphia, Pennsylvania. I was also performing contemporary, jazz, tap, and modern dance forms in multiple regional- and national-level dance competitions every year. As a dance major, I expected to take as many technique classes as I did in high school and to continue to be the best dancer I could be.

Much to my disappointment, this was not the case. I was in technique class 3 days a week with dancers who had greater flexibility, strength, and artistic ability than I did—and who I immediately compared myself to during class. I was conflicted; I wanted to take more ballet classes, and I thought my only option was to transfer to a school where

I could. A professor noticed my anxiety and asked, "Alyssa, do you want to become a professional ballet dancer?" I agreed that my final goal was not to be in a ballet company, and decided to continue my studies by broadly engaging with dance at a university.

I see myself as fortunate to have waited before transferring. I recognized later into my first year that I could become the dancer I wanted to be by asking myself what that actually was. In answering myself, I found out that in order to improve my technique and develop my creativity, maintaining a curious and open mind was the most important factor. For the following 3 years, I continued to make an effort to meet other dancers in the community, get to know other kinds of artists, and put time into the relationships I cared about. I learned how to focus on myself in a healthy way, which led me to exploring alternative movement forms and making dance in new ways.

Photo by Elizabeth Bates.

Types of Dance Classes

While studying dance on campus, you will learn more about the intelligence of the moving body through your movement and technique classes as well as courses in dance science and somatic practices. **Movement and technique courses** are those courses that address movement concepts of dance through physical exploration. **Creative, compositional, and performance courses** address the creative components of dance making such as the creative process, improvisation, composition, and performance. In these classes, you will explore how movement can be shaped to express your ideas. Your skills as a performer will be developed through rehearsals and performances as well as viewing works created by your peers, faculty, and professional dance companies. **Contextual courses** that focus on the educational, scientific, philosophical, historical, and cultural aspects of dance will broaden your knowledge of dance. Assessing your previous dance experiences can provide insight into these areas and how they can be developed during your time on campus.

Expanding Definitions of Dance

Your definitions of dance will expand while studying dance on campus. In order for this expansion to occur, you will frequently be asked to think about dance in new ways, to approach movement from a different perspective, and to academically engage with dance through reading, writing, and talking about dance. This can be intimidating to some students, because they might think that their previous dance understanding is being disrespected. Remember, your previous dance experiences are valuable, but it is through constantly challenging yourself as a mover, thinker, and dancemaker that you grow. It is helpful to think of your time on campus, especially your first year, as an opportunity for your current dance understanding to evolve. This evolution can lead to increased opportunities on campus and beyond that reflect what you personally value in dance, but it requires a wide understanding of the art form. Think of your time studying dance on campus as a bridge between your previous dance experiences and your dance future.

FUTURE APPLICATIONS

Your journey of studying dance on campus will eventually lead to a career in dance, in the arts, or in another creative field. As you start your journey on campus, it is helpful to identify and contextualize your current dance interests and goals. Identifying your interests helps you stay motivated to learn more about dance. Naming your goals can help you see how your past dance experiences relate to your future so

Engaging WITH Dance

Andrew Sanger (Wayne State University)

Dance is a field dominated by passion and talent. When I began my audition for class placement at Wayne State University, doubt clouded my thoughts. My original choice of major had been biochemistry, and I planned to go to medical school eventually; but I had forsaken both of these to delve into my true passion, movement. I had passion enough to soar to New York City, but I doubted that I had talent enough to succeed. That audition was the first time I had ever laid my hands on a ballet barre. I was eventually placed into both a level one ballet technique course and a level one modern technique course. However, I also

Kate Phinney of just kate photography

auditioned for Company One at WSU. Against all my presumptions, I made it into the company, and my experiences with them have helped shape my future and my dreams. I discovered throughout that semester that even though I was very behind in technique, I was dedicated. Being a member of Company One helped me be more involved with my department. It provided multiple performance opportunities, most of which were for children whose smiling faces and clapping hands spoke volumes to me. I had decided to follow my dream, and through trial and tribulation, my passion and my dedication would see me through to the end.

that you can determine how to best link your past to your future through engaging with an academic study of dance. Lastly, by reassessing your future goals throughout your time on campus, you can begin to see how your dance understanding continuously expands.

Expansive Dance Careers

Most young dancers aspire to become performers, teachers, or choreographers. As the field of dance continues to change, dancers are likely to work in all three of these areas as well as others. More than ever, many dancers engage in **community dance,** where movement works are communally created and facilitate the expression of a diverse group of people or specific community. In **dance therapy,** professionals use dance movement to help clients overcome psychological difficulties. **Arts administration** (the business or management end of an arts organization) is an emerging field, and many dancers find it satisfying to work with a variety of dance companies or arts organizations. Others find writing about dance, whether it be an educational textbook, a scholarly research article, or a biography of a famous choreographer, to be a rewarding way to share dance with the world. Dancers who have a knack for visual and technical design frequently enjoy designing **production elements,** the nonmovement elements that contribute to a dance performance, such as lighting and set design for dance works. They also enjoy working as graphic artists either independently or for other choreographers. In today's dance world, most professionals have one or two areas of expertise but are able to contribute to the field of dance in many ways. The ability to think about dance from diverse perspectives is part of being a successful

a dancer, but it is also needed in order to advance the field of dance. An academic study of dance helps you create a wide understanding of dance.

Expansive Life Skills

An academic study of dance can lead to careers outside of dance too. Through engaging in an academic study of dance, you learn additional non–dance-specific skills that can transfer to many other disciplines. You learn leadership through choreographing dances for your peers. Through working on group projects and providing peer feedback in your classes, your collaboration and community-building skills are strengthened. All of your classes will challenge you to develop creative problem-solving skills through activities such as making dances, embodying different performance intents, learning to teach, and giving creative presentations about dance. Critical-thinking skills will be developed as you complete written assignments for your classes, and you will become more self-aware and confident as you grow as a dancer. An academic study of dance not only gives you the skills needed in order to succeed in dance, it gives you the skills you need to succeed in all areas of your life.

CONNECTING YOUR PAST, PRESENT, AND FUTURE DANCE EXPERIENCES

As you identify your current dance goals, it is helpful to relate them to your past experiences. Doing so helps

Photo courtesy of JMU.

• • • Community dance works are communally created and facilitate the expression of a specific community.

you establish your time studying dance on campus as a bridge between your current dance understanding and your dance aspirations. For example, if you want to become a performer but you have only performed in choreographed group dances for the stage, you might look for or create opportunities to perform improvisations, solos, or site-specific dances. If you are interested in teaching, you might consider the places where dance education happens (e.g., private studios, community centers, public schools, colleges) and research the teaching methods used in each of these settings. It is important that you personalize your academic study of dance so that it aligns with your values and provides a larger understanding of what is possible in dance.

Studying dance on campus is your opportunity to learn to dance, to learn about dance, and to learn about yourself through dance. An academic pursuit is exciting, because you are learning about dance technique, theory, history, science, and pedagogy all at the same time. Your experience studying dance on campus truly is a comprehensive one. Your time on campus is an opportunity to expand your current understanding of dance. It is a chance to build on the physical expertise you bring to dance so that you can grow intellectually and creatively into a well-versed dance artist.

SUMMARY

You are about to embark on an exciting educational journey that will challenge you creatively, intellectually, and physically. Studying dance in an academic setting is incredibly rewarding and will provide you with a well-rounded understanding of dance. While studying dance on campus, you will continuously build on your previous and current dance understanding to navigate new problems, gain new information, and grow as an artist. It is important that you recognize the skills you bring to your academic pursuit of dance; these are the skills that led you to study dance on campus. You are now ready to build on the passions and interests that you have discovered through previous dance experiences. Your dance goals, values, and definitions will be challenged and will expand while studying dance on campus. Although you should have your own specific areas of interest, it is essential to gain a wide comprehension of dance during your time on campus. Doing so allows you to see how all areas of dance are interrelated and better prepares you for a successful future in dance.

REVIEW QUESTIONS

1. What are the differences between studying dance on campus and your previous dance training?
2. What are some of the skills you will gain through academically studying dance? How do these skills relate to your previous dance experiences and future dance goals?
3. What types of classes can you expect to enroll in while studying dance on campus? How do these classes provide a broader understanding of dance?

GLOSSARY

arts administration—The business or management end of an arts organization. Arts administration includes both for-profit and not-for-profit arts organizations. An arts administrator's duties can include managing staff, marketing, budget making, fund-raising, public relations, and developing and evaluating arts programs.

community dance—A movement work that is communally created and facilitates the expression of a diverse group of people or specific community. Community dance projects are usually led by an individual or group of individuals, but the finished project reflects the creative contributions of all participants. Additionally, community dance projects usually take place outside of traditional dance performance venues and involve performers who do not identify themselves as dancers.

contextual courses—Courses that focus on historical, philosophical, pedagogical, cultural, or scientific aspects of dance. Some examples include dance history, dance kinesiology, dance teaching methods, and dance ethnography.

creative, compositional, and performance courses—These courses address the creative components of dance making such as the creative process, improvisation, and composition.

dance education—Learning experiences that educate students physically, intellectually, and artistically about dance as an art form; a holistic approach to learning about dance.

dance genre—A specific type of dance with its own unique history, aesthetics, and ways of moving.

dance therapy—A field in dance that uses dance movement in a psychotherapeutic way to help patients integrate emotionally, behaviorally, cognitively, and physically.

dance understanding—A dancer's personal practice of dance as an art form. It can include taking dance classes, teaching dance, performing, choreographing, or writing about dance and the knowledge gained through those activities.

movement and technique courses—Courses that address movement concepts of dance through physical exploration. Movement courses can address specific dance techniques or general movement concepts.

production elements—Nonmovement elements that contribute to a dance performance. Production elements can include, but are not limited to, the lighting design, set design and construction, costumes, props, music editing, and media used in a dance performance.

BIBLIOGRAPHY

Byrnes, W. (2009). *Management and the arts*. Oxford, UK: Elsevier.

Kuppers, P. (2007). *Community performance: An introduction*. New York: Routledge.

2

Getting to Know Your Campus

LEARNING OUTCOMES

After reading this chapter, you will be able to do the following:

- Differentiate between types of campuses.
- Describe and distinguish between various types of dance degree programs.
- Identify campus and department resources.
- Design strategies to become more connected to your degree program and campus community.

From classes to research to community engagement, college, university, and school campuses provide tremendous resources for people to learn more about their specific passions. Although academic institutions and dance programs vary from campus to campus, an academic study of dance always promotes learning, discovery, and innovation. Studying dance on campus affords you numerous opportunities to expand your dance understanding. The dance studio in the photograph is a place where students who are enthusiastic about dance come to develop their dance knowledge in new ways. It is where your dance understanding will grow as you learn more about the art form, discover more about yourself, and find inventive approaches to dance.

Chapter 2 helps you relate your personal dance goals to your current **dance degree program,** which refers to your required dance curriculum. The chapter describes various academic settings and types of dance degree programs. Your campus and department websites are introduced as ways to learn about the culture of your dance degree program. After completing this chapter, you will have a greater awareness of how your dance interests can expand on your campus.

The empty studio in the photograph represents the resources and structures that studying dance on campus provides. It is a place that is ready to be filled with students who are curious about dance, interested in expanding their comprehension of dance, and ready to be challenged in new ways. While studying dance on campus, it is essential that you take advantage of campus resources so that you gain the fullest dance education possible. When you understand the goals and atmosphere of your campus, you can proactively broaden your dance understanding in many new directions.

TYPES OF CAMPUSES

Your academic pursuit of dance will be similar to other students' experiences studying dance on other campuses. You will take classes, make and perform dances, engage with dance in new ways, and interact with your larger campus community. The goals and atmosphere of your campus will partially depend on its size and location as well as its academic purpose. Knowing the academic purpose of your campus can help you determine the best approach to personalizing your dance education.

- **Liberal arts colleges** primarily enroll undergraduate students and focus on areas in the liberal arts, which includes the arts, humanities, social sciences, and physical sciences. They can be either public or private institutions, and they usually offer four-year degree programs. Typically, students have an area of specialization, such as dance, but they are encouraged to pursue a broad range of interests during their time on campus. In general, the enrollment at these schools is smaller than in universities, which can create a sense of camaraderie on campus. Studying dance at a liberal arts college gives you the chance to learn about dance deeply while broadening your education in a tight-knit campus community.

- In contrast to liberal arts colleges, **universities** enroll graduate and undergraduate students, offer several types of degrees, and usually include several smaller colleges, such as fine arts, liberal arts, engineering, and business. Universities are concerned about teaching, but they are also involved in cutting-edge research in the arts, sciences, and various other fields. University campuses tend to be larger in scope and population than liberal arts colleges, which can make them feel like small cities at times. Studying dance at a university allows you to pursue an undergraduate degree in dance while interacting with students seeking graduate degrees and potentially participating in creative and scholarly dance research projects.

- **Two-year colleges** prepare students to continue their education at another institution or to immediately enter a vocational field. In addition to recent high school graduates, two-year colleges also enroll working adults, returning college students, retirees, others who are interested in continuing their education one or two courses at a time, and those who want to pursue lifelong learning. Community colleges are the most common type of two-year school, although two-year vocational colleges and private colleges do exist. Studying dance at a two-year college gives you a strong foundation to build on at a four-year school while working with a variety of people from your local community.

Each of these types of campuses creates an opportunity for a comprehensive dance education. To varying degrees, each campus is set up so that you can study dance intensely while interacting with your larger campus community. In a liberal arts setting,

• • • Your campus is set up so that you can study dance intensely while interacting with your larger campus community.

you may find that you want to connect dance with another area in the liberal arts to create your own area of specialization. If at a university, you might seek circumstances to perform with graduate student choreographers or become involved in research connecting movement and the sciences, other disciplines, or arts. On all campuses, you should be aware of the resources and structures that your degree program and institution offer so that you can be proactive in broadening your dance understanding.

TYPES OF DEGREES

All undergraduate dance degree programs encourage you to find a balance in gaining breadth and depth in your dance education. Dance degree programs range from intensely focusing on performance, choreography, or education to framing dance in a larger study of the liberal arts. The connection between different areas of dance as well as how dance connects to the larger world is emphasized in all dance degree programs. Depending on your type of degree program, one approach to studying dance may be stressed more than the other. Recognizing the expectations and goals of your current degree program can help you understand how your personal interests in dance will develop in your academic study of dance.

• In **liberal arts degree** programs, students focus on broadly learning about the liberal arts with a specialization in dance. Dance coursework makes up about one-third to one-half of students' degree requirements. Liberal arts programs typically offer **generalist degrees,** which are college degrees that allow for a wide range of coursework. Depending on the degree program, students can earn a bachelor of arts (BA) or bachelor of science (BS) in dance, dance education, dance professions, dance administration, or other areas. It is not uncommon for BA and BS students to pursue two degrees while on campus or to select a complementary minor such as theater, health and wellness, or nutrition. Students in BA and BS programs are often naturally curious about how dance connects to other interests such as math, psychology, or anthropology. The structure of BA and BS programs gives students room to explore and develop these connections. Earning a BA or BS in dance gives students a wide comprehension of dance in a liberal arts framework. It provides the skills for a lifelong engagement with dance.

• **Bachelor of fine arts** (BFA) degree programs focus more specifically on dance and less on general studies. Although students in BFA programs are still required to enroll in general education courses, dance coursework comprises about two-thirds of students' degree requirements. Dance coursework is geared toward developing the knowledge and skills required to succeed as a dance artist. Some programs offer a BFA in dance, while others allow for specific concentrations in dance, such as a BFA in choreography or a BFA in dance performance. Pursuing a BFA degree leads to an intense investigation of dance.

• **Associate degrees** are commonly offered at community colleges and relate to degrees offered at four-year schools. An associate of arts (AA) or associate of science (AS) in dance is similar to a BA or BS in dance in that they are both generalist degrees and provide a liberal arts education with dance

as a specialization. However, there are some differences between the two degrees. An AS degree in dance aims to prepare students to start their careers after graduation, whereas an AA degree in dance is directed toward students who would like to move on to a BA degree or another four-year dance degree program. Similar to BFA degree programs, associate of fine arts (AFA) degree programs consist of an in-depth study of dance. An AFA degree in dance provides intense training so that students can continue on to pursue a BFA in dance or begin a professional career performing dance upon graduation. If you plan to continue your dance education through a four-year degree program, you should research how various four-year dance degree programs align with your AA, AS, or AFA program, both in terms of course requirements

© Karen Schupp

• • • All undergraduate dance degree programs encourage you to find a balance in gaining breadth and depth in your dance education.

and the curricular focus. Doing so will allow you to make a smooth and successful transition into a BA, BS, or BFA program.

- **Dance minor degree programs** provide a way for students who are curious about dance but passionate about other areas to academically engage in dance as a secondary focus while on campus. Dance minor degree programs vary greatly from campus to campus. Usually, dance minors are required to complete about 15 to 24 credit hours in dance to complete their dance minor requirements. Coursework can range from studio classes to lecture courses in a variety of dance styles. Pursuing a dance minor is a great way to learn more about dance while intensely engaging in another area of study.

Each type of degree program has unique strengths that you can use to deepen and expand your dance understanding. Becoming aware of the expectations of your specific dance program and campus can help lay a foundation for a successful academic study of dance.

RESOURCES AT YOUR FINGERTIPS

Once you have oriented yourself to the type of campus and degree program you are enrolled in, it is time to get even more specific. All campuses and dance degree programs have their own websites that provide insight into their atmosphere and goals. Familiarizing yourself with these websites can provide not only pathways to meeting new people and creating new opportunities in dance but also ideas about how to connect dance to various personal interests.

Campus Websites

It is likely that you have already visited your campus website to find information about applying to your degree program, arranging a campus visit, or assessing tuition and related costs. Now that you are an enrolled student, you should revisit your campus website on a regular basis. It provides the latest campus headlines, information on upcoming events (such as athletics, performances, and cultural events), as well as information for alumni and faculty. In other words, it is your connection to your campus community. Additionally, your campus website can link you to a variety of resources, includ-

ing your campus writing center and library as well as a variety of student organizations. Most campus websites include a video or photo gallery that gives a clear picture of campus life, as well as articles about student projects taking place across campus. The goals and values of your campus are shown on your campus website. Familiarize yourself with your campus website so that you can be informed and prepared to succeed during your time studying dance on campus.

Department Websites

Your department website is similar to your campus website. It includes information about your dance program, upcoming performances and events, the latest department news, as well as resources for students and faculty. As a student new to studying dance on campus, visiting your department's website is a fantastic way for you to learn about your program and interact with fellow students and faculty.

Most department websites will have an "About" page, where you learn about the philosophy and history of your department as well as areas of emphasis and find information about various degree programs. Some may have a message from the department chair, interviews with current or former students, or answers to frequently asked questions, all of which are great ways to learn about your program's values and expectations.

Department websites also have a page titled "Faculty." This page can be a tremendous resource to new students. Often students know only the faculty members they see daily, and they only know them as teachers. Your faculty members are tremendous resources for you, so it is essential that you get to know them. Collectively, they have a variety of backgrounds, research interests, performance histories, and choreographic approaches that can play an important role in shaping your dance education. You may find that your specific interest in dance relates to a faculty member's work outside of class or off campus. Knowing the areas of expertise of your professors can assist you in creating opportunities to learn more about your personal interests.

Additional webpages available on your department's website might include information about students, events, alumni, or facilities, all of which contain specific and useful information to you as a student. Acquainting yourself with your department's website—and frequently checking it—is a great way to stay up-to-date about your campus dance community.

GET INVOLVED

Of course, the best way to learn about your campus and your department is to interact with your campus community. Students who are more proactive in meeting with their faculty, getting to know upper division students, and joining campus organizations have a better awareness of the expectations of their departments and campus. Additionally, getting involved in your department and campus communities is a way for you to create opportunities in your dance education.

Know Your Faculty

You will work closely with your faculty members in each dance class you take. They will design dance phrases, assign readings, create choreographic prompts, and provide a variety of learning experiences for you and your classmates. While faculty members enjoy working with students in the classroom, most are also available to meet with students outside of class time, willing to formally and informally mentor student projects, and ready to offer scholastic and career advice. It might seem intimidating to approach your faculty members about an individual meeting, but proactively connecting with your faculty can be a valuable step toward shaping your dance education and widening your dance practice.

Most faculty members are required to hold office hours. **Office hours** are a time set aside for indi-

vidual meetings between a faculty member and a student. Few students take advantage of office hours, but taking the initiative to meet with your faculty members during their office hours helps you to get to know them (and they get to know you better, too!). Visiting your professors during office hours with questions about class material or to follow up on something discussed in class that piqued your interest demonstrates that you are curious about dance and your coursework. Meeting in person with your faculty members outside of class is a great way to learn firsthand information about your dance program.

Many dance faculty members have won awards for their work; are active as performers, choreographers, or researchers; and have occasional presentations of their work on and off campus. You may find that one of your instructors has choreographed a dance for a regional dance company, or that a professor of yours is having a book reading and signing at a local bookstore. Attending these types of events lets you learn more about your faculty members while also learning more about particular areas of dance that are new to you. Also, these events may give you new ideas about what you can pursue in your dance education.

Know Your Fellow Students

As a new student on campus, you will initially be surrounded by other new students in your dance and general education courses. You will spend a lot of

Engaging WITH Dance

Tess Listick (Moorpark College)

I started to get involved with Moorpark College's dance program by taking a couple of basic dance classes. I wanted to start off simple to get a sense of what dancing in a college environment was like. I assumed that it would be different from taking dance classes at a dance studio, which I had spent my last 14 years doing. I instantly fell in love with everything about the classes. They were structured to teach you more about the style of dance and the history behind it, and the teachers encouraged students to get involved with the classes by participating and asking questions. One of the most important things I learned throughout my experience was to build a great relationship with my teachers. They have so much insight and provided me with lots of helpful tips and suggestions. Because of my relationship with my teachers, I have gained so much knowledge about dance. If it weren't for them, I would not have had the confidence to choreograph and be the dancer I am today.

Photo courtesy of Tess Listick.

Engaging WITH Dance

Gracie Corapi (American University)

During "Welcome Week" of my first semester, I attended placement auditions for the American University dance department. I was probably overly eager to be back in a dance studio, but jumping head-first into the dance program was the best decision I made during my freshman year. I was placed into a higher-level modern class, where I met and became friends with junior and senior dance minors. They became my mentors as well. They encouraged me to do everything I could in the program. As a result, I felt more like a dance major than just a minor. I was part of two department shows, two club shows, the department repertory company, and most important, a tight-knit group of dance minors who whole-heartedly opened their arms to me. I think leaving fears and intimidation behind and diving into the dance program made my freshman year truly incredible.

© Gracie Corapi

time together, and friendships will quickly develop. While sharing experiences with other new students helps develop community, it is important to meet upper division undergraduate students.

Some campuses have formal and informal buddy systems in which upper division students mentor new students. The term **upper division** refers to coursework typically taken in the third and fourth years of college, so these third- and fourth-year students can help you navigate the academic study of dance from a student's perspective. Even if your campus does not have a buddy system, it is advantageous to connect with at least one upper division student. Upper division students will likely have plenty of tips to offer, ranging from information about how to best approach your instructors with questions to the best place to get pizza after a dance performance, so it is a smart idea to seek out their advice. Connecting with upper division students can help you feel more secure in studying dance on campus.

You can also think of meeting upper division students as a networking opportunity. If your campus does not have a formal mentoring program, look for opportunities to initiate casual conversations with upper division students at various campus events. Frequently, upper division students are more established as part-time teachers in local dance studios, choreographers and performers in department productions, and leaders in the campus community. Meeting upper division students can assist you in finding and creating enriching out-of-class experiences that enhance your dance education.

Know Your Campus Community

You will develop a close-knit community in your dance program. At the same time, it is essential that you connect to your larger campus community. All campuses have a variety of student-run organizations that allow for like-minded students to connect. Campus clubs and organizations range from academic clubs, to cultural, ethnic, and religious organizations, to associations that promote social awareness, to honor and professional societies. Chances are that if you have a specific interest, your campus has a club related to it. Getting to know students outside of dance can help create new connections in your campus community.

Additionally, meeting students from outside of dance can help generate interest about dance on your campus. As nondance students hear you talk about the value of dance, what you learn through dance, and the innovative approaches you are learning about as a dance major, they may be more inclined to attend an upcoming dance performance or even enroll in a dance class. You might find that your nondance friends have skills or interests that dovetail nicely with a particular dance focus of yours. Getting to know students outside of dance helps you learn more about different areas of study, social and cultural activities, or volunteer opportunities on

Engaging WITH Dance

Rachel Keane (The College at Brockport)

For me, the best way to get involved was to simply keep my eyes open and ask as many questions as possible. By paying attention to signs in my dorm and around campus, I learned about a lot of opportunities. These opportunities then turned into more and more opportunities, until after a while I did not need to look half as much as before. My favorite involvements have been the ones through my resident assistants. I live in a community with many other first-year danc-

ers, and my resident assistants have offered many programs catering to this population. We have done programs ranging from ballroom dancing to seeing the Rochester Philharmonic Orchestra. It was also through my dorm that I learned about Bill Nye the Science Guy's visit to Brockport. This, in turn, led to my most current project of building a permanent sundial on campus. It is amazing how many opportunities you can create for yourself by simply reading signs posted on campus.

campus; furthers your awareness of dance; and creates potential future collaborations.

FILLING THE DANCE STUDIO

The dance studio remains an empty room until it is used to make, rehearse, or teach something. Likewise, your campus and department resources are only valuable when you use them in a way that expands your dance education and dance understanding. Your campus and department offer numerous resources in the form of faculty, classes, organizations, and student support. It is up to you to take advantage of these resources during your time on campus.

The best way to fill the studio is to personalize your dance education. As you learn more about your campus and department, it is important to be proactive in determining how their resources relate to your goals and interests. Throughout your time studying dance on campus, you will have opportunities to personalize your dance education. For example, if you are curious about community dance, you may seek an apprenticeship with a faculty member who is working on a community dance project. Students who are interested in performing may offer to dance in upper division students' choreography projects. As you are introduced to various global dance genres, you may want to pursue an independent study to learn more about the music and visual arts of a specific culture. The more you know about your department's faculty, students, and resources, the more you can personalize your dance education.

Once you have an awareness of your campus community, you can also create your own opportunities to expand your dance experiences into other areas. For example, if you are involved in a campus club focused on social awareness, you may be inspired to create a performance that includes dances about equality and justice. As you become friends with students pursuing other majors, you might challenge yourself to work on an interdisciplinary project that combines your areas of expertise. Your time studying dance on campus is an opportunity to expand and deepen your dance understanding. The more you seek and create opportunities to interact with dance in various ways, the more your dance knowledge will evolve in a way that is unique to your specific interests.

SUMMARY

Your academic pursuit of dance will be similar to other students' studying dance on their campuses. All dance students take a variety of dance classes, take general education courses, and interact with their larger campus communities. While the basic structure of an academic pursuit of dance is similar on all campuses, each campus and degree program is unique. The more you understand the goals, values, and atmosphere of your campus and degree program, the greater success you will have in your dance education. Additionally, it is up to you to proactively tailor your dance education into something that is relevant to your unique interests. Doing so not only helps you develop your dance understanding, it helps the field of dance to expand into new areas.

REVIEW QUESTIONS

1. What are the various types of campuses and degree programs for studying dance? Which campus and degree program best describes the academic program you are enrolled in? How will your campus and degree program's approach to studying dance on campus strengthen and expand your dance understanding?

2. What are the goals and values of your degree program? How do they relate to your dance education goals? Use examples from your department's website and your personal experiences to support your answer.

3. How do the goals and values of your campus reinforce your academic pursuit of dance on campus?

GLOSSARY

associate degrees—These degrees are commonly offered at community colleges and relate to degrees offered at four-year schools. In dance, the associate of arts (AA), associate of science (AS) degrees, and associate of fine arts (AFA) are the most common types of associate degrees.

bachelor of fine arts (BFA)—These degree programs focus more on dance and less on general studies.

dance degree program—The dance courses and curriculum required for a degree in dance or dance education.

dance minor degree programs—Dance programs that provide a way for students to academically engage with dance as a secondary focus while on campus.

generalist degrees—College degree programs that allow for a wide range of coursework.

liberal arts colleges—Colleges that primarily enroll undergraduate students and focus on areas in the liberal arts, which includes the arts, humanities, social sciences, and physical sciences.

liberal arts degrees—Dance degree programs where students focus on broadly learning about the liberal arts with a specialization in dance. In dance, the bachelor of arts (BA) and bachelor of science (BS) are the most common types of liberal arts degrees. Liberal arts degrees can be obtained at both liberal arts colleges and universities.

office hours—Specific time set aside for individual meetings between a faculty member and his or her students.

two-year colleges—Colleges that prepare students to continue their education at another institution or to immediately enter a vocational field.

universities—Institutions that enroll graduate and undergraduate students, offer various types of degrees, and focus on professional degree programs, such as engineering and computer science, in addition to liberal arts programs. Universities are concerned about teaching, but they are also involved in cutting-edge research in the arts, sciences, and various other fields.

upper division—Refers to 300- and 400-level coursework typically taken in the third and fourth years of college.

BIBLIOGRAPHY

Carnegie Foundation for the Advancement of Teaching. (2001). *The Carnegie classification of institutions of higher education.* Menlo Park, CA: Author.

College Board. (2012). Types of colleges: The basics. https://bigfuture.collegeboard.org/find-colleges/college-101/types-of-colleges-the-basics.

National Association of Schools of Dance. (2012). *National Association of Schools of Dance handbook 2011-2012.* Reston, VA: Author.

Roberts, A.L. (2010). *The thinking student's guide to college: 75 tips.* Chicago: University of Chicago Press.

Dance as an Academic Discipline

LEARNING OUTCOMES

After completing this chapter, you will be able to do the following:

- Comprehend and explain the goals and requirements of studying dance as an academic discipline.
- Evaluate the importance of writing, technology, and research in studying dance on campus.
- Formulate and articulate your role in studying dance as an academic discipline.

Studying dance on campus gives you the opportunity to connect your current dance understanding to future possibilities in dance. Because dance is a multifaceted discipline that is always evolving, your academic pursuit of dance will be comprehensive, multilayered, and interconnected. In the photograph, students are engaging in dance as an academic discipline. On campus, learning takes place in the dance studio, by attending general education courses with students from across campus, and by interacting with your campus community. Each one of these experiences contributes to a comprehensive dance education. Recognizing the scope and aims of studying dance on campus better prepares you for a fruitful dance education and forthcoming accomplishments in dance.

Chapter 3 focuses on dance as an academic discipline and helps you grasp the various components and expectations of studying dance on campus. You will examine the importance of academic and creative rigor in your dance studies, both in your dance and general education courses. To help you better understand the academic requirements of studying dance, you will learn about dance and college curricula and the roles of writing, technology, and research in the study of dance on campus. You will assess your own approach to studying dance on campus and articulate the importance of studying dance as an academic discipline so that you can fully engage in your dance education. Taking time to learn about what studying dance on campus entails, situates you for success throughout your time on campus.

A college dance education involves taking classes with other dance students, enrolling in general education coursework, seeking assistance from and interacting with your professors, and learning in many distinct contexts. Each of these experiences and classes is valuable for completing your education; although they may seem separate, they are interrelated. Studying dance on campus is exciting, because you get the opportunity to gain depth in your comprehension of dance as well as a broad knowledge base, both of which you can build on after you graduate. The skills and information you learn while studying dance on campus will prepare you for various achievements in dance. Therefore, it is important to recognize the goals and comprehensive nature of dance as an academic discipline early in your college dance education so that you can continually build your dance expertise.

DEPTH AND BREADTH OF YOUR CAMPUS DANCE EDUCATION

Studying any subject on campus necessitates dedication, curiosity, and responsibility, but this is especially true for dance. Successfully studying dance on campus as a dance major, dance minor, or dance enthusiast requires you to push yourself as a student. Because dance is a versatile field, you need to fully invest and do your best work in your dance, general education, and elective courses. Equally essential is the willingness to embrace new frameworks for thinking about dance and other subjects as well as new teaching and learning methods. Approaching

Engaging WITH Dance

Jessica Lesar (University of Montana at Missoula)

Studying dance on campus is a unique experience. It is different from the studio world that most students come from. You are pushed past your comfort zone in ways that allow you to accomplish things you never thought you could. You are constantly exposed to new dance forms, new ideas, and new people who will eventually become your family away from home. You and your peers are creating and performing new works throughout the semester. You are able to do almost anything you could imagine doing onstage or offstage, as long as you are able to find willing collaborators. There are multiple performance opportunities each year, chances for you to teach your peers, and opportunities to engage with dance in new ways. Your answer to the question *What are you doing tonight?* is almost always *Dancing; I have rehearsal.* I think it is worth it beyond words.

Photo courtesy of Amelia Hufsmith.

your studies in this way will help you create a solid bridge between your current dance understanding, developing dance interests, and prospective opportunities in dance.

Today's dance professionals are articulate movers and speakers, proficient as artists and writers, and able to apply dance-specific knowledge to other disciplines and vice versa. At the same time, dance learning cultivates multiple types of knowing and interacting with the world. Because dance involves the whole person and is a comprehensive area of study, you can expect to be challenged in numerous ways while studying dance on campus. You should expect to be challenged physically, artistically, and intellectually as you make and perform dances, write papers about your experiences relative to new knowledge, give presentations, and work individually and collaboratively in both your dance and general education courses. These multiple experiences not only mirror the expectations of working as a dance professional, they provide diverse means for you to learn about dance.

Your college education will include a combination of discipline-specific courses and general education courses. Dance and other **discipline-specific courses** focus on your major or minor area of interest. For students interested in dance, these courses may include technique, dance history, and choreography classes to name a few. **General education courses** are designed to provide a wide academic foundation. English, mathematics, humanities, and science courses are some common examples of general education courses. The ratio of discipline-specific courses to general education courses will vary depending on your degree program. It is also likely that your degree program will require elective courses. **Elective courses** are courses that students can select to fulfill either a general education or discipline-specific degree requirement. Successfully studying dance on campus depends on recognizing that all of your coursework, inside and outside of dance, is interrelated and relevant.

Discipline-Specific Courses

The academic study of dance examines the interconnected aspects of artistry, culture, education, history, science, entrepreneurship, and research in dance. No matter what area of dance you think you will pursue upon graduation, you must have experience with and an understanding of dance as a distinct yet broad discipline. Dance performers need to be conscious of the historical and cultural contexts of the dances they perform. Dance educators may draw on reviews of research literature, such as research about best teaching practices, new information about how to safely execute movement, or recent findings about child development, in their teaching. Community dance practitioners need to constantly reflect on how their teaching and choreographic methods relate to emerging artistic and educational trends so that their work stays relevant. As a small business owner, the private studio owner needs both marketing and business management skills. Fully investigating all areas of dance helps you achieve a wide and interwoven knowledge of dance so that you appreciate how much there is to the discipline.

Engaging WITH Dance

Sarah Escobedo (University of Texas at El Paso)

Dancing in college is an opportunity to expand your knowledge and experience in all aspects of dance before immersing yourself in the dance world. It gives you a taste of what is to come and prepares you for your dance journey by introducing you to not only movement technique but also dance history, anatomical and somatic knowledge of the body, pedagogy, theory, and choreography. Studying dance in college provides more in-depth study than what you may have experienced in your studio or high school dance training because of the various performances, projects, assignments, and coverage of the many aspects of dance, which provide other options and outlets for you to further your career. Through your academic study and participation in one or several areas of dance, you are able to work on your weaknesses and further your strengths while discovering what interests you about dance before entering the professional dance world.

Photo courtesy of Gil Arias.

Your movement and technique courses; creative, compositional, and performance courses; and context courses are the places where you will delve into dance-specific content. You will learn how to expand your movement abilities and to develop your creative voice as well as various philosophies, histories, and practices of dance. Although each course has a distinct purpose, you must recognize how these courses work together to provide you with a wide and interconnected comprehension of dance. Each dance course you enroll in, regardless of whether it immediately connects to your current dance interests, is equally important to your dance education.

General Education Courses

Balancing depth and breadth is central to any college education. Whereas your dance courses provide depth into a specific discipline, your general education courses provide you with breadth, or general knowledge. This wide understanding is important in many ways. First, these classes give you a broad educational foundation to build on within and outside of dance. For example, English courses cultivate your writing and reasoning skills, and math courses foster logical problem-solving abilities. These aptitudes can be applied in dance, other disciplines, and everyday life. Because general education courses can introduce you to new areas of study such as anthropology, psychology, women's studies, and fine arts, you may find new areas to connect to dance that will influence your dance education and future career pursuits. Lastly, regardless of your interest in dance, all successful dance professionals possess not only an incredible understanding of dance but also a keen awareness of dance's relationship to other disciplines, inside and outside of the arts, and diverse communities and cultures. In your campus dance education, this wider awareness is cultivated through general education courses.

As a dance student, you should take your general education courses just as seriously as your dance courses. The more you fully invest in your general education courses, the more apparent the connections to dance become. You may have some choice in which general education courses you take. It is to your advantage to stay open minded about what you might learn in these courses and how they relate to your evolving dance interests. The more knowledge you gain from your general education courses, the more foundational information you have to build on in your study of dance and as a young dance professional.

ROLES OF WRITING, TECHNOLOGY, AND RESEARCH

Throughout your studies, certain expectations and requirements will be present in most of your classes. Writing, both to gain proficiency and as a method of learning, is a large part of the college experience. Technology is everywhere on campus, and its use in college goes beyond social networking and communication. Because colleges and the learning process both value inquiry, research is frequently present and used in a variety of college courses. Writing, technology, and research will be regular parts of your dance and general education courses.

Writing

In all of your dance and general education courses, you will write. The types of papers you write may range from short reflective assignments, to essays, to in-depth research papers. Writing serves many purposes in your dance education. Most writing assignments are created to help students develop writing skills as well as learn more about themselves or about a given topic. Through writing reactions to new information, you are more likely to understand and remember the information. In some cases, writing gives you an opportunity to figure out confusing ideas or to consider how new information can be applied to your own interests. And, the more frequently you write, the more familiar you become with writing, sharing your ideas, and the writing expectations of your discipline. The more you can embrace writing as a pathway to learning, articulating your thoughts, and sharing new information with others, the more valuable each writing opportunity will be. As you progress through your dance education on campus, you may be surprised by how much you learn about yourself and dance through writing.

Technology

The use of online and mobile technologies will also be a large part of your education, both in dance and general education courses. Some classes may use an online course management system, such as Blackboard, Moodle, or eCollege, where the syllabus, assignments, and additional course materials are posted for easy student access. Additionally, there may be videos, websites, and articles you need to find and read or view online for class assignments.

© Karen Schupp

• • • Online and mobile technologies will be a constant presence in your college dance education.

At times, online and mobile technologies provide unique learning experiences. For example, course discussion forums allow students to interact with one another and with course content outside of class time and teach you to listen to peers in a different way. You may even enroll in an online class, where all of instruction takes place online instead of in a physical classroom. The use of online and mobile technologies will vary from class to class and subject to subject, but it will be a constant presence in your college dance education. Therefore, it is important to familiarize yourself with the online and mobile technologies at use in each of your courses and to fully engage in all online learning activities.

Research

To varying degrees, research is a part of most students' campus experiences. Along with the materials instructors provide in class, you can expect to bring additional content into each of your classes. This can range from finding an academic article to analyze in a general education class, to researching various choreographers for a dance class, to preparing research papers or presentations. Research-related assignments and learning experiences not only help students stay abreast of current research in their specific subject areas, they also assist students in developing a process of inquiry.

College campuses have tremendous resources relative to research. The most common research tool you will likely use is your campus library. Your campus library website can connect you to databases where you can search for academic articles on just about any subject, give access to the library's catalog and specialized collections, and put you in contact with research and subject area librarians. The physical library provides books, quiet study spaces, and areas for collaboration. It is likely that you will use your library's services on a regular basis in both your dance and general education courses while studying dance on campus. The more you can view the library's resources as a pathway to gaining more knowledge about subjects that interest you, the more you can learn through various research assignments and activities on campus.

PERSONALIZING YOUR STUDY OF DANCE AS AN ACADEMIC DISCIPLINE

Even though your program of study may be outlined for you by your campus, you will have the opportunity to cultivate your own voice and interests as a dance student. The first step to personalizing your study of dance on campus is to familiarize yourself with the required curriculum for your degree program. Most campuses have major or minor curriculum check-sheets or program of study documents available online. These materials outline the dance, general education, and elective requirements of your degree program. Identifying the balance between dance and general education requirements can help you realize opportunities to connect your learning across disciplines. Whenever possible, select general education courses that pique your interests.

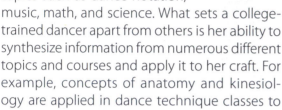

Engaging WITH Dance

Maia Stam (Goucher College)

Studying dance on campus is about so much more than mere performance and technique, regardless of the school or program of study. The college dancer studies dance history, composition, anatomy and theory, and in many cases a slew of other topics such as dance notation, music, math, and science. What sets a college-trained dancer apart from others is her ability to synthesize information from numerous different topics and courses and apply it to her craft. For example, concepts of anatomy and kinesiology are applied in dance technique classes to achieve a better understanding of alignment and muscle use. Personally, I've chosen to study communications in addition to dance. My communications courses have shown me how to take advantage of technology in the creation and promotion of dance, and they have allowed me to become more articulate in both my verbal and nonverbal communication. Dance on campus is no longer about the act of dancing; it is about the process of it—the history, the culture, the information, and the training that go into making dance the amazing, versatile commodity that it is.

Euphoric Shutterbug Photography

For example, if you are interested in choreography, you might enroll in a design or visual arts course so that you can learn new compositional ideas while fulfilling your fine arts requirement. Courses such as women in other cultures or urban anthropology would benefit students interested in dance ethnography, and they would count as social sciences classes. Enrolling in general education courses that are potentially interesting to you and satisfy your degree requirements ensures that you are getting the most of your study of dance on campus.

Because writing, technology, and research will be a large part of studying dance on campus, it can be helpful to assess your familiarity and comfort with each. Although these elements will be present in most of your courses, there may not be much time devoted to explaining how to write, how to use technology, and how to find resources for research projects. If you know that you have challenges in one of these areas, it is to your advantage to be proactive and to seek assistance. Many campuses have writing centers where students can get peer assistance with writing mechanics. Campus librarians are able to help students navigate the library and various research tools, and campus computer centers frequently have help desks to assist students. And, of course, you can always ask your instructors for assistance. Because these three elements are a large part of learning on campus, you should find ways to develop these skills as needed. This will guarantee that you are getting the full benefits of studying dance on campus.

Lastly, a beneficial way to personalize your academic study of dance is to talk about it with other campus community members. When someone asks you what you are interested in or what your major is, use that as an opportunity to articulate your specific dance interests. You will find that over time you are not only clarifying to yourself your dance interests by explaining them to others, you are promoting the value of dance as an academic discipline. Dance is an incredibly rich area of study, and studying dance on campus gives you the opportunity to experience breadth and depth in your college education, and that better prepares you for success in the future.

SUMMARY

It is important to recognize the value of dance as an academic discipline. Because dance is a multifaceted discipline that demands both a high level of knowledge in and about dance and a wide educational foundation, studying dance as an academic discipline ensures that you are ready for a career in dance. Understanding the role of discipline-specific and general education coursework allows you to proactively shape your dance education in response to your evolving dance interests. Increasing your proficiency in writing, technology, and research allows you to deepen your dance knowledge while also providing you with skills needed for success after graduation. It is up to you to fully engage in all of your coursework so that your dance education is rich, complete, and relevant to your future in dance.

REVIEW QUESTIONS

1. Briefly define and explain the goals of general education courses, discipline-specific courses, and electives. Then explain how these courses work together to provide a complete dance education.

2. Why are writing, technology, and research important aspects of learning on campus? How do writing, technology, and research relate to your future success inside and outside of dance?

3. What are the benefits of selecting general education courses that interest you? Why is it beneficial to assess your comfort with writing, technology, and research? How do these work together to personalize your academic study of dance?

GLOSSARY

discipline-specific courses—Courses focused on a major or minor area of interest.

elective courses—Courses that a student can select to fulfill either a general education or discipline-specific degree requirement.

general education courses—Courses designed to provide a wide academic foundation.

BIBLIOGRAPHY

Bazerman, C., Little, J., Bethel, L., Chavkin, T., Fouquette, D., & Garufis, J. (2005). *Reference guide to writing across the curriculum*. West Lafayette, IN: Parlor Press.

Success Strategies

LEARNING OUTCOMES

After completing this chapter, you will be able to do the following:

- Comprehend your responsibilities as a student.
- Demonstrate skills needed for effective learning of and critical engagement with class material.
- Understand the significance of and strategies for time management.
- Evaluate the importance of balancing schoolwork, employment, and a personal life.
- Construct personal strategies for success.

tudying dance on campus is a rewarding and enriching adventure that requires you to call on and develop many skills. As with most new experiences, it will take some time to discover what is expected of you and how things work, and to find your place in the campus community. The students in the photograph are visibly happy because they are successfully studying dance on campus. Along with learning new things about dance, they are implementing strategies for success. Taking the time to unpack the habits needed for student achievement provides you with powerful learning tools and frameworks for studying dance on campus.

Chapter 4 introduces various blueprints for academic success. You will learn about your responsibilities and what is expected of you as a college student. The capacities needed for effective learning and critical engagement are outlined so that you are better prepared to excel in your coursework. Time management is discussed to help you determine how to efficiently budget your time. Because many students balance numerous obligations, such as family, work, and a social life, the importance of life balance is addressed. You will evaluate your current approach to studying dance on campus and formulate a new plan for academic success. Being proactive about how you study dance on campus ensures that you are getting the most out of your college education.

The students in the photograph are proud of their recent accomplishments. Perhaps they just aced an exam, or they were selected for a guest artist's residency, or they were just accepted into a selective summer dance workshop. Regardless of the achievement, success takes hard work. Often that sense of working hard is what makes an achievement rewarding. Success on and off campus happens through persistent dedication and effort. Developing the competencies needed for academic success on campus will also serve you well as a young professional. As such, it is important to fully understand and practice these skills while studying dance on campus.

STUDENT RESPONSIBILITIES AND CONTRIBUTIONS

For most students, studying dance on campus comes with a great sense of independence. As a college student, you have much more freedom in determining your classes, how you spend your time, who you interact with, and how you prioritize your obligations. With this greater independence comes increased responsibility. You will find that you need to be more self-responsible inside and outside of the classroom and that you are expected to contribute to your campus community in a more mature way. This newfound sense of adult responsibility can be overwhelming at times, but developing self-responsibility and the aptitudes needed to meaningfully participate in classes and campus activities is central to your overall education.

With most things in life, the more you put into an activity, the more you gain from it. This is certainly true while studying dance on campus. In both your dance and general education coursework, what you learn is dependent on how much effort you invest in your studies. Although your teachers will provide you with learning experiences and new content, it is your responsibility to digest this knowledge, demonstrate what you have learned, and apply it. In all of your coursework, you need to be proactive about your learning so that you can continuously shape your dance knowledge in a relevant and meaningful way.

Behaviors for Success

It is likely that you have already experienced some of the differences between high school and college classes. At the collegiate level, professors expect students to be more self-responsible in their learning. This shift in responsibility is reflected in student–teacher dynamics, how you interact in the classroom, how you complete assignments and progress in a course, and how you seek assistance. College professors are seen as facilitators of knowledge. They each have expertise in their respective disciplines to share with students, but they expect students to be very active in learning and understanding that knowledge.

One of the most notable distinctions between high school and college courses is the change in student and teacher dynamics. In college settings, teachers assume that you are enrolled in a course because you are interested in the subject matter, you are there to learn as much as possible, and you value their expertise. Therefore, it is to your advantage to be respectful, polite, curious, and focused on the process of learning instead of solely focusing on your grade in the course. Remember, whether you are in a seminar class with 12 students, a technique class with 25 students, or a lecture class with over 300 students, you are responsible for your own learning. College professors want students to invest in their own learning because it leads to student achievement. Practicing some common-sense approaches to your classes can assist you in making the switch from high school to college learning expectations.

Read Your Course Syllabus

A **syllabus** is a detailed outline that includes the learning outcomes, expectations, assignments, required course resources, and evaluation criteria for a given course. Each course you enroll in will have its own syllabus, and you need to read each one carefully so that you are prepared. Many students find that the answers to their day-to-day questions about a course, such as when assignments are due, what the attendance policy is, or what dance shoes and clothing are expected, are listed in the syllabus. Taking the time to familiarize yourself with your course syllabus gives you a basic understanding of the course's expectations, which is essential to doing well in a course.

Go to Class

Unlike high school, the attendance policies will differ for each of your classes. Some professors will not take attendance, yet you are responsible for everything covered in class even if you are absent. In other courses, you may be permitted a certain number of absences, which, if exceed, reduces your grade in the course. Regardless of the attendance policy, attending class allows your comprehension of a subject to consistently grow, such as understanding how one era of dance history influences the next generation of innovators or learning how basic vocabulary and grammar rules lead to conversational fluency in a foreign language class. Besides, going to class provides a chance for you to engage more fully in the coursework and to get to know your faculty and peers better.

Submit Your Assignments

In college classes, each out-of-class assignment, whether it is a response essay, research paper, or choreographic study, is critical to your progress. Usually these assignments provide a way for students to synthesize their learning and for professors to respond to that through written evaluations or in future classes. Because college faculty expect you to be responsible and mature, it is assumed that your assignments will be thoughtfully completed and submitted on time. Failure to do so not only will affect your learning in the course, it will likely impact your grade as well.

Check Your Online Learning Platform Daily

Try to think of your online learning platform as "information central." Here, professors post announcements about upcoming class changes. Your department may have a section that includes information on visiting artists, performances, and auditions. In addition, your campus might use it to disseminate essential information about class registration, tuition due dates, and graduation. As a responsible student you need to stay informed, and frequently checking your online learning platform is critical to staying informed.

Avoid Digital Distractions

Remember, class time is tremendously valuable to your learning, which means you should avoid the temptation to text your friends, check social media,

● ● ● Attending class allows your comprehension of a subject to consistently grow.

or surf the web. While some classes permit or require the use of laptops and other digital devices for note taking, in-class research, audio playback, and recording and viewing videos, the expectation is that your full attention is focused on the task at hand. Constantly checking digital devices distracts you from your learning and disturbs those around you, including your professor. Additionally, some faculty members view this behavior as disrespectful, and it can affect your course grade negatively.

Ask for Help

Being a mature student does not mean that you know everything. It means that you are proactive in seeking additional information, resources, and assistance. In some courses, you may have teaching assistants. **Teaching assistants** are graduate students assigned to assist in the teaching of a course. They, as well as your professors, are often willing to assist students outside of class. It is advantageous to proactively ask for assistance. Professors would prefer that you ask for clarification or assistance on an assignment before it is due rather than not complete the assignment or do it poorly. When you reach out for help, be sure that you are organized, open to suggestions, and respectful of your professor's or teaching assistant's time. Knowing when you need assistance is central to being a self-responsible student.

Get to Know Your Professors

There are a few ways to get to know your professors, and doing so demonstrates that you are invested in your learning and interested in their area of expertise while also providing you the opportunity to find possible mentors and new areas of interest. You can start by reading your faculty members' biographies on departmental websites to give you a quick survey of their research areas, creative work, teaching interests, and history. You could also visit faculty during their office hours. Most faculty members have office hours that are woefully underattended. Because office hours are time specifically set aside for one-on-one student–teacher interaction, it is a great time to get to know your faculty, seek assistance, and learn more about your emerging interests.

Aptitudes for Success

Being a responsible student means that you are ready and eager to partake in all aspects of college learning. Inside and outside of the studio and classroom, you need to call on certain aptitudes to fully participate in and benefit from your courses and extracurricular activities and to interact with your peers. Leadership, collaboration, initiation, and negotiation are skills to use daily as you study dance on campus and as a young professional.

- **Leadership and stewardship. Leadership** is the ability to enlist and direct the help of others to achieve a shared goal. **Stewardship** refers to the management and care of resources, which can include people for whom a person is responsible. As you can see, leadership and stewardship are closely related. Both require a person to inspire others, focus a group's attention around a specific task, enable people to work toward success, and reinforce jobs well done. They also require constant learning and communication. The academic setting provides opportunities to practice leadership and stewardship. Perhaps you recognize the need to start a study group in your biology class or a new student club in response to shared student interest. For class assignments, you may be assigned to lead a project such as choreographing a dance or teaching a movement phrase. Leadership and stewardship are aptitudes that can be developed, and college is a great place to enhance them.

- **Collaboration.** Closely related to leadership and stewardship, **collaboration** refers to working with others, sharing ideas, and creating something as a group. Perhaps you have already worked collaboratively in your classes. When collaborating, it is essential that you respect other people's ideas, find ways to acknowledge all viewpoints, and keep the common good in mind. In some collaborative situations, there will be a clear leader who makes the final decision; in other situations, you may make decisions democratically. Some collaborative projects involve students from other disciplines, and others might take place in a dance course such as developing a group presentation on a renowned choreographer or co-creating a duet for your choreography class. Working collaboratively is a great way to expand your own thinking about a subject, because you will constantly hear other people's opinions, relate them to your own, and find new ways to communicate your ideas.

- **Negotiation.** Negotiation is part of leadership, stewardship, and collaboration. **Nego-**

tiation is the exchange of viewpoints on and solutions to a problem as a means to find an answer that satisfies all parties involved. Because your education is a social experience, meaning you are always learning and working with others, negotiation will be part of your everyday life. For example, as a choreographer, you will need to negotiate a variety of things with your fellow dancers, ranging from rehearsal times to actual sections of the choreography. When working collaboratively on a class presentation, you will need to negotiate ways of organizing content, determining responsibilities, and how the presentation will proceed. Viewing negotiation as a way to find a common solution is critical to developing leadership, stewardship, and collaboration skills.

• **Initiation.** Leadership, stewardship, collaboration, and negotiation all require you to be proactive, and the best way to do that is to take initiative. **Initiation** is the act of getting something started. As a leader, collaborator, or negotiator, someone needs to take the first step. In terms of self-responsibility, initiation is central. The ability to take action in direct relationship to your needs and interests will ensure that you are getting the most out of your dance education. Of course, following through is also critical. Once you put a plan in action, you need to follow up and see the creative project, the request for assistance, or the opportunity to learn more through to completion. The ability to initiate and then see something through to completion is incredibly satisfying and will be an essential component of your study of dance on campus.

DIFFERENCES BETWEEN HIGH SCHOOL AND COLLEGE LEARNING

One of the most exciting, and sometimes intimidating aspects of starting college is the realization that college-level work is more challenging than what you experienced as a high school student. In college, the majority of your learning time is spent outside of the classroom, and you—not your teachers—are primarily responsible for what you learn. Recognizing how high school and college learning differ can help you develop strategies for success so that you can meet these new expectations.

In high school, you spent about 40 hours per week learning; about 30 of those hours were at school and 10 hours were spent on homework. In college, you will likely still spend about 40 to 45 hours per week learning but only 15 to 25 hours in class. To put it another way, at most campuses, a 3-credit-hour, semester-long course comes with the expectation that students will spend 9 hours a week on that course. If the course meets twice a week for

---

Engaging WITH Dance

Hannah Fischbeck (Arizona State University)

In my first week of classes on campus, I found I had a lot of time! Unlike high school where classes happen back to back in a consistent time period, college classes left my schedule with huge gaps and, sometimes, only one class in a day. I found myself having nothing to do. I could get ahead on assignments, but because they weren't due for another week, I quickly fell into the habit of procrastinating and taking naps. However, I soon realized that just because I did not

have any assignments due did not mean that I was homework free. In college suddenly drafts were not requested, readings required no written submission, and so on. These steps in completing an assignment became an expectation in college, and it was up to me to make time to actually do them. Learning how to use your free time while taking classes on campus can be very helpful in ensuring that you make time for necessary steps in your education.

1.5 hours each session, students should expect to spend about 6 hours a week on homework, studying, reviewing movement phrases, and creating work. Although the overall time spent learning does not change that much from high school to college, the ratio of in-class to out-of-class learning can change substantially. Unlike in high school, where teachers planned most of your learning time, you are now responsible for organizing the majority of your learning time. Understanding and acting on this change in responsibility is one of the best things you can do to ensure that you flourish while studying dance on campus.

Differences exist also in how in-class time is used. In college, professors expect that everyone has competed the assigned readings, creative projects, and homework before coming to class. If you come to class unprepared, it is unlikely that the professor will set aside class time for you to catch up, so it is essential that you are prepared for each class. Additionally, class time will mostly be dedicated to building on previously established knowledge, discussion, and applications of new material, so failure to complete assignments, projects, and readings can quickly set you back. Although the learning expectations are different in high school and college, you can succeed if you stay on top of assignments and readings and seek assistance as needed.

Because the format and expectations of learning in college are different from high school, you may need to refine some of your study habits. Understanding critical thinking and knowing and how to actively read texts, effectively take lecture notes, strengthen your writing, and alleviate assessment anxiety will help you better engage in your learning and empower you toward academic success.

Critical Thinking

Critical thinking involves the examination of thought and how arguments are presented. When critically thinking, the purpose, assumptions, reasoning, implementations, and consequences of an argument are actively considered. Critical thinking requires you to go beyond simple memorization of facts, movements, and acquisition of skills and to examine how the information is constructed and applied. The ability to critically think will both be cultivated by and required for studying dance on campus. You will have many opportunities to practice this in all of your coursework.

Active Reading

You may find that college requires much more reading in both your dance and general education courses than high school, and that much of the information you need to learn about a topic is initially presented in readings instead of being explained by your professors. Therefore, the ability to actively read is beneficial to your overall learning. Active reading requires you to create a dialogue with what you are reading. Asking the text questions and trying to answer them can help you pull out essential information, more readily connect that information to your own experience, and practice critical thinking. You might start by asking yourself some pre-reading questions, such as *What is the topic?* and *What do you know about it?* to help you situate your current understanding. Then, it could be beneficial to identify and then define unfamiliar terms and somehow indicate the thesis of the reading so that you can readily refer to them. As much as possible, resist the urge to highlight text; instead, make notes or comments in your own words that summarize the text, provide commentary, or ask questions. As questions arise, it might be helpful to write them in the margins of printed reading materials or to annotate electronic formats using the "comments" or "notes" feature, and then to answer them in a notebook or a separate electronic document. Writing a summary, devising your own practice exam questions, and teaching what you have learned to someone else are excellent ways to synthesize what you have read. All of these pointers keep you active in and responsive to your reading, increase your reading comprehension, and prepare you well for class.

Effective Note Taking

Taking notes in class is a useful way to retain essential information, clarify questions that have come up in the readings, track what you are learning in a course, remember movement phrases and choreography, and critically participate in a lecture. Although note-taking methods vary, there are some common tips on taking effective notes, and they are discussed here. Before class, make sure that you are prepared. This means that you have completed the assigned readings, you have reviewed your notes from the previous class, and you have the required materials for taking notes. When you get to class, sit or stand toward the front of the classroom, where fewer distractions are likely, and come to class with an enthusiastic attitude. Start each lecture's notes

• • • Active reading requires you to create a dialogue with what you are reading.

on a separate page, date the notes, and leave room in your notes to add additional information later. During class, listen and watch the speaker very carefully. He or she will often give clear clues about what information is essential. Listen to the introduction so that you can hear the outline of the lecture. Be brief in your note taking. Whenever possible, take notes in your own words instead of trying to write down each word a speaker says. If something is written on the board or presented in slides, write it down. Often professors use the board and digital presentations to emphasize key points in a lecture. Pay special attention to the summary, and at the end of class ask questions about points you are unclear about. After class, review your notes soon, and take some time to match your lecture notes with your reading notes. It may be helpful to review your notes regularly—perhaps weekly—so that you are continuously scaffolding your learning and are prepared for any upcoming exams or papers. When you view note taking as a way to stay engaged in classes and to connect your in-class and out-of-class learning, you can learn as much as possible in each class.

Writing

In college, writing takes many forms and purposes. You may be required to complete research papers and analytical essays in which you analyze a given text, argumentative essays in which you have to articulate an informed opinion on a given topic, synthesis essays in which you synthesize information from various sources, summative essays in which you summarize an article, reflective essays in which you reflect on an experience, and research papers. In most cases, professors view the act of writing as an essential component of your learning. In college, writing is a way for you to better comprehend and critically think about a topic. Just as it is important to stay invested in your reading and note taking, it is critical to stay engaged in the act of writing. Perhaps you can start with some prewriting exercises where you use free-writes, brainstorming, and pictures to generate idea. You might use index cards to jot down ideas from outside resources so that you can experiment with different ways of organizing your ideas. After you have gathered your thoughts, you want to schedule enough time to complete at least two drafts, which you can revise based on feedback from yourself, peers, or teaching assistants. As you edit each draft, you want to be sure to proofread. Some proofreading approaches include reading the paper aloud, having someone else read it to you, and using your computer's spell-checker. You also want to read your paper to ensure that your ideas are well organized and that your thesis or argument is clear and connected to the assignment's prompt. Your thesis should be clearly stated and supported with ample evidence and examples. To help with this, you can think of each paragraph as a place to make a point, explain your point, and provide an example. The introduction and conclusion, which are essential parts of each type of essay, should provide cohesion to the essay. Finally, be sure that your paper is properly formatted, includes your name and the essay's title, and uses proper citation. Writing in college gives you numerous opportunities to learn more about a topic while also formulating and articulating your thoughts about a subject matter. As such, it might be helpful to view each written assignment as another way to present yourself and your ideas. This will ensure that you are putting your best work forward each time.

Alleviating Assessment Anxiety

At times, a little bit of nerves can give you an extra boost to do your best, but at other times, anxiety can be overwhelming. In addition to completing papers and projects, your learning will also be measured through tests, exams, and performance assessments as you study dance on campus. There are a few ways that you can avoid or minimize assessment anxiety. Try to avoid cramming for exams and assessments. It is better to consistently review and apply information throughout the semester so that studying for exams is an opportunity to refresh your learning. Stay engaged with your studying by asking yourself sample test questions, and then answering them with material from your readings, notes, and papers. Try to stay positive about assessments. Sometimes it is helpful to remind yourself that a test is only a test, and that there will be others. Try to avoid thinking in all-or-nothing terms, and remember that the only reasonable expectation is to try your best. Be sure to get enough rest, to eat well, and to relax. The healthier you are emotionally and physically before a test, the better you will do. On the day of the test or assessment, be sure to have breakfast, to show up to the test site early, and to avoid students who make you feel nervous. If it is a written test, review the entire exam before starting and consider reading the directions twice. For multiple choice questions, consider all the answers before selecting one, and for essays, create a short outline before starting to write. Take your time. After the assessment, reward yourself! Go to the movies, go out for lunch, and visit with friends. Usually, assessments are milestones in your learning, and completing them should be celebrated. While most assessment anxiety can be eased through proper preparation, there may be times when you need to seek additional assistance to deal with assessment anxiety. In those cases, your campus counseling center can provide strategies to assist with test anxiety.

MANAGING YOUR LIFE

As you are probably realizing, college involves hard work, consistency, and dedication. Success in college also requires a great deal of organization and creating a rich and full life. Knowing how to efficiently budget your time and to create room for family, work, and a social life while in school can help you succeed academically and enjoy your time on campus.

Time Management

Studying dance on campus can sometimes feel like you are trying to manage a variety of tasks and obligations all at the same time. Classes, homework, and rehearsals all compete for your attention, and you want to do well in each scenario. Learning to manage your time is a highly effective way to make sure that you complete everything you need to with a minimum amount of stress.

For starters, it is never too early to make a plan. Many students find it advantageous to use a planner or digital calendar to block out class, rehearsal, and study time (yes, you need to schedule time to study) as well as list due dates for assignments, readings, and exams. Do this as soon as you get your course syllabi. It is also beneficial to determine whether you are a morning, daytime, or night person so that you can schedule your study times for when you feel best. Because college assignments can be comprehensive, it is a good idea to start an assignment log where you track how long it takes to complete assignments and readings for each class. This will help you best determine how to prioritize the completion of assignments and readings as workloads increase throughout the semester. Finding ways to break large assignments and projects into smaller chunks can make them more manageable, relieve the anxiety of trying to complete a big project the day before it is due, and create a greater sense of accomplishment as you are working on the project. Especially around midterms and finals, you will need to prioritize your coursework, but remember to give each course enough attention. It is tempting to spend your study time on the class you like the best, but remember each course contributes to your overall learning. Finally, be consistent. The first time you skip a study session or rehearsal will only make it easier for you to skip the next one and easier for the work to pile up. With planning and consistency, you will find that you are more able to focus on your schoolwork, instead of using your energy to figure out how you will get everything done.

Engaging WITH Dance

Destinee Smith (University of North Carolina at Greensboro)

College is no easy feat, so congratulations for considering the challenge. Generally, college is a time of endless social opportunities, continuous assignments, and countless e-mails. The easiest way to be a successful college student and socializer is to keep an organized agenda. Keep everything written down. Even those events and assignments that are tentative should be written on a sticky note until they are confirmed and can be written under an actual date. Organization is key for dance students. For example, keeping an organized schedule is helpful when you have three papers due the week of tech week. You will know that the weekend before tech week is your opportunity to get caught up on your assignments so you avoid exhaustion and stress. Giving your mind time to relax will only help your body and help you succeed in college.

inTown Photography by: Heather Groves

Life Balance

Although academic success is a large part of studying dance on campus, there are other components to campus life. Finding balance between all aspects of your life, such as family, friends, and work, ensures not only that you are getting the most out of your campus experience but also that you are leading a full life.

Spending time with friends and family is very important. It keeps you connected to those you care about and can help you relieve stress through doing fun activities. College is a great time to meet new people, but it can also be beneficial to stay in contact with those you already know. If you live on campus, you may find that communicating with friends and family through phone calls, text messages, and e-mails keeps you grounded. These people know you very well, and can offer a great sense of support as you encounter new things on campus. If you live off campus or at home, meeting new people is a way for you to develop and follow new interests that you have found on campus. Many campuses have specific centers or clubs for commuting students to help them get involved with campus life. It may make sense to join a religious or community center if you were active in a similar organization before coming to college. Connecting with people outside of your discipline but with similar values creates a full and rich life. Students who work while studying dance on campus need to really use their time management skills to the fullest. Working while studying dance on campus is a way to gain additional knowledge, such as people skills and leadership experiences, that can be particularly useful in dance. While your primary goal in studying dance on campus is to get the fullest dance education possible, that does not mean that other aspects of your life should be ignored. Have a social life, visit with your friends and family, work a part-time job, join a student club or volunteer organization. Creating a vibrant life assists you in dealing with the challenges of studying dance on campus, keeps you emotionally healthy, and makes life more meaningful.

PERSONAL STRATEGIES FOR SUCCESS

Of course, understanding different strategies for success is important, but the frameworks only become beneficial when implemented. Now that you understand your responsibilities and contributions as a student, how learning in college is different from learning in high school, and the significance of time management and life balance, it is time to develop and implement personal strategies for success. Taking the time to assess your current approaches to studying dance on campus, addressing your strengths and challenges as a student, and reflecting on how you manage your life can help you develop a more proactive and focused manner to studying dance on campus.

A good place to start is to objectively assess your behaviors and aptitudes as a student. Consider the approaches you use that best serve you as a student.

For example, maybe you read each of your course syllabi before classes start and you consistently attend classes. Also consider the approaches that you can improve. Maybe it is difficult for you to ask for assistance from your teaching assistants and professors, or perhaps you feel very shy about setting up a meeting with your professors. Next, consider how different aptitudes for success relate to your strengths and challenges as a student. For example, consistently showing up for class requires leadership, whereas setting up a meeting with a professor requires initiation. As you assess your approaches to school, you will find which aptitudes you are more comfortable calling on and which ones you could develop more. Remember, college is not only an opportunity to learn in the classroom, it is also an important time to learn about yourself. Knowing your strengths and weaknesses and how to use and improve on them is a key step in knowing yourself and maturing as a person.

Next, take some time to reflect on your study skills and consider how they can be strengthened. If you are in the habit of reading only for information instead of engaging in a dialogue with a text, you might find it helpful to develop an active approach to reading. If you have difficulty paying attention in lecture classes, you may find that developing a new way of note taking keeps you on task as an active listener in your classes. Active reading, effective note taking, and confident and clear writing all contribute to developing critical thinking. The more you can see each of these individual approaches to learning as part of a complete educational experience, the more well-rounded your education can be. Of course, remember that you should also ask for assistance as needed. Many campuses have online resources, such as PDF files with tips for note taking, writing centers where peer tutors provide feedback on your writing, and seminars and workshops about how to improve your learning. Upper division dance students can offer advice about how to best review phrase work, approach faculty for assistance, and balance the academic demands of studying dance on campus. Taking advantage of these resources not only helps you succeed academically, it contributes to developing lifelong learning skills.

One of the biggest challenges for students new to studying dance on campus is time management and life balance. You will frequently feel that you have a million things that you want and need to do. Besides your coursework and rehearsals, you might have work obligations, family commitments, and a social life. Remember, achievement in dance requires expertise in dance, but it also requires a supportive network of family and friends. Most students find it helpful to sketch out their days and obligations in a calendar and to plan ahead. Doing so provides a framework that allows you to meet your obligations without having to worry about how and when things will get done. In your planner, be sure to leave room to see friends and family, rest, and take care of yourself, which includes time to prepare and eat meals and some downtime. Each aspect of your life contributes to your overall success studying dance on campus, so it is beneficial to acknowledge this fact early in your dance education.

SUMMARY

Understanding what is expected of you as a student, the aptitudes needed for success, the differences between high school and college, and the importance of time management and life balance is critical to your college dance experience. Taking the time to familiarize yourself with each of these areas, to assess your approaches to learning, and to reflect on your strengths and challenges as a student, and knowing how you can improve will ensure that you are getting the most out of studying dance on campus. It will also ensure that you are enjoying your educational journey. Developing the skills needed to succeed academically on campus will also benefit your growth as a young professional and will allow you to continuously learn about yourself and about dance, and develop new interests while studying dance on campus and beyond.

REVIEW QUESTIONS

1. How do leadership, stewardship, collaboration, initiation, and negotiation work together? How does each of these aptitudes contribute to academic success?

2. In your own words, define critical thinking. How do active reading, effective note taking, and writing assignments relate to critical thinking?

3. Why is it important to balance schoolwork with friends, family, work, and other obligations? How does this contribute to successfully studying dance on campus? How does this contribute to leading a full and balanced life?

4. Explain why it is necessary to be a self-responsible student while studying dance on campus. How does this relate to academic success and success as a young professional in your selected career?

GLOSSARY

collaboration—Working with others, sharing ideas, and creating something as a group.

critical thinking—The examination of thought and how arguments are presented. When critically thinking, the purpose, assumptions, reasoning, implementations, and consequences of an argument are actively considered.

initiation—The act of getting something started.

leadership—The ability to enlist the help of others to achieve a shared goal.

negotiation—The exchange of viewpoints on and solutions to a problem as a means to find an answer that satisfies all parties involved.

stewardship—The management and care of resources, which can include people for whom a person is responsible.

syllabus—A detailed outline that includes the student learning outcomes, expectations, assignments, required course resources, and evaluation criteria for a given course.

teaching assistants—Graduate students assigned to assist in the teaching of a course.

BIBLIOGRAPHY

College of Saint Benedict. (2012). Lecture note-taking. www.csbsju.edu/academic-advising/study-skills-guide/lecture-note-taking.htm.

Jacobs, L.F., & Hyman, J.S. (2009). Top 12 time-management tips. www.usnews.com/education/blogs/professors-guide/2009/10/14/top-12-time-management-tips.

McGraw Center for Teaching and Learning. (2013). Active reading strategies. www.princeton.edu/mcgraw/library/for-students/remember-reading.

New Paltz State University of New York. (2012). Difference between high school and college. www.newpaltz.edu/advising/highschool_college.html.

Pendleton, D., & Furnham, A. (2012). *Leadership: All you need to know.* London: Palgrave Macmillan.

Roberts, A.L. (2010). *The thinking student's guide to college: 75 Tips.* Chicago: University of Chicago Press.

Scriven, P., & Paul, R. (1987). Defining critical thinking. www.criticalthinking.org/pages/defining-critical-thinking/766.

University of Illinois at Urbana-Champaign. (2007). Test anxiety. www.counselingcenter.illinois.edu/?page_id=114.

University of North Carolina at Chapel Hill. (2012). Keys to successful college writing. www.unc.edu/~twtaylor/success.html.

PART two

Dance as a Discipline

CHAPTER 5

Dance and Artistry

After reading this chapter, you will be able to do the following:

- Compare modern dance, ballet, jazz dance, tap dance, and urban dance genres.
- Understand the artistic roles and careers in dance.
- Differentiate and discuss performance opportunities in dance.
- Evaluate current trends in dance.
- Assess your current dance artistry.

When we think of great artists, we think of people who can take ordinary materials and objects and transform them into distinct, innovative, or beautiful expressions of their ideas. A sculptor might use clay and her hands to communicate her ideas through an abstract statue. When that statue is presented in a gallery, viewers gain a glimpse into the artist's thinking and experiences. **Dance artists** are people who make art through and with movement. They use their bodies, movement, and the performance space to communicate their ideas. The stage space in the photograph provides one place for you to express your ideas to others. It is by sharing your ideas through movement, either onstage or in other performance spaces, that you present yourself as a dance artist.

Chapter 5 introduces you to dance and artistry. Although all dance artists express their ideas through movement, the styles of movement vary greatly. In this chapter, you will learn about five dance genres that you may study on campus, roles and careers in the artistic realm of dance, and various opportunities for performance. You will also assess the ways that your current dance studies are artistic preparation, and you will formulate personal goals to advance your artistry. By the end of the chapter, you will have a greater understanding of what it means to be a dance artist and how your academic study of dance can best prepare you as a dance artist.

Throughout the ages, dance artists have continuously found new ways to transform their bodies, movements, and the performance space to communicate their ideas. Although the technology, performance spaces, and movements have changed, the drive for dancers to artistically express themselves through movement has remained constant. The stage space represents the history of dance as a performing art and as a means of entertainment as well as a place where you can communicate your ideas with others. It is important that you use your time studying dance on campus to broaden your awareness of dance as a performing art while developing your unique directions in dance. Doing so will ensure that you have the desire and skills to communicate your ideas through movement onstage and beyond.

DANCE GENRES

As a dancer, you probably prefer some dance genres and styles more than others. Each dance genre has its own **aesthetics,** which refers to the philosophical ideas that guide the work of a particular artist or dance genre. In many cases, there are many

dance forms or methodologies in a larger genre of dance, such as the techniques that exist in ballet. Additionally, dance genres are constantly changing in response to societal shifts and evolving through fusions between dance genres. Studying dance on campus affords a tremendous opportunity for you to gain in-depth knowledge in a particular dance genre while also gaining a larger understanding of various dance genres and how they are interrelated. Learning and experiencing how these genres are intertwined yet distinct allows you to further your dance understanding and creates numerous chances for you to develop as a dance artist through studying both preferred and unfamiliar dance genres.

Each dance genre has its own technique or movement vocabulary. The set of physical skills and intellectual understanding required to embody dance movement in a specific dance genre is called **technique. Movement vocabulary** builds on a genre's technique and includes common aesthetics, attributes, stylistic preferences, and dance movements linked to a given dance genre, choreographer, or dancer. Although the terms are interrelated, some genres use the word *technique* and others use the term *movement vocabulary* when discussing movement characteristics of the genre.

Just as each dance genre can include diverse movement, where and why the dance is performed can also vary. **Concert dance** refers to dance genres or specific dance works that are intended to be viewed by an audience in a formal theatrical setting. **Commercial dance** refers to dance genres as well as choreography that are entertainment oriented and can be seen in musicals, theme parks, movies, music videos, television, and industrial shows. Dances in which the main purpose is to interact with others in a social setting are called social dances, and dances that are not intended for public performance and are highly influenced by cultural traditions are called folk dances. Both folk and social dances can be adapted for concert or commercial dance settings. As you learn more about the history of various dance genres, you will see how these categories of dance are interrelated and influence each other.

Modern Dance

Modern dance is a concert dance genre that emerged in the early 20th century and continues to develop today. Throughout the history of modern dance, each generation has built on or challenged ideas of the previous generation to explore new directions in dance. Today, while studying dance on campus,

Tim Trumble.

● ● ● Exploring how the body creates movement and the inherent expressivity of movement are recurring themes in modern dance.

you may encounter several distinct styles of modern, postmodern, and contemporary modern dance.

Exploring how the body creates movement and the inherent expressivity of movement are recurring themes in modern dance. These ideals have manifested themselves in many expressions of movement, including the free and frolicking movements of Isadora Duncan, Martha Graham's use of contraction and release, the dynamic efficiency of Trisha Brown's movement, and the raw physicality of Elizabeth Streb's dance works. Floor work is common, as is a pronounced and dynamic relationship to gravity.

The technique and movement vocabulary of modern dance is vast and depends on the era and choreographer of a given style. Modern dance techniques developed out of choreographers' desires to create movement specific to their choreographic aims in the mid-1900s. Codified techniques, such as those developed by Martha Graham, José Limón, and Merce Cunningham fall into this category. The postmodern era began in the 1960s as choreographers questioned who could dance and where dance could take place. The movement vocabulary of this period incorporated pedestrian movements and embraced a tasklike, energetic quality. Today, modern dance is in the contemporary modern or postmodern contemporary era. Now, codified modern dance techniques and postmodern movement ideologies are combined with somatic methodologies and movements from

other dance genres to create eclectic movement vocabularies. Each strand in modern dance is seen as valuable and interrelated, and you will likely come across elements of each era when studying modern dance on campus.

Modern dance emphasizes experimentation and improvisation in creating choreography or movement compositions, although the object of experimentation varies. Modern dance choreographers explored how dance could communicate a variety of social and psychological themes. Postmodern choreographers questioned who could dance and the purpose of technique. Today's choreographers test the full range of human movement used in dance works from extremely minimal to extremely physical movement. Narrative, abstract, literal, and symbolic works all have a place in modern dance. In addition, choreographers and dancers often question the performance space. Today, modern dance works are created for public and virtual spaces as well as for the stage. The relationship between modern dance and music, sound, or silence is also open to experimentation. As the next generation of dance artists, it is up to you to help shape the next phase in the evolution of modern dance.

Ballet

Ballet is a concert dance genre that developed across the European courts in the 15th and 16th centuries. Ballet was formalized in France during the late

• • • Although ballet has a long history, it is constantly evolving.

1600s, which is why ballet uses French terminology. It gradually emerged as a concert dance genre across Europe. Ballet now exists in many parts of the world, with each geographic region adding its own distinct flair to the genre.

Most ballet movement emphasizes the external rotation of the legs at the thigh joint (called *turnout*), musicality, precision in shape and line, and creating the illusion of defying gravity. These characteristics can be seen in the use of pointe shoes starting in the romantic era, Marius Petipa's collaborations with composer Pyotr Ilich Tchaikovsky, the clarity and syncopation of George Balanchine's neoclassical movement, and the agility of contemporary ballet.

Ballet technique has evolved over several centuries. During that time, a general understanding of ballet technique has developed; in other words, a shared terminology and aesthetic exist in the genre. However, particular styles or teaching methodologies in the genre vary in movement quality and subtle differences in body positions and poses. For example, when performing an arabesque (a body position in which the dancer stands on one leg with the other leg extended behind the body), dancers trained in the Cecchetti method work to keep their shoulders directly above the hips, while dancers trained in the Balanchine technique open their hips to facilitate a larger range of movement, while contemporary ballet dancers may spiral or contract the torso. Even though the technique of each ballet style is still distinctively

ballet, the look and feel of each one reflects the range of ballet's history.

Although ballet has a long history, it is constantly evolving. Repertory includes works that are hundreds of years old, reinterpretations of the classics, and brand new pieces. Choreographically, ballet works include storybook narratives, dance works that explore structure and musicality, and dance works that are more abstract or experimental in nature. Typically, choreography aims to feature ballet technique and is designed to be performed on a proscenium stage. Contemporary ballet tends to incorporate more movement in the torso, parallel alignment of the legs, and movement from a range of dance genres, and it is currently gaining popularity. During your time studying dance on campus, you will be exposed to many different ideas about ballet and its application to your own dancing.

Jazz Dance and Tap Dance

Although jazz dance and tap dance are separate genres, they share a common history. Both are American dance genres that emerged from the blending of West African, Afro-Caribbean, and European dance genres in minstrel shows, vaudeville, and musical theater. They are both concert dance forms as well as commercial dance genres. In addition, they both emphasize a complementary relationship between movement and music.

Jazz Dance

Jazz dance's movement vocabulary is syncopated, propulsive, explodes outward from the center of the body, and is performed with a *weightedness* (clear connection to gravity). The movement's connection to music is always clear, and it can range from physically highlighting aspects of the music to having dancers contribute to the musical score through body percussion and vocalization.

Jazz dance includes many diverse approaches. Some companies and choreographers have been highly influenced by principles of modern dance and ballet. Luigi combined balletic movements with jazz dance to create what some call the first systematic approach to teaching jazz dance. Jack Cole, and later Gus Giordano, studied with many modern dance choreographers, which is reflected in their movement styles and choreographies. Still, other choreographers were inspired by popular culture. This can be seen in Bob Fosse's incorporation of popular dances, such as the frug, watusi, monkey, and other dances from the 1960s, into his choreography. Contemporary jazz dance expands on the attributes of earlier eras while still valuing the syncopation and musicality of earlier jazz dance styles. Essentially, jazz dance movement is characterized by its energetic and athletic qualities. It is likely that you will learn contemporary jazz dance as well as older jazz dance styles while studying jazz dance on campus.

Jazz dance choreography varies widely depending on where and why it is performed. In musical theater, choreography might be used to advance the musical's plot or to reveal additional information about a character. In commercial settings, jazz dance is viewed as entertaining and spectacular. When jazz dance is presented as concert dance, there may be a sense of experimentation present. Musicality is probably the most common thing jazz dance choreography shares across approaches and contexts. Although it can vary greatly, the relationship between the music and movement is usually clearly defined by the choreographer.

Tap Dance

Tap dance's most recognizable characteristic is perhaps its sound. As dancers move, the sounds of their shoes striking the floor provides a textured audio accompaniment to the movement and music (if used). The movement in tap dance is percussive, highly energetic, and rhythmically complex.

The tap dance genre has two main styles. The Broadway style focuses on the design of the whole body, meaning that the upper body is choreographed so that the head, arms, and torso are active in a stylized way. Broadway tap dancing is mostly used in musical theater, and it is featured in musicals such as *42nd Street*, *Anything Goes*, *Thoroughly Modern Millie*, and *Newsies* to name a few. While the Broadway style tends to be more *lifted* (upward in the use of

• • • Some jazz dance choreographers, such as Bob Fosse, have found inspiration in popular culture.

weight), rhythm tap is more *grounded* (downward in the use of weight). Rhythm tap, which is sometimes referred to as *jazz tap* or *hoofing,* focuses more on musicality and less on the design of the whole body. Many rhythm tap dancers consider themselves to be musicians as well as dancers. Notable rhythm tap dancers include Savion Glover, Sammy Davis, Jr., and Gregory Hines. Throughout tap dance's history, dancers have incorporated other styles of movement, such as Gene Kelly's integration of ballet and the Nicholas Brothers' incorporation of acrobatics. Today, tap dance continues to evolve, and it is common for tap dancers to be comfortable in both styles of tap dance as well as other dance genres.

Choreographically, tap dance embraces a wide range of approaches. Some choreographers, such as Brenda Bufalino, have made tap dance works for the concert stage. Savion Glover continues to experiment with musicality by improvising with musicians in live performances to test the boundaries of tap dance as a responsive, musical form. Tap dance remains a fundamental part of musical theater, where it helps to advance the plot of the musical by building energy and allowing characters to interact in new ways. Tap dance is also used as entertainment in theme parks; revues; and occasionally music videos, movies, and commercials. Depending on the context, tap dance can be seen as a concert dance, commercial dance, or even a social dance. While studying tap dance on campus, you will likely encounter a full range of styles and experiences.

Urban Dance Forms

Urban dance forms are part of urban culture, which includes graffiti art, emceeing, deejaying, and dance. Urban dance forms developed primarily in densely populated urban areas such as New York and Los Angeles. They emerged from disenfranchised populations and functioned as a mouthpiece for expression beginning in the 1970s. Urban dance forms can occur onstage, in community events (such as battles and festivals), in music videos, in movies, and on television. Although it is very entertaining to watch, it is important to remember the sociocultural aspects and purpose of self-expression in urban dance forms.

The range of styles in the urban genre is very wide; however, each style values precision, isolation, clear connection to the music, and the importance of freestyling (improvisation sets). It is expected that dancers will have their own movement signatures, which are expressed both through the styles they study as well as the development of personal movement vocabularies.

The urban dance genre includes breaking, waacking, and house dancing, among others. Breaking, sometimes referred to as b-boying or b-girling, started as a street dance and involves performing top rocking, power moves, freezes, and other movements, typically to the break beat of a hip-hop song. Waacking, which uses complex and fast arm and upper-body movement and footwork, was originally performed to disco music. Although waacking developed in the gay com-

"Yes, Indeed!" by Bill Evans; courtesy of The College at Brockport (photo: Christopher Duggan)

• • • The movement in tap dance is percussive, highly energetic, and rhythmically complex.

EPIK Dance Company. Photo by Nightfuse.com.

● ● ● Urban dance forms can occur on stage, in community events, in music videos, in movies, and on television.

munities of the 1970s and '80s, today it is performed by diverse communities. House dancing developed alongside house music in the post-disco era. House dancing can be characterized by its complex and fast footwork, "jacking" movement in the upper torso, and a sense of buoyancy in the spine.

Freestyling plays a large role in urban dance forms. In community settings, cyphers commonly occur. A **cypher** is a circle of dancers that allows space for one or more dancers to freestyle in the center. As dancers enter the cypher, they improvise in response to the music, other dancers, and the energy of the event. Often dancers start their freestyling with a short choreographed phrase that emphasizes their individuality. Choreography varies widely from style to style, but it is frequently used to feature the dancers' personal movement vocabularies and exhibits a heightened sense of musicality. When studying urban dance forms on campus, you can expect to learn about specific forms of urban dance as well as additional aspects of urban culture.

ARTISTIC ROLES AND CAREERS IN DANCE

In each dance genre, common artistic roles are present in the development and performance of a dance work. Most dance performances involve dance performers, choreographers, artistic directors, and performing arts presenters. Each person involved in the development and presentation of a dance work has a different yet equally important contribution to the overall product. Although the roles can be distinct, at times significant overlap exists and it is not uncommon for a person to assume multiple roles simultaneously. In fact, the ability to "wear multiple hats" is incredibly beneficial because it permits you to more fully engage in the development of a dance work from the initial inspiration to the final performance. Fully understanding the responsibilities of dance performers, choreographers, artistic directors, and performing arts presenters gives you an awareness of how each role contributes to the making and performing of dance works.

Dance Performer

Dance performers execute choreographies, structured improvisations, or movement compositions in performance settings. They are involved in the rehearsal, development, and performance of work, either onstage or in another venue. Some dance performers find it incredibly rewarding to work with one dance company for years, while others prefer to work with multiple choreographers simultaneously.

Dance performers need the facility to quickly learn and embody dance movement with attention to nuance, qualitative accuracy, and musical sensitivity. It is important that performers be able to make the choreography their own while also maintaining the integrity and intent of the original material. In some situations, dance performers are expected to create and contribute movement phrases and ideas to the choreographic development of a work. Additionally, dance performers need a

Engaging WITH Dance

Adrian Skrentny (Dance Performer)

As a dancer in Los Angeles, I have many opportunities with varying levels of stability, compensation, and recognition. The music industry employs dancers for music videos, tours, and television performances. Hundreds of dance performers compete for very few spots, and although the pay can be great for tours, a dance performer needs to book gigs frequently to make a decent living. Stage productions and theme parks offer more consistent employment for dance performers. The onslaught of television talent shows can garner a dancer individual notoriety and career opportunities.

Dance performers often begin taking classes in Hollywood and performing with rising choreographers in local nightclubs. After paying dues, performing, and making connections, dance performers can become assistant choreographers and eventually choreographers or directors. Often dance performers with a good business sense also make great agents.

Los Angeles is extremely competitive. Success is based on image, personality, and skill. Timing is everything; agents fill their rosters with the type of dance performer that is in demand. There are many dance studios for adults with high-quality classes and a variety of options for studio rentals.

While in college, you can prepare yourself by taking technique classes in a variety of dance styles. Viable competitors have excellent technique, a repertoire of stunts, and perform frequently. It is critical to build stage presence and personality early on; this allows a dancer to stand out and be noticed by agents, choreographers, and casting directors.

© Dina Petringa

high level of performance presence and the abilities to work well both with their fellow performers and independently. The life of a dance performer can be very demanding, making time management, organization, self-responsibility, and follow-through essential skills for success.

Choreographer

Choreographers are people who take a dance from an image or idea to a completed performance. They are constantly called on to communicate their ideas and movements to others, such as dance performers, production designers, and audiences. Some choreographers start their own dance companies, whereas others prefer to work on a project basis. Fundamentally, choreographers, or dance makers, are people who create dances to share with others.

The talent to create movement, establish positive rehearsal environments, engage an audience, and articulate a distinctive viewpoint is essential. Because choreographers are constantly developing and explaining their ideas, they need excellent communication and leadership skills. Additionally,

choreographers must be able to relate to others so that they can create an open rehearsal environment for dancers and other collaborators.

Artistic Director

In general, an **artistic director** is responsible for imagining, developing, and implementing the artistic goals of an organization such as a dance company. The artistic director makes important decisions about the evolution of a dance company in terms of artistic vision, and communicates with administrators within and outside the organization. Briefly, the artistic director shapes the artistic goals of a dance organization.

Some artistic directors have been performers or choreographers. The important qualities for this job are leadership, the ability to collaborate, and vision. Artistic directors are primarily responsible for sustaining and evolving the artistic content and creative approach for their organizations, so they need to be able to implement artistic plans, develop audiences, and seek out new artistic talent to meet their organizations' goals.

Engaging WITH Dance

Kristy Schupp (Musical Theater Choreographer)

As a freelance musical theater choreographer, you must be able and willing to work on any project that comes your way. There are times when I am choreographing two high school musicals and working on a professional show at the same time. You need to understand the level of dance ability that each cast presents. Making sure that you choreograph for your cast is important. Not all professional actors are dancers; you have to learn how to make the choreography work well for your cast.

The more styles of dance you know, the more jobs you will be hired for. You could be hired to choreograph anything from a waltz in a Shakespeare play, to a pub dance in a classic Irish play, to a full musical. Dance in a musical theater piece helps push the plot along and tell the story. You always have to remember that your job as a musical theater choreographer is to tell the story. Therefore, you need a wide understanding of dance styles so that you can work on a variety of musicals and successfully tell the story.

In college, make sure you perform in musicals while developing your dance technique. Explore different types of dance; you never know what may pop up in a musical. Be sure to study the great musical theater choreographers. Many times you will be hired to work on a show that is known for its original choreography, and you will need to make sure that your work reflects that. Also, keep up on your dance history. Again, choreography needs to help tell the story, so if hired to work on a show that takes place in the 1950s, your work needs to be faithful to that time period.

Besides dance skills and choreography, people skills are a must. In musical theater, you are not working by yourself; you are part of a team. The ability to work well with the director and designers is important. Directors usually get to pick their choreographers, so establishing good working relationships will help get you jobs in the future. Time management is also important. You have to share rehearsal time with the vocal director and stage director, so you need to make sure you can teach what is needed in your allotted time.

Working as a musical theater choreographer takes a lot of time and hard work. However, when you get to sit in the audience on opening night and see your work onstage, it is all worth it.

Chris Cavanagh

Performing Arts Presenter

A person who connects performing artists with audiences is called a **performing arts presenter.** Performing arts presenters may select different dance works for festivals or dance companies to perform as part of a performing arts season. Some performing arts presenters also connect dance artists to different educational opportunities such as residencies and cultural exchanges. A performing arts presenter usually works for a presenting agency, such as a theater or performing arts organization, and not a dance company.

Performing arts presenters need strong artistic visions and the aptitude to design and implement plans to promote that vision. Additionally, the ability to respect the individual artistic values of each artist they work with while also balancing the obligations of their presenting agencies is essential. Performing arts presenters provide opportunities for artists to share their work with a larger audience, so the capability to communicate with audiences as well as dancers is a necessity.

PERFORMANCE OPPORTUNITIES

The range of performance opportunities in dance demonstrates the breadth of dance as an artistic discipline. Performance opportunities in dance range from creating and performing concert dance works for the

Engaging WITH Dance

Matt Pardo (Dance Performer)

Each dance company operates within its own structure. Most begin their rehearsal days with company class. This time not only serves as a physical warm-up for the body, it also allows the dancers a chance to come together as a cohesive unit. The day continues with rehearsal for whatever project the company is working on at that time. If you dance for a repertory company and are not working with a new choreographer, you will most likely spend the day learning old or current repertory from either the rehearsal director or videos. This rehearsal process is where you work to present yourself as an artist in the context of a choreographer's vision, making deliberate choices to make the piece your own. Developing your individual involvement in a piece is one of the most exciting journeys you will embark on as a dancer as you experience the piece from

Photo courtesy of Ruben Graciani.

the first rehearsal to the finished product that appears before audiences on opening night.

If the company you are working with is a pickup company (company that hires dancers per project as opposed to a contract of length), then company class will most likely not be given and the structure of the rehearsal itself may change based on the needs of the choreographer setting the piece or the dancers learning it.

Whatever the daily structure of the company, it is important as a prospective dancer to realize that although we all love performing and being onstage, most of a professional dancer's life is spent in a rehearsal studio. Performing may be fun, but the collaborative experience of bringing a piece of art to fruition with the other dancers or choreographer you are working with, is a truly profound experience.

stage as a member of a dance company, to working on a project basis, to performing in industrial shows and music videos. Each type of performance experience is valuable to the development of dance as an art form and can enhance your dance understanding.

Concert Dance

In previous generations, many dancers aspired to either join or start a dance company. Although dance companies continue to exist, and several are well established, many of today's dancers work project to project as freelance artists instead of as company members. As you familiarize yourself with the roles and careers in dance, it is helpful to become aware of the various performance opportunities available.

Dance Companies

A **dance company** is a group of dance performers, other artists, and administrators who work together to create and perform dance. Dance companies exist across dance genres and serve numerous purposes in the field of dance and in society.

Dance companies can range in size from 4 dance performers to over 70. Many dance companies were created to facilitate the vision of a choreographer. In this model, the majority of the work performed is created by the company's namesake. There are also repertory dance companies, where the work performed comes from a variety of choreographers. Some dance companies make and perform work exclusively for the stage, while others are equally active in community dance projects. There are dance companies that tour nationally and internationally, dance companies that present four or five performances a year in their regional community, and companies that perform once a year. Dance companies can be unionized, meaning that dance performers are members of the American Guild of Musical Artists, but most are not unionized.

Nationally and internationally known dance companies are diverse in size and purpose, but they are characterized by a large amount of performing. Dance performers who work with a nationally or internationally known dance company can expect perform on tour as well as in the company's local community. Performing or working with a nationally or internationally known dance company is very time intensive, but is also tremendously rewarding.

Throughout the United States, you will find a variety of regional dance companies. They range from established and well-known dance companies to emerging, loose collectives of dance performers and choreographers. Regional companies can also tour, but they tend to focus their energy on performing in their local communities and geographic regions. The work can be just as challenging as the work in a nationally or internationally known company.

Many university and college dance programs have dance companies that serve as a training ground for college students who want the experience of performing and working in a dance company. In university or college dance companies, students have the opportunity to perform works created by guest artists, faculty, and their peers. Being a member of your college dance company gives you the chance to hone your performance and choreography skills in a challenging and safe way.

Project-Based Dancing

Working on a **project basis** means that you are commissioned to collaborate, as a performer or choreographer, on a single project rather than joining an established dance company. This way of working can create more diverse dance experiences. Some dancers are able to work on multiple projects at the same time. Working as a freelance artist on a project basis might allow you to act as a choreographer of your own project while dancing in another project, to dance in multiple projects at the same time, or to work as a performer while pursuing another dance interest. In a commercial dance context, dancers might pursue several short-term opportunities and find themselves performing on a cruise ship for 9 months, then dancing in a series of industrial jobs, and then joining a national tour.

Dancers who work on a project basis must be adaptable. In the company model, dancers frequently perform with the same company for many years and as a result become highly proficient in that company's movement vocabulary. Project dancers have to quickly adapt from the style of one choreographer to the next. Dancers who work on a project basis often develop their own means of maintaining their technique, which allows them to be versatile movers.

Working as a freelance dancer or choreographer on a project basis can lead you to a wealth of artistic experiences. You can replicate this experience while studying dance on campus by working on a variety of dance performance projects with your peers, faculty, and guest artists. Self-discipline, time management, and adaptability are central to success. Therefore, it is important to develop these skills while on campus.

Engaging WITH Dance

Catherine Baggs (Dance Performer)

Roy Cox - photographer

I traveled the world at 22 while performing for thousands of people during my time at Disney Cruise Lines (DCL). On each cruise, I performed a rotating repertoire of shows and witnessed the joy of cruisers while escorting Disney characters around the ship. I took that energy with me on my daily breaks, which was when I was able to explore whatever port we were docked in or take advantage of most guest amenities—a perk for entertainment.

DCL holds auditions throughout the year. To prepare, I recommend attending as many dance auditions and classes as possible and being comfortable singing. I attended a dance call, in which I learned a short jazz combination. Following two cuts, the remaining dancers were asked to sing. I made it through the final cut and signed preliminary paperwork that day. I received my official contract offer 3 months later.

Contracts are nonunion; however, some of the cast had equity permission contracts. A typical contract is 8 to 10 months, and the first 2 months are spent rehearsing in Toronto. Housing, travel, and health care during rehearsal are covered; once on the ship, meals are also included. A contract completion bonus is awarded at the end of a successful contract. Working for DCL broadened my horizons as a performer and allowed me to fulfill a lifelong dream of traveling the world as a performer.

Commercial Dance

Commercial dance can be performed in musical theater, film, television, music videos, theme parks, cruise ships, and industrial shows. Although some of these jobs can provide consistent work and good pay, many dancers interested in working commercially find that they need to book several short-term or one-time performance opportunities to feel fulfilled artistically and financially.

Dance performers who work in commercial dance tend to be "triple threats," meaning that besides dancing, they also sing and act. Additional skills, such as acrobatics and advanced partnering, are commonly required. If you are interested in pursuing commercial dance, you should take advantage of classes in other departments, such as theater and music, while studying dance on campus.

It is common for dance performers interested in musical theater, film, or television to have an agent. An **agent** is either a person or business that represents you to choreographers and directors to help advance your career. Dance performers who work in commercial dance sometimes join unions—either Actors' Equity Association or SAG-AFTRA (formed through the merging of the Screen Actors Guild and the American Federation of Television and Radio Artists)—as they book jobs that take place in a Broadway theater or on screen. Building a career in commercial dance takes keen business sense, so it is best to develop networking, budgeting, and marketing skills while on campus if you are interested in commercial dance.

CURRENT TRENDS IN DANCE AND THE ARTS

New trends in dance are constantly emerging, and there are plenty of opportunities for you to make and discover in the artistic realm of dance. Today, many dance artists are interested in assuming a variety of roles in dance, blurring the lines between dance genres, questioning assumptions about dance, and creating new opportunities. Gaining an awareness of these trends better prepares you for your future in dance.

Wearing Different Hats

In dance, it is increasingly common for artists to work as dance performers and choreographers, choreographers and artistic directors, or in any combination of artistic roles. For some, the artistic roles they assume changes from project to project or evolves over the span of their careers. Other dancers find themselves simultaneously in two or more artistic roles due to interest or necessity. As the dance field continues to advance, the lines between these artistic roles are dissolving. Furthermore, dancers frequently find themselves engaging with dance in other ways such as teaching or working in an administrative capacity while pursuing careers as dance performers and choreographers. Fully investigating many areas of dance during your time on campus will prepare you to create your own opportunities as a professional artist.

Blurred Lines

Today, more and more dance artists are intentionally or unintentionally blending dance genres to better express their ideas. Although dancers may deeply identify with one particular dance form, most are curious about or practice more than one. In the contemporary dance field, this diversity of interest is reflected in the work that is made and performed. This fusion ranges from studying multiple genres of dance to gain a fuller understanding of dance movement to actively blending dance genres to create a personal movement vocabulary.

The fusion of dance genres has long existed in dance, but it is more common today than ever before. Choreographers and dance performers frequently create movement vocabularies that reflect their personal dance interests and training through combining distinct dance genres. Some dancers are able to find success in multiple dance genres. Gaining a broad understanding of dance genres and styles while on campus can provide you with wider knowledge of dance movement as well as increased career opportunities in the professional field. As much as possible, you should study dance widely, even if there are one or two dance genres that you study deeply, to expand your knowledge of dance.

Questioning Assumptions

Artists are always questioning the rules of their art form to challenge themselves and to contribute to the progression of the art form. Today, many dance artists find themselves questioning what is and what is not dance, or what belongs and does not belong in a specific dance genre or style. It is often easier to appreciate the evolution of dance in retrospect, but it is important as a young artist to start questioning your assumptions about dance and different dance genres. This questioning allows your dance artistry to mature.

Some dance work created today actively addresses these questions. Classical ballet fans may question

Engaging WITH Dance

Jordan Kriston (Dance Performer)

As a college dance student, it is important to believe not only that studying dance teaches you about the art but also that it has a real place in the professional world. I've learned from working in the field that having an "intention" is essential. When I have an intention in dance I know what I'm doing, what I want, and what I'm trying to say, which also serves as a reflective learning tool. I've found the more I practice this in dance, the more it carries over to my everyday life. Each person finds his or her reasons to choose a career in dance, and I think being aware of this is crucial in staying focused.

Take advantage of all the courses you are curious about inside and outside of dance. Take improvisation classes as much as you can. Being interested in multiple things broadens your perspective and gives you more inspiration. Many choreographers rely heavily on their dancers to generate movement, so you must know how to contribute artistically. You have to learn to think for yourself and add to the process. Improvisation helps this immensely.

Taking summer workshops is a great way to boost your dancing. Aside from being a lot of fun, this concentrated dose of dance will strengthen your technique and artistry and provide a taste of what your days will feel like as a professional dancer. Workshops and festivals will connect you to people in the dance world and give your dance career a head start. The dance world is small, and the people you meet at these places will most likely end up being your professional colleagues, so the relationships made here are important.

After graduating, there are many avenues a dancer can take. The two avenues I can speak on from experience are dancing for a major dance company and working on a project basis.

Dancing for a major touring dance company is nice in that it is your only job and it is stable as

long as your body and relationship with the company stay intact. This is an amazing opportunity to see the world and have job security, but it comes at a price: for those touring years, your job is your entire life. What makes it worth it is having the chance to inspire thousands of people each week while on the road. It feels good to hear audiences tell you about how much your show meant to them. Your life will always have movement, and getting to meet people from all over, teaching master classes, and learning a lot about yourself and others are a few of the many benefits of dancing with a major company.

Working on a project basis, or freelancing, involves working for two or more choreographers at once and doing single projects rather than entire seasons. It is typical for choreographers to rehire you if they like you, and as time goes on, work will get steadier. Freelancing requires a lot of schedule shuffling and planning ahead. The great thing about it is that you are always working on something new with new people, and the schedule is flexible because you may say yes or no to any project. The hard part is that work isn't always available, so you have to stay on your toes as far as securing yourself financially. It forces you to be comfortable in unpredictable situations and creative in how you build your schedule; I actually found this exciting.

Your college years fly by! Be wise enough to take advantage of what is available while you are in school. Once you graduate, the main thing propelling you forward is going to be you. Understand that there is not just a want for dance in the world—there is a need. You have to believe in this idea, believe in yourself, and believe in what you are doing. Figure out your truth about why you dance, and as long as you have tenacity, passion, and persistence it will lead you to your ever-evolving place in the world of dance.

Photo by Oriel Pe'er.

contemporary ballet works as too modern because of the use of improvisation, modern dance movements, and spoken text. Yet others may not recognize contemporary jazz dance as jazz dance because the use of isolation and syncopation is very different from the jazz dance of 30 years ago. Some urban dance forms did not even exist 20 years ago. In each of these examples, dancers and choreographers are taking artistic risks, which lead to inventive choreography and movement. Challenging your assumptions about dance and art is central to growing as an artist. It is also directly in line with contemporary dance trends, which are focused on pushing the boundaries of what is permissible in dance.

New Opportunities

Of course, numerous opportunities exist in dance that cannot be described because they have not yet been created. This is where you, as a future member of the professional dance world, need to be proactive.

The trends and career types discussed in this chapter rely on a shared set of characteristics and abilities. Developing a successful career strategy takes creativity, leadership skills, the ability to relate to others, self-knowledge, and entrepreneurial awareness, as well as a solid understanding of what has happened and is currently happening in the professional field. A constant drive to challenge yourself artistically and to learn more about dance is imperative to your artistic growth. Cultivating these skills will allow you to use your dance knowledge in a variety of ways in a diversity of settings.

Luckily, studying dance can implicitly and explicitly enhance these skills. This is why it is important that you pay attention to what skills you are using as you take classes. Each time you choreograph dances for your peers, teach young children, and write dance research papers you are developing creativity, critical thinking, leadership skills, people skills, and the ability to thoughtfully self-reflect. Every experience you have studying dance on campus contributes to your dance knowledge and skills.

TAKING THE STAGE

Each time you perform dance, whether it be in a technique class or onstage, you are expressing your personal artistry. As you choreograph dances and organize dance performances or events, you are developing essential artistic skills. You are currently active as a dance artist, but it is necessary that you actively seek opportunities to expand your artistic development while studying dance on campus.

Your Artistic Development

If you are interested in performing as a dancer, you should actively seek and create situations to practice your performance skills. As you take technique and movement classes, you can look for chances to enhance performance skills related to musicality, nuance, and qualitative sensitivity when performing class material. You can volunteer to dance in works choreographed by your peers, and you can audition for guest artists' residencies. As you assess your current strengths as a dancer, look for ways to challenge your weaknesses. While challenging yourself in this way can be difficult at first, the more you proactively seek ways to increase your dance understanding, the more you will learn about yourself and about dance. If you are primarily comfortable performing solo work, you should find opportunities to dance as part of a group. If you are only familiar with performing set choreography, you should find or create projects that require improvisation. As a student studying dance on campus, some dance performance opportunities will be made available to you. Supplementing these performances with opportunities that you seek and create will give you a wealth of experiences to learn from.

Students interested in choreography should also be proactive. Most students studying dance on campus will be required to enroll in choreography, composition, or other creative classes. If you are truly interested in becoming a choreographer, you should consistently make and share dances. These can range from a series of small studies to an ongoing project that you are constantly revisiting and revising. As an emerging choreographer, you need to assess your strengths and then challenge your weaknesses in composing dances. If your experience has been focused on making short dances for the stage, it would be a good challenge to create a longer piece for a different performance space. If you are comfortable improvising in response to music, you may benefit from improvising and choreographing in silence. The more you can challenge yourself creatively in and outside of your choreography and creative classes, the broader a foundation you will have to build from upon graduation.

Students who are interested in artistic direction or performing arts presenting can benefit from producing or working on dance events both within and outside their dance departments in a variety of capacities. Taking the initiative to solicit, organize, and produce a dance event requires vision, organization, and follow-through. Additionally, working on a dance performance or event is an excellent way to collaborate with students interested in performance, choreography, or other disciplines. Many schools have organizations that bring students from different artistic disciplines together to discuss, collaborate on, and present student works. Becoming involved in an interdisciplinary student organization provides a wide awareness of the arts to build on as a future performing arts presenter or artistic director.

Relating to Current Trends

Even though you are just beginning your academic pursuit of dance, you are already involved in the current dance field. Many students tend to think of the professional dance field and current trends as outside of their study of dance on campus. The more you can think of yourself as an active participant in the current and future field of dance, the more beneficial your study of dance on campus can be.

As you learn about contemporary trends and artists in dance, there will be some with which you closely identify. Your dance curriculum aims to give you a broad understanding of dance, which means that at times there is not enough class time to go into great detail about an artist that really speaks to you. Try to view this as a chance for you to independently learn more about artists and ideas that interest you. Take the time to personalize your dance education on your own outside of class so that your dance education is rich and personally relevant.

This chapter has mentioned many dance artists' roles and dance genres or styles. It is likely that you know very much about some of them. However, it is probable that one or more of these roles or genres piqued your interest. If that is the case, you can learn more about these artists and dance styles through asking your instructors or exploring via the Internet. Your faculty are often eager to help you learn more about individual artists and artistic trends that inspire you. Pay attention to what excites you, and then follow through. This is the best way to develop as a dance artist in a way that is specific and meaningful to you.

SUMMARY

Artistry is central to dance. Many students studying dance on campus aspire to work as dance performers, choreographers, or both; or to contribute in another way to the artistic realm of dance. Regardless of the dance styles that you are interested in, maturing as a dance artist depends on understanding the various artistic roles in dance, how dance genres relate, and current trends in the professional dance world. The more opportunities you can find and create to learn about dance genres, to practice performing and choreographing, and to learn more about current artists who interest you, the more rich and rewarding your dance education will be. Additionally, taking this approach will allow you to continuously deepen your dance artistry while on campus and beyond.

REVIEW QUESTIONS

1. What are the main similarities between modern dance, ballet, jazz dance, tap dance, and urban dance forms? What makes each dance genre unique?

2. Briefly summarize the responsibilities of each of the following: dance performer, choreographer, artistic director, performing arts presenter. What aptitudes are needed in order to be successful in each area?

3. Discuss the benefits and challenges of working with a dance company, on a project basis, and commercially in the field of dance. How do these approaches relate to your dance career goals?

4. Give two examples of how a contemporary dance artist or dance company is challenging your expectations of a dance genre. In your opinion, are these challenges strengthening or weakening artistic development in that dance genre? How do these challenges relate to the current trends discussed in this chapter?

GLOSSARY

aesthetics—The ideas that guide the work of a particular artist or dance genre.

agent—A person or business that represents you to choreographers and directors to help you advance your career.

artistic director—The person responsible for imagining, developing, and implementing the artistic goals of an organization such as a dance company.

choreographers—People who take a dance from an image or idea to a completed performance; people who make dances.

commercial dance—Dance genres as well as choreographic works that are entertainment oriented and can be seen in musicals, movies, music videos, television, and industrial shows.

concert dance—Dance genres and dance works that are presented to an audience in a formal theatrical setting.

cypher—A circle of dancers that allows space for one or more dancers to freestyle in the center.

dance artists—People who make art through and with movement.

dance company—A dance company is a group of dance performers, other artists, and administrators who work together to create and perform dance. Dance companies exist across dance genres and serve numerous purposes in the field of dance and in society.

dance performer—Someone who executes choreographies, structured improvisations, or movement compositions in performance settings.

movement vocabulary—The common aesthetics, attributes, stylistic preferences, and dance movements linked to a given dance genre, choreographer, or dancer.

performing arts presenter—An arts administrator who connects performing artists with audiences.

project basis—A commission to collaborate, as a performer or choreographer, on a single project rather than joining an established dance company.

technique—The set of physical skills and intellectual understanding developed and used to embody dance movement in a specific dance genre.

BIBLIOGRAPHY

Anderson, J. (1992). *Ballet and modern dance: A concise history*. Princeton, NJ: Princeton Books.

Bales, M., & Nettl-Fiol, R. (Eds.). (2008). *The body eclectic: Evolving practices in dance training*. Chicago, IL: University of Illinois Press.

Banes, S. (1994). *Writing dancing in the age of postmodernism*. Hanover, NH: Wesleyan University Press.

Banes, S. (1987). *Terpsichore in sneakers: Post-modern dance*. Hanover, NH: Wesleyan University Press.

Chang, J. (2005). *Can't stop won't stop: A history of the hip-hop generation*. New York: St. Martin's Press.

Fletcher, B. (2002). *Tapworks: A tap dictionary and reference manual*. Princeton, NJ: Princeton Books.

Noisette, P. (2010). *Let's talk about contemporary dance*. Paris: Flammarion.

Stearns, M., & Stearns, J. (1994). *Jazz dance: The story of American vernacular dance*. New York: Da Capo Press.

CHAPTER •••• **6** ••••

Dance and Culture

LEARNING OUTCOMES

After reading this chapter, you will be able to do the following:

- Define and describe key terms in the study of dance and culture.
- Examine ways that dance can reflect culture.
- Discuss contemporary trends relating to dance and culture.
- Identify careers that advance the understanding of dance and culture.
- Outline steps to proactively explore dance and culture.

Throughout human history, people have danced to connect with each other, to celebrate, to mourn, and to develop a sense of identity. Dance can portray countless stories and ideas, occurs in a variety of settings, and is performed by people of different ages, abilities, communities, and cultures. As you study dance on campus, you may be surprised by the diversity of dance genres performed around the world. Studying dance on campus gives you the opportunity to deepen your dance studies through examining how dance reflects or challenges cultural values while also learning about dance genres from around the world.

Chapter 6 introduces you to dance and culture. You will learn key terms and definitions for discussing dance and culture. This chapter introduces ways to examine the relationships between dance and culture. You will learn about careers that advance the understanding of dance and culture as well as contemporary trends. Lastly, you will determine ways to increase your knowledge of dance and culture while studying dance on campus. By the end of the chapter, you will be better prepared to consider how the dance genres you study as well as dance genres from around the world relate to culture.

Dance is an important part of many cultures. Cultural traditions, including dance, demonstrate the values of their communities and provide a way for people to connect. All people have traditions and customs that they associate with their families, cultural heritage, and local communities. For example, step dancers, such as those in the photograph, dance to express solidarity, whereas lindy hoppers socialize with each other through dancing. Folkloric dance provides a way for dancers to convey pride in their cultural heritage, and liturgical dance is a way for dancers to express their religious beliefs through dance. Each of these dance genres illustrates a different purpose for dance and expresses cultural values. While studying dance on campus, you have a tremendous opportunity to learn about the intersections of dance and culture while learning about dance genres from around the world. This will help you see how all dances are cultural dances, including the dance genres you currently study. Gaining a global understanding of dance will prepare you to engage with dance in diverse ways.

LINKING DANCE AND CULTURE

When considering the scope of dance genres around the world it is important to use a broad definition of dance. Joann Kealiinohomoku, a dance anthropologist and ethnographer, provides a definition of dance that is inclusive of the differences in dance genres around the world. Kealiinohomoku defines dance as a "transient mode of expression" performed by humans through deliberately selecting movements in a specific dance genre; the resulting dance is acknowledged as such by both the performer and the observers of a given culture (Kealiinohomoku 1983, p. 541). The breadth of this definition does not privilege the stylistic attributes of one dance genre over another and can help you start to see how dance genres connect to culture.

Kealiinohomoku's definition of dance recognizes the link between dance and culture. **Culture** consists of the symbolic aspects, beliefs, behaviors, and customs of a specific group of people. The term **cultural** denotes arts, traditions, and ways of life that relate to a specific culture. By integrating a broad definition of dance, such as Kealiinohomoku's, with a comprehensive definition of culture, you can see how different aspects of dance genres, such as the movements, music, and themes of a dance, mirror the values, traditions, and ways of life of a specific group of people.

Learning how dance reflects culture and how culture shapes dance is critical to gaining a full awareness of the multifariousness of dance. The cultures around the world are diverse, which means the dance genres performed across the globe are equally rich and varied. Identifying and understanding different purposes and ways that dance connects to culture provides a gateway to respecting the diversity of dance genres present in a multicultural world.

CULTURAL CATEGORIES OF DANCE

Although dance genres are varied across the globe, some shared categories of dance exist across cultures. Some dance genres clearly fall into one category, while other dance genres may cross categories. Still other dance genres may change from category to category throughout history. Therefore, it is important to recognize that considerable overlap can exist between the categories. Familiarizing yourself with cultural categories of dance assists in your investigation of dance in a given culture.

Ceremonial Dance

Dance is often used to highlight the importance of an occasion or to solidify a group identity. In **cer-**

Matt Crossick/Press Association Images

● ● ● The cultures around the world are diverse, which means the dance genres performed across the globe are equally rich and varied.

emonial dances the primary purpose is to display a group identity as well as individual rank in a secular or sacred setting. Performers are usually limited to a specific social or cultural group. Ceremonial dances can be performed to celebrate rites of passage; to demonstrate national, regional, or local identity; or to honor political events.

Stepping, also known as step-dancing, can be considered a ceremonial dance. Stepping is a percussive and intricate dance genre that uses the body and voice as percussive instruments. Dancers clap, stomp, use spoken word, and execute precise full body movement to simultaneously create dance and music. Usually performed in groups, stepping draws on African American traditions of using movement and sounds to demonstrate loyalty to a group. Stepping has been part of African American fraternity and sorority life for decades, although it is now expanding to new communities. Through stepping, dance performers express their solidarity as a group to others.

Ritual Dance

In some cultures, **ritual dance** serves as a way for people to connect with the spiritual realm and is used in religious ceremonies. This connection can occur in many different ways. Dancers may portray characters from sacred teachings, or they may become possessed by supernatural beings through dancing. Regardless of how dancers create a union with the spiritual realm, dance can have a powerful place in religious ceremonies.

An example of a ritual dance is liturgical dance. Liturgical dance refers to a dance that is part of a worship service. Although dance has a long historical presence in churches and synagogues, liturgical dance is currently increasing in popularity across various Christian and Jewish religious ceremonies as a way to create moving experiences for congregation members. Movement in liturgical dance is drawn from a variety of sources, including modern dance, ballet, and jazz dance, as well as elements of acting and mime. The dance performers and congregation members recognize liturgical dance as a way to communicate with the divine and to express their religious beliefs.

Social Dance

Many cultures recognize that dancing is a way to socially interact with others. **Social dance** refers to dance genres that occur in social, secular settings. From birthday parties to weddings to formal balls, social dance genres typically use an agreed-on set of movements that dancers, either individually or with a partner, can perform as they wish. **Folk dance** refers to dances that were developed and performed by "the folk" (the peasant citizens of a society). Many folk dances are considered to be social dances. Social and folk dances can be learned informally or formally, and they can be performed by novices and professionals alike.

The lindy hop, sometimes referred to as swing dance, is an American social dance genre that is known worldwide. Performed in pairs, traditionally

Engaging WITH Dance

Chareka Daniel (Liturgical Dance Performer)

Unlike many other dancers, I did not start my training at a studio, school, or recreational center; I started in my living room. Growing up with many disadvantages forced me to miss out on so many opportunities to engage with dance. Attending high school was life changing for me, because that was when I was first introduced to liturgical dance. Liturgical dance became my foundation. It allowed me to freely express myself without having any expectation or pressure to look a certain way. One thing I enjoy about liturgical dance is that it incorporates several dance genres, such as West African and jazz dance. In addition, having a strong community was something I longed for as an adolescent, and participating in liturgical dance created a bond among the dancers that has lasted a lifetime. Before any rehearsals or performances we would always pray and check in with each other, and there was always a strong sense of unity among the group. Having this mindset not only empowered us as a group but allowed us to dance with so much joy, freedom, and passion.

Photo courtesy of Chareka Daniel.

by a man and woman with the man leading, the lindy hop uses a shared set of movements as well as improvisation. The lindy hop started in 1920s Harlem, and it drew from previously popular social dances and blossomed alongside jazz music. Although the lindy hop is over 90 years old, people young and old still participate in this fun and, at times, acrobatic dance genre as a way to socially interact.

Theatrical Dance

The intent of many dance genres is to present dances in a theatrical setting. **Theatrical dance** includes dance genres and dances that aim to entertain an audience, to articulate an artistic viewpoint, or to educate an audience. The concert and commercial dance genres discussed in chapter 5 are considered theatrical dance, as are many dance genres around the world.

Folkloric dance (called *baile folklórico* in Spanish) is a Mexican dance genre that draws on indigenous dances to create dance performances for an audience. Established in 1952, Ballet Folklórico de México is one of the most famous folkloric dance ensembles in the world. Founder Amalia Hernández creates dance works based on traditional dances from various historical periods and regions but reshapes them for theatrical settings and contemporary audiences. Most folkloric dance ensembles and choreographers follow this model. In the United States, folkloric dance is performed as a way to demonstrate respect for and awareness of Mexican heritage. Audience members and dance performers recognize that folkloric dance creates a sense of pride, can be educational, and is enjoyable to perform and observe.

VALUING DIVERSITY

When you recognize dance as a part of culture, you can discover how a given culture's values and traditions shape dance, dances, and the various roles of dance in a given society. You will see how dance genres evolve over time in response to shifting cultural values, how fusions abound in dance, and how the boundaries between dance genres and categories are very porous.

Situating dance in a culture can help you appreciate diverse dance genres that may be unfamiliar to you. The more you can keep in mind that each dance genre has a deep history and reflects its cultural heritage through movements, purposes, music, and participants, the less likely you are to dismiss a dance genre as "weird" or "not dance." Opening yourself up to the wide range of cultural contexts and dance genres can help you respect unfamiliar dance genres.

Viewing and participating in dance through a cultural lens prepares you to effectively function in the world. As the human population becomes increasingly diverse and technologies connect people from all parts of the world in real time, the ability to recognize and value diversity is essential. Not everyone has the same experiences, values, and expectations that you do, and that is what makes the world interesting. While studying dance on campus, you will be introduced to dance genres from different parts of the world. The same skills you use to navigate diverse dance genres can assist you in your understanding of diverse cultures.

Lastly, recognizing that dance is a part of culture allows you to see how dance is used in other academic disciplines of study. Cultural anthropology, geography, ethnomusicology, and other humanities disciplines include dance when analyzing a society's cultural knowledge. The saying *Dance is a universal language* holds much truth, especially if you embrace the connections between dance and culture. Linking dance and culture opens up your dance studies to a more integrated awareness of dance and its rich and complex diversity.

EXAMINING RELATIONSHIPS BETWEEN DANCE AND CULTURE

Dance is fully woven into and emerges from cultures. Although some dance genres may be currently practiced outside of their originating cultures, dance genres often indicate the values and traditions of the cultural context in which they developed. Movements may illustrate ways of living or working that are common in a culture or ethnic group or accepted ways of interacting with one another. Cultural values are perhaps revealed through the purpose of and stories related to a given dance. Clothing, costumes, and musical instruments for a given dance genre can represent a specific geographic region or specific dance type. Examining the breadth of intentions and purposes, the themes and stories, the participants, and the location of dance events of various dance genres provides information about an incredible wealth of knowledge about dance genres practiced around the globe.

Intent and Purpose

The intent and purpose of a dance can vary greatly from culture to culture and within cultures. The intent can be specific to a particular dance, to a dance genre, or to the general role of dance in that culture. Examining the purpose of dance in a culture is a good way to start understanding the dance and the culture, and it may lead you to investigating the intentions of other cultural traditions. Some purposes include religious worship, demonstrating national identity or status, socializing, celebrating life events, entertainment, and personal expression, among others.

One way the Yoruba people, a West African ethnic group found primarily in Nigeria, use dance is to

Richard B Levine/Photoshot

• • • In the United States, Mexican folkloric dance is performed as a way to demonstrate respect for and awareness of Mexican heritage.

express social status and organization. For example, the leader of the Yoruba illustrates his command and prestige in formal dances; if his dancing does not meet expected standards, his authority may be questioned. Lesser chiefs and the leader's wives also dance to demonstrate their rank and renown. For the Yoruba, one purpose of dance is to categorize and illustrate the roles of individuals and groups in their culture.

Themes and Stories

After identifying the larger purpose of a dance, the next step is to identify the background story and theme, if one is present. If the dance has a religious purpose, the movements may depict a specific religious story. Dances that focus on entertainment may reenact or reference stories that are well known to

a culture, such as fables or children's stories. Identifying the themes and stories of a dance can give insight into why certain movements or movement qualities are embodied in a dance as well as introduce ways that dance connects to other aspects of culture.

Bharata natya is an Indian dance genre that was first danced by female temple servants (called *devedasis*) but is now presented in theatrical settings. Nrtya, one aspect of bharata natya, focuses on pure storytelling. Besides moving the whole body, bharata natya dancers use a series of codified hand gestures (called *mudras*) to communicate the story's meaning. In many bharata natya dances, a clear correlation exists between the movements used in the dance and the story being portrayed. Bharata natya demonstrates how identifying the stories present in a dance can help you to contextualize movement choices and give insight into other cultural aspects.

• • • Besides moving their whole bodies, bharata natya dancers use a series of codified hand gestures, called mudras, to communicate the story's meaning.

Participants

Looking at who participates or performs, who does not participate, how people relate to others, and what movements are used in a dance can echo cultural ideas about how people should interact and larger cultural beliefs. The way men and women move in a dance genre may stem from how men and women behave in the larger culture. Dances that are only performed by men or only performed by women can highlight cultural expectations about gender. Some cultures may view some dance genres as appropriate for one age group but not for others, or as germane for certain members of society but inappropriate for others. Each dance genre has expectations, some explicit and some implicit, regarding participation. Becoming aware of these expectations can assist in knowing why certain people participate in specific dance genres within a given culture.

The Tiwi, an aboriginal Australian population, embrace a holistic worldview, which unites past and present. Through dancing, the Tiwi reclaim a sense of wholeness that "existed in the past when one could move between different realms of existence" (Grau 2003, p. 174). Although there are distinct behavioral expectations for men and women, men are thought to be "mothers' of their sisters' children" and women are thought to be "fathers' to their brothers' children" (Grau

2003, p. 176). These ideals are represented through dances where men perform movements related to nursing and labor, and women perform movements representative of male behavior. In some ways, genders are interchangeable in Tiwi culture, and this is represented in their dances. Tiwi dances illustrate how expectations about men's and women's movements in a dance genre can reflect cultural values.

Place

To fully comprehend dance in a culture, you must consider where and when a dance occurs. Usually, the place of the dance is directly connected to the intent, themes, and participants of the dance. Dances for religious purposes can happen in temples, churches, or open spaces depending on where the culture communicates with the divine. Dances with a social purpose tend to take place in settings that foster community, such as school gymnasiums, recreational and social settings, and family gatherings, whereas dances that require a clear distinction between the audience and performers commonly occur in theaters and other performance venues. Looking at the physical location where the dance occurs and the time of day the dance takes place provides information about the role of dance in the larger culture.

Flamenco dance is recognizable by its hand clapping, rhythmic footwork, and detailed, spiraling arm movements. In the late 18th and early 19th centuries, this Spanish dance genre was performed as a means of personal expression in gypsy communities in southern Spain. It has since moved into cafés, cabarets, and formal theatrical settings. Although personal expression is still important, flamenco dance now also serves as entertainment and as a way for people to learn about some aspects of Spanish culture. Flamenco dance is an example of a dance genre that has been performed in many different places in response to the evolution of the dance genre's purpose.

CAREERS IN DANCE AND CULTURE

Regardless of the dance genres or world cultures that interest you, certain careers specifically advance the understanding of dance and culture. Careers in performing, choreographing, and presenting dance genres beyond concert and commercial dance genres help promote cultural awareness of diverse dance genres and cultural heritage. Studying other research-based disciplines, such as anthropology and ethnography, also increases knowledge of specific cultures and cultural behaviors. All of these careers work together to promote the importance of dance and culture.

Artistic Careers in Dance and Culture

Working as a performer, choreographer, or performing arts presenter is one way to increase appreciation for diverse dance genres. Dance companies in the United States and around the world feature a variety of dance genres, such as flamenco dance, tango, folk dance, West African dance genres, and others. In many countries, dance festivals present various dance genres from a given region or regions. The artistic and cultural aspects of dance are not separate, which means it is possible to work as a performer, choreographer, or performing arts presenter in most dance genres.

Cultural Research

Dance is one way to learn about a specific culture's values and ways of working. Two related research fields provide methods to deeply examine dance as an aspect of cultural knowledge. **Anthropology** looks at the ways that humans are unique but also similar through studying the evolution of human behavior, including social and cultural development. **Ethnography** is an aspect of anthropology that involves a thorough examination of a specific social and cultural group. Ethnographers study cultures up close through participating and observing the daily life of a culture. Because dance exists across cultures, it is clear to see how studying dance through either of these academic lenses gives insight into the shared behaviors, values, and symbolic aspects of a culture.

Dance ethnographers and dance anthropologists need strong research skills and advanced written and oral communication skills. Students interested in these areas need advanced abilities in recognizing movement patterns and vividly describing movement. A sense of adventure is helpful, as you may have the opportunity to travel to unfamiliar parts of the globe. The abilities to empathize with others, to work as a leader and collaboratively, and to create your own opportunities are also essential skills for success in this field.

Engaging WITH Dance

Erica Nielsen Okamura (Dance Ethnographer)

Dance ethnographers aspire to learn about various peoples and cultures through the lens of dance. They strive to understand dance practices from the perspective of cultural insiders—the people who claim the dances as their own. Interviewing and fieldwork skills are essential, because dance ethnographers must immerse themselves in the communities they want to research. To establish rapport with cultural insiders, dance ethnographers also should familiarize themselves with the history, values, and beliefs of a given community.

Dance ethnographers can conduct research anywhere in the world. If you are interested in becoming a dance ethnographer, I suggest that you take anthropology classes for research methods, and practice interviewing. In college, I took an ethnographic interviewing course and that helped a lot. Later, as a dance graduate student, I went to Bulgaria to learn how people danced. I attended performances as well as social dance events, and I wrote about how social and political trends affected Bulgarian dance practices throughout the 20th century. Soon after, at age 27, I wrote a book about folk dancing and square dancing in the United States. Fieldwork can be expensive, so aspiring dance ethnographers should look for grant and fellowship opportunities. Furthermore, they should take advantage of online resources such as YouTube, blogging, and social networking sites to conduct research as well as promote their work.

Photo courtesy of Nicholas Okamura.

CONTEMPORARY TRENDS

Both culture and dance are dynamic—they are constantly changing and evolving in response to contemporary life. Some dance genres developed from ancient rituals and practices, and some are less than 20 years old. It is important to remember that dance genres reflect the cultures and times in which they developed. This means that a dance genre may represent or preserve an older way of life even though the current culture is contemporary. At the same time, many traditional dances embracing contemporary trends are evolving into new sub-genres of dance. As dancers are exposed to new dance genres and cultures, they may appropriate ideas and movement into the dance genres they perform. This in turn contributes to the development of new dance genres. The idea that dance and culture are dynamic and constantly changing applies across dance genres and is essential to understanding dance as a cultural practice.

Choreographers around the globe have been influenced by multiple dance genres. It is not uncommon for theaters to present dance companies focused on diverse dance genres such as Brazilian dance, Chinese dance, and Irish step dancing. Dances that were once practiced in nontheatrical contexts are now expanding into presentational contexts.

Today, choreographers are fusing different dance styles to create a movement vocabulary that is specific to their unique identities and choreographic aims. This is true across dance genres, as is questioning what is or what is not dance and what does or does not belong in a specific dance form. For example, take contemporary Bollywood dance, which frequently fuses classical Indian dances and contemporary dances. Just as contemporary and commercial dance genres continue to advance and expand, so do dances around the world.

YOUR EXPLORATION OF DANCE AND CULTURE

Your dance experiences already connect to culture. Whether or not you are cognizant of it, your dance preferences, in terms of genres and the ways you like to move, reflect the values of cultures and communities you are part of inside and outside of dance. Studying dance on campus gives you a tremendous opportunity to consider how your own dancing relates to culture and how cultural values are present in dances around the world.

To begin to see how your dancing links to culture, take some time to learn about the history and development of the dance genres you practice. You might discover that the movement expectations of these dance genres mirror the cultural expectations of their times, and that this connection challenges or reinforces your own ideas. As you learn more about the historical and cultural aspects of the dance genres you are interested in, you will start to see how dance movements have cultural significance.

Modern media make it increasingly easier for us to communicate with others, regardless of geographic limitations, and to learn about dance and cultures around the world. While this is a valuable way to increase your exposure to diverse dance genres, it is important that you create opportunities to physically participate in new dance genres. Taking the time to learn about diverse dance genres is one way to widen your cultural knowledge. The more dance genres you experience, the broader your understanding of dance. You should proactively pursue opportunities to learn about new dance genres while studying dance on campus. And, if a dance genre really speaks to you, take your education one step further by learning about the foods, music, and customs of that culture. Perhaps plan for a semester abroad! In any case, it is important that you view dance as a gateway to learning about different cultures and not as an end in itself. Learning about diverse dance genres can increase your ability to empathize with others, expand your habitual ways of moving, and increase your overall proficiency in

Engaging WITH Dance

Kayt MacMaster (Oakland University)

I first became interested in traveling to Ghana after attending a class at the American College Dance Festival. The instructor, who currently teaches at Ohio University, is a musician from Ghana, and he mentioned that every year he took a group of students to Ghana to study African culture through the arts. I have always been an advocate of the universality of dance as a nonverbal language, and as I started to plan my honors thesis, it seemed the most authentic approach to deciphering the communicative and coalescing power of organized movement would be to travel to a country in which dancing is an integral part of the culture. While my first trip to Ghana was the basis for my thesis research, it was only the beginning of a project that would carry through the end of my undergraduate degree and into my professional career. Upon returning to the United States, I choreographed a dance for 12 dancers titled **Agbevivina: Life is Sweet,** with the live accompaniment of 5 musicians who generously composed an original score for the piece. As a group we were invited to come to Ghana to teach the music and move-ment of **Agbevivina: Life is Sweet** to the Sakaamu Dance Troupe in the summer of 2012. My research culminated with a presentation at the annual conference of the National Dance Education Organization Conference in October 2012.

My advice to dancers beginning their undergraduate studies is to make an effort to connect with students and professors from a variety of fields of study. Join a world music ensemble, take an art class, do yoga, and make friends with engineers! Nothing is more intellectually or artistically satisfying than an interdisciplinary collaboration. The dance world can become mundane if it is constantly perceived as an exclusive art form. Make connections in college, and allow the connections to broaden your experience. The purpose of academia can be just earning a degree, or it can open the mind to a new realm of possibilities in the field of dance. Think of your undergraduate years as time to practice traveling and researching, as well as technique and performance, under the academic umbrella where funding, mentors, research facilities, and opportunities abound.

dance. All of these factors are essential to success in all aspects of your current dance education and future dance career.

Locally, you can broaden your dance education by participating in dance genres from around the world. Many campuses have student groups that celebrate and educate others about a specific culture. There may be a capoeira, Bollywood, folk dance, or contra dance club or group on your campus where you can learn an unfamiliar dance genre. You can look to your local community to participate in new dance genres. If there are organizations in your community that focus on preserving and celebrating cultural heritage, there is likely to be an opportunity to learn an associated dance genre. Proactively look for opportunities to experience diverse dance genres in your own community. You might be surprised by the diversity that surrounds you.

If you are interested in becoming a dance ethnographer or dance anthropologist, you should look for courses specific to those disciplines. Each of these fields requires a particular knowledge set based on a wide range of research methods, ways of contextualizing experiences, and relating disciplines. Combining dance with either anthropology or ethnography allows you to fully investigate dance practices in your local community and around the world with a comprehensive view of dance. Finding the time to attend dance events and workshops in unfamiliar dance genres will increase your knowledge of diverse dance genres. Doing so develops an awareness of dance practices around the world, helps you recognize that dance genres have specific purposes and intents, and reinforces that all dance genres are valid.

SUMMARY

Recognizing how dance relates to culture is critical to gaining a complete comprehension of dance. No matter what your dance interests are, identifying the connections between dance and culture allows you to acknowledge the diversity of dance genres present around the world. Examining dance and culture enhances your ability to discuss the various purposes, themes, participants, and places of a dance genre, which deepens your understanding of the dance genres you are interested in as well as your awareness of dance around the world. Appreciating the role of dance in cultural research and recognizing contemporary trends in dance and culture can better prepare you for a successful dance career in an increasingly diverse world. Recognizing how your dance experiences reflect culture encourages you to

continuously contemplate the role of dance in your life and diverse cultures while leading to a richer engagement with dance.

REVIEW QUESTIONS

1. Restate Joann Kealiinohomoku's definition of dance in your own words. How does Kealiinohomoku's definition of dance connect dance to culture? How does her definition challenge or support your own ideas about dance?

2. State the key characteristics of ceremonial dance, ritual dance, social dance, and theatrical dance. Provide examples for each category in your answer.

3. What areas should you examine when looking at dance and culture? How are these areas related, and how do they correspond to different aspects of culture?

4. Describe in detail one career that promotes the understanding of dance and culture. Supplement your answer by using the Internet to find an example of a person, dance company, or group that does this. What makes this person, company, or group unique, and how are they advancing the understanding of dance and culture?

GLOSSARY

anthropology—An academic discipline that studies the ways in which humans are unique but also similar through studying the evolution of human behavior, including social and cultural development.

ceremonial dances—Dances in which the primary purpose is to display a group identity as well as individual rank in a secular or sacred setting.

culture—The behaviors, beliefs, and practices of a specific ethnic, social, or geographic group.

cultural—A term that denotes arts, traditions, and ways of life that relate to a specific culture.

ethnography—An subfield of anthropology that involves an extremely thorough examination of a specific social and cultural group.

folk dances—Dances that were developed and performed by "the folk" (the peasant citizens of a society).

ritual dances—Dances that serve as a way for people to connect with the spiritual realm and are used in religious ceremonies.

social dances—Dance genres that occur in social, secular settings.

theatrical dance—Dance genres and dances that aim to entertain an audience, to articulate an artistic viewpoint, or to educate an audience.

BIBLIOGRAPHY

Brainard, I., Schneider, G., McDonagh, D., & Sommer, S.R. (2005). Social dance. In *The international encyclopedia of dance*. Oxford, UK: Oxford University Press. www.oxford-dance.com/entry?entry=t171.e1627.s0003.

Dance Exchange. (2012). Dance Exchange: Mission and vision. http://danceexchange.org/about/mission-vision.

Devi, R. (2005). Bharata Natyam. In *The international encyclopedia of dance*. Oxford, UK: Oxford University Press. www.oxford-dance.com/entry?entry=t171.e0219.

Erikson, T.H. (2010). *Small places, large issues: An introduction to social and cultural anthropology* (3rd ed.). New York: Pluto Press.

Fine, E.C. (2003). *Soulstepping: African American step shows*. Chicago, IL: University of Illinois Press.

Friedland, L. (2005). Folk dance history. In *The international encyclopedia of dance*. Oxford, UK: Oxford University Press. www.oxford-dance.com/entry?entry=t171.e0626.

Grau, A. (2003). Tiwi dance aesthetics. *Yearbook for Traditional Music, 35,* 173-178.

Grossman, C. (2000). Religion and ethics newsweekly. Feature: liturgical dance. https://web.archive.org/web/20130310155436/http://www.pbs.org/wnet/religionandethics/week332/feature.html.

Hammersley, M., & Atkinson, P. (2007). *Ethnography: Principles in practice*. New York: Routledge.

Kealiinohomoku, J. (1983). An anthropologist looks at ballet as a form of ethnic dance. In Copeland, R. and Cohen, M. (eds.), *What is dance?* (pp. 533-549). New York: Oxford University Press.

Reynolds, W.C. (2005). European traditional dance. In *The international encyclopedia of dance*. Oxford, UK: Oxford University Press. www.oxford-dance.com/entry?entry=t171.e0584.

Sevilla, S., Dallal, A., Martinez, C.D., Axtmann, A.M., & Aulestia, P. (2005). Mexico. In *The international encyclopedia of dance*. Oxford, UK: Oxford University Press. www.oxford-dance.com/entry?entry=t171.e1155.s0003.

Stearns, M., & Stearns, J. (1994). *Jazz dance: The story of American vernacular dance*. New York: Da Capo.

Step Afrika. (2007). What is stepping? www.stepafrika.org/stepping.htm.

Thompson-Drewal, M. (2005). Yoruba dance. In *The international encyclopedia of dance*. Oxford, UK: Oxford University Press. www.oxford-dance.com.ezproxy1.lib.asu.edu/entry?entry=t171.e1883&srn=1&ssid=797681969.

Dance and Education

LEARNING OUTCOMES

After completing this chapter, you will be able to do the following:

- Evaluate the comprehensive nature of dance education.
- Differentiate and discuss dance education sectors.
- Identify and describe sectors and careers in dance education.
- Recognize current trends in dance education.
- Assess your current dance studies in relation to education.

Dance and education intersect in many ways. Some people start learning dance at a very young age, others may be introduced to dance through a college dance appreciation class, while others become dance enthusiasts as adults. Just as a wide range of dance genres and artistic aspects of dance exists, there is an equally large range of places and ways that dance education can occur. Through engaging in dance education as a student, you have the opportunity to learn about the comprehensive nature of dance while also learning about yourself and how you interact with others. Dance educators create and provide these opportunities for learning dance.

Usually, a person's education is fueled by curiosity and the sense of accomplishment that stems from the aha moment of an idea clicking. The acquisition of new skills, knowledge, and awareness causes you to mature as a person, a dancer, and an artist and is part of your daily experience. Like you, the people in the photograph are discovering the expansive nature and personal relevance of dance in empowering ways.

As your dance experience expands, so will your comprehension of the breadth of dance education. You will encounter various methods of teaching dance, places where dance education can occur, and motivations for learning dance. In this chapter, you will discover how dance educates the whole person and learn about different dance education sectors. After completing chapter 7, you will be able to evaluate your current dance and educational experiences from various perspectives so that you are better pre-

pared to engage in your own dance education and, potentially, in the dance education of others.

While studying dance on campus and beyond, at times you will likely be both a dance student and an instructor. Whether you take daily technique class, attend professional development workshops, or informally learn about dance through the Internet, your dance education will continue after graduation. Statistically, the majority of people who work in dance teach dance to children, adults, or both at some point in their careers. Therefore, it is essential that you understand and value the educational process of learning dance. Studying dance on campus gives you the chance to gain exposure to dance education so that you can enhance your own passion and understanding of dance and then potentially share that joy and expertise with future generations of dance students.

EDUCATIONAL NATURE OF DANCE

You are actively pursuing your individual dance education through studying dance on campus. Becoming cognizant of how you are learning dance enables you to see the effectiveness and purposes of different teaching methods. While on campus, you will be actively increasing your comprehension of dance education from a student's perspective, but it is necessary that you proactively expand your awareness from an educator's viewpoint as well. This will

• • • Because people engage their bodies, minds, and spirits while learning to dance, dance can educate the whole person.

ensure that you have a solid grasp of dance educational practices.

As a dance student, you are well aware that dance teaches you to move in a personally and artistically expressive way. However, learning to dance and learning about dance develops much more than movement coordination. Dance education is a broad term that refers to the transmission of dance knowledge from one individual to another and includes several models of dance teaching, such as early childhood dance lessons, studying dance on campus, and learning to dance in community programs. A comprehensive dance education cultivates and calls upon people's kinesthetic abilities, intellect, and emotional intelligence while learning to dance, about dance, and through dance.

Because people engage their bodies, minds, and spirits while learning to dance, dance can educate the whole person. The holistic nature of dance places it as a discipline at the heart of learning. Learning the movements, aesthetics, theory, history, science, and traditions of various dance genres will certainly enrich your knowledge of dance as a discipline. Additionally, because learning dance involves the whole person, studying dance can develop valuable life skills such as leadership, empathy, adaptability, critical and reflective thinking, and creative problem solving.

To facilitate dance learning in a sequential, scaffolded, and assessable way, many dance programs address core understandings of dance in their curricula and lesson plans. **Curriculum** refers to the total courses or lessons that a student completes in a given area of study, such as dance. **Lesson plans** are outlines for daily classes with clear learning outcomes that relate to one or more curricular goals. In dance education, many dance curricula and lessons focus on developing competencies to create, perform, and respond to dance; comprehending the place and role of dance in history and culture; and the capacity to understand and critically evaluate dance and dances in an informed way. All of these components are embedded in your dance curriculum. Your role while studying dance on campus is to learn how these aspects are interwoven and engrained in dance so that you can deepen your dance knowledge and share it with others.

LEARNING THEORIES AND DANCE LEARNING

Throughout history, people have engaged in informal and formal learning processes to survive, to fully function in society, and to gain in-depth understanding of personally relevant topics. Learning occurs in many ways, and various theories explain how learning happens. Because dance is a discipline reliant on inquiry and contextualization, the process of learning dance is well aligned with current theories about learning and intelligence. Gaining an awareness of how dance learning and learning theories are linked can help you see the range of learning possible through dance education.

Constructivist Approaches

Imagine yourself in a dance improvisation class. In this class, the teacher provides an improvisational prompt for you to respond to through movement. There is not a right or wrong answer to the teacher's prompt, and through the improvisation you have a chance to select and perform movements that are meaningful to you, perhaps draw on previous dance experiences, and possibly include new movements. After the improvisation, the teacher asks you to reflect on how and why you made your improvisational choices while dancing and how that relates to the ways you make decisions outside of class.

In this example, you are constructing your own knowledge and experience of dance improvisation. The teacher provides an open-ended prompt that allows you to build on previous dance experiences to find new ways of working with and comprehending dance while practicing dance improvisation. **Constructivism** is an educational approach that requires students to build their own knowledge while gaining specific skills and information about a subject. Constructivist approaches embrace problem solving, structuring learning around primary concepts, seeking and valuing students' unique points of view, adapting lesson plans to address students' current understanding, and assessing student learning in the context of teaching. Constructivism situates students as active learners and knowledge constructors. As you can see, constructivist approaches are well aligned with dance learning.

Embodied and Somatic Learning

Dancers are aware that the body and mind are connected and that moving the body is one way to make sense of the world. Theories of **embodiment** assert that the mind and ways of thinking are largely influenced by the existence of the human body. In other words, how you interact with the world through your body shapes what you know and how you came to know it. In dance, somatic practices are frequently used to promote embodiment. **Somatic practices** are modalities that aim to fully integrate the body and mind to increase an integrated sense of wholeness, movement awareness, and expressivity. Being fully present inside your movement and body gives you confidence and an increased capacity to respond to others, as well as increased movement potential.

Embodied and somatic learning approaches emphasize the ability to notice and process information perceived through the body and mind as people interact with their surroundings. These approaches respect the whole person as a learner and focus on experiential knowledge that involves strengthening and honoring the connections between the mind and body, and perception and action. Dancers have the advantage when it comes to sensing embodiment and unifying the mind and body, because this is inherently part of learning to dance. As a student of dance, it is important that you become aware of these approaches so that you cultivate a sense of wholeness for yourself and your future students.

Photo taken @ LASALLE College of the Arts by Dorothy Png

• • • Because dance calls on and values different ways of thinking, many important skills can be gained through learning dance.

Theory of Multiple Intelligences

Most people agree that dancers are smart movers. Nondancers are often amazed by dancers' abilities to learn dance movement and to remember choreography. However, dancers are smart in multiple ways. Consider what happens when you perform group choreography. Besides physically executing the choreography, you are relating to music, responding to other performers, navigating different formation changes, and keeping track of yourself. To remember the choreography, you may use a logical or numerical approach, such as counting the movements, or you may make up a story of what the dance is about. Learning and performing dance is much more than executing movement; it involves the entire person and a variety of intelligences.

Howard Gardner, an American developmental psychologist, developed the theory of multiple intelligences to explain the ways people process information. There are eight independent intelligences that people use to navigate their daily experiences. The intelligences are bodily-kinesthetic, spatial, musical, interpersonal, intrapersonal, linguistic, logical-mathematical, and naturalistic (Gardner 2006). The more you are able to notice and foster the intelligences you use while participating in dance, the wider and more personally significant your own dance education can become. Additionally, knowing how the intelligences are activated in dance learning allows you to appreciate the comprehensive and empowering nature of dance education.

Dance Learning and Life Skills

Regardless of a person's area of expertise, there are certain life skills that cross disciplines and are fundamental to success. Because dance calls on and values different ways of thinking, many important capabilities can be gained through learning dance. Through learning to make, perform, analyze, and talk about dance, you are gaining expertise that is valuable in many careers inside and outside of the arts.

Competencies such as creative problem solving, critical thinking, collaboration, communication, leadership, and social engagement can all be components of arts learning and are certainly embedded in a dance education. Through using student-centered learning approaches such as constructivism, fostering an awareness of how dance involves multiple ways of thinking, and valuing embodiment, dance educators are able to cultivate these aptitudes in students as they learn dance.

CAREERS IN DANCE EDUCATION

Within dance education, careers are geared toward making quality dance education available to as many people as possible. Careers in dance education include dance educators, teaching artists, and careers outside of the classroom. In each of these career paths, people have the opportunity to spark a passion for dance in others while also continuously learning more about dance as an educational force.

Dance Educator

A **dance educator** teaches dance to others in a way that values the comprehensive nature of dance. Dance educators are responsible for sharing dance with others through empowering students to engage with dance in an embodied, artistic, analytical, emotional, creative, and physical way. The sector a dance educator selects to work in can greatly vary, and dance educators are present in all dance genres.

Besides a broad comprehension of dance and a deep mastery of specific dance genres, dance educators must have pedagogical knowledge. **Pedagogical knowledge** refers to the *how* and *why* of teaching and learning. Effective dance educators are conscious of how and why they are teaching dance and of the ways their teaching methods affect student learning. Dance educators are dedicated and respectful, and their love of dance is usually contagious. Time management, organizational skills, empathy, leadership experience, and creative problem solving are vital to dance educators.

While it is essential that dance educators have an extensive comprehension of the dance genres or dance topics they teach, additional required competencies exist that are specific to teaching dance. Dance educators need supportive knowledge, which includes knowing the history and culture of a dance genre, knowing what equipment is used to teach a dance genre, and awareness of any standards or assessment methods used in their institution. Because dance is a physical art form, dance educa-

tors need an understanding of kinesiology, and physiological training is essential. A keen knowledge of the movement vocabulary and choreographic methods of the dance genres they teach as well as the skills to develop age-appropriate and developmentally appropriate lesson plans to ensure that students receive a comprehensive dance education are necessary. Classroom management skills, knowledge of various teaching methods, and a wide understanding of education theories and psychosocial development are required to create vibrant classroom learning communities. While you are studying dance on campus, it may be informative to observe your current dance educators to see how these competencies are present in their teaching and to consider how they relate to your experiences in the classroom or studio.

Teaching Artist

A **teaching artist** is a professional artist who also has talent as an educator and creates arts-centered learning activities for a variety of people. Teaching artists may work on short- or long-term residencies with schools or community organizations; may perform for students, teachers, and community members; or may help establish additional programs for schools, school districts, or in the community. In dance, teaching artists can work in any dance genre.

Teaching artists must maintain active profiles as artists and be informed educators. Successful teaching artists are organized, have exceptional people skills, and comprehend the social and organizational contexts in which they work. Most teaching artist residencies focus on creative aspects of dance, such as improvisation and creating movement phrases, so teaching artists need a wide appreciation of the creative process along with movement and aesthetic expertise about a given dance genre. The capability to work with diverse ability levels and age groups is also beneficial. Because teaching artists sometimes work on multiple projects at once, such as creating a new dance while leading a teaching artist residency at a local community center, time management is essential. While on campus, you may offer to teach a series of classes that relate to a dance project of yours to a student organization. This way, you can sample being a teaching artist.

Nonclassroom Careers

Along with teaching dance are careers that promote effective dance education by developing and assessing curriculum or by advocating for dance education.

Usually, people enter these careers after an extensive career as a dance educator. Two examples of this type of career are an arts curriculum specialist and an arts education advocate.

An **arts curriculum specialist** develops and assesses the effectiveness of arts curricula for schools or other organizations. Arts curriculum specialists work in schools and school districts; for local, state, and federal government agencies; and for nonprofit and private consulting firms. Arts curriculum specialists possess a broad understanding of dance, music, theater, and visual arts and of the role of arts in society, and have extensive pedagogical knowledge. Great sensitivity to the educational and sociological context of their schools, school districts, and communities is required so that they can prioritize students' learning in an informed way. Working with curriculum requires the capacity to see the big picture as well as the details that make up the big picture, an awareness of research and assessment methods, and a background as an arts educator. Leadership experience, creative problem solving, and the ability to collaborate with people in other arts and outside of the arts are highly beneficial.

Even though the arts are essential to a well-rounded education, arts programs are frequently in danger due to budget challenges. An **arts education advocate** encourages public policy makers to include arts education in schools through demonstrating the scholastic benefits of student engagement in the arts and the importance of arts in the larger society. Arts education advocates can be active at the local, state, or federal level, and they usually speak on behalf of arts education organizations. In addition to possessing a wide understanding of the arts, arts education, and pedagogy, arts education advocates are persuasive. Knowing how to concisely articulate the value of the arts in schools in a factually supported way is essential. Comprehension of how public policy is determined and implemented is also required. Leadership experience is a necessity, as are advanced oral and written communication skills, the ability to collaborate with people outside of the arts, and creative problem solving. If you are interested in arts

Engaging WITH Dance

Sara Stewart (Arts Curriculum Consultant)

When I enrolled as a dance major at Arizona State University in 2000, I wouldn't have predicted that today I would be the education services director at Arts Integration Solutions (AiS), a nonprofit organization that provides professional development to teachers in aligning the arts and academic standards to affect student achievement. As the education service director I create arts integration resources; provide professional development; coach teachers in their practice; and serve as the education face of AiS by helping to shape the educational system and keeping AiS current with educational policy, needs, theories, and practices.

In 2000, I knew that I loved to dance but didn't know all of the opportunities that my passion and skill set could be applied to. Thankfully I kept an open mind and risked being involved in as much as possible. In my freshman year I was a member of Dance Arizona Repertory Theatre (DART), a performing and community-project–oriented dance company. My experiences teaching with DART began my gravitation toward dance education. Next I grabbed the opportunity to be an ArtsBridge scholar. ArtsBridge was my introduction to arts integration and directly relates to what I do today.

Although I decided early on to work toward a bachelor's degree in dance with a teaching certificate, I didn't limit my involvement to dance education, nor did I limit it to the university. I took technique classes, performed, invested time researching dance history, and taught at the local parks and recreation center.

I'm constantly applying all of these experiences and perspectives to the many hats I wear at AiS, and I'm still expanding my involvement. I participate in professional learning communities and conferences, and I also perform with two dance companies. I feel so fortunate to be challenged at AiS, doing what I love to do and continually growing with each new opportunity.

education advocacy, you would benefit from taking courses in political science, sociology, and public speaking while studying dance on campus.

DANCE EDUCATION SECTORS

Your dance education started before you came to campus. You may have studied dance in a private studio, taken weekly classes at your local community center, or participated in your high school dance classes. Each sector of dance education is valuable and has distinct purposes that reflect the interests of its students. Some of the dance education sectors you may have already encountered include dance studios, K–12 programs, preprofessional conservatories, community and recreational centers, and postsecondary education. Learning about the commonalities and distinctions between sectors illustrates the breadth of dance education and allows you to consider which sector best aligns with your interests.

Dance Studios

It is likely that your local community has one or more dance studios where people of all ages and experiences come to learn dance. Some dance stu-

dios chose to focus on one or two related dance genres, while some offer classes in a variety of dance genres. Some dance studios may have competitive teams that perform locally and nationally. There are dance studios that address creativity within dance or offer drop-in classes for professional adult dancers. Dance studios can follow a for-profit or a nonprofit model, enroll fewer than 50 students or more than 5,000, and exist in small towns and large cities. For example, in your hometown, there may be a dance studio, run by a local teacher as a small business, that enrolls a large number of students who come in for weekly lessons and then perform in an annual showcase. On the other hand, in cities with large dance communities, such as New York, San Francisco, and Chicago, dance studios exist that are financed through grants and donations in addition to class revenue and in which professional and pre-professional dancers can take classes at their convenience. There are diverse goals among dance studios, but what they share is the desire to provide a place for people in their community to learn to dance.

Dance teachers in private studios come from a wealth of dance backgrounds. Although no official certification is required to teach dance in a private studio, more and more often private studio teachers have degrees in dance. Others have opted to become

Engaging WITH Dance

Tori Rogoski (Private-Sector Dance Educator)

Photo courtesy of Smith Photographic Arts.

The role of a private-sector dance educator is the most significant contribution to a dancer's training regarding the path he or she chooses after high school. Many dancers fall in love with dance in the studio setting during childhood and teenage years, and because studio educators often work with dancers for a decade or more (sometimes even as many as 15 years), the instructor becomes the trusted guide to further dance training and higher education. Studio dancers look to their instructors for advice when choosing summer programs, higher education, or professional study. The private-sector dance educator holds the responsibility to best guide each individual to a role in the dance field best suited to his or her strengths and desires. Studio teachers should then hone and train their teaching skills with the same intensity and commitment as one prepares for a career as a performer. For the private-sector dance educator, courses in educational psychology, human development, business, arts management, anatomy, biomechanics, exercise science, dance history, and teaching theories and pedagogy must supplement his or her technical dance training. Study in these areas and continued professional development provide a strong foundation for the studio teacher to have the knowledge to help direct each dancer's passion which, in turn, creates a more complete dancer and directly affects the quality of our profession.

certified through professional organizations, such as Dance Masters of America and the National Registry of Dance Educators. To work in a private studio, dance educators should be comfortable working with a variety of ages and abilities. Comprehension of multiple dance genres, specifically ballet, jazz, tap, contemporary, and urban dance forms, is a plus. Business savvy is fundamental to owning a private studio regardless of the population served and the dance genres offered.

Public School Dance Programs

The arts have long been a component of public education, and dance is no exception. As of 2010, approximately 6,000 public schools in the United States included dance in their curriculum. Many public school dance curricula offer students a dance education centered in the arts, although the dance genres offered and learning intents vary from school to school. Most states offer a dance or theater teaching certification to teach dance in public schools, and many implement standards-based curricula. A **standards-based curriculum** outlines academic benchmarks at different age levels that relate to

what students should know and demonstrate by a specific point within a given discipline. Some states have mandatory statewide or district standards that guide each school's curriculum. Other schools may voluntarily use nationally recognized standards such as those developed by the National Dance Education Organization or SHAPE America (Society for Health and Physical Educators). Regardless of the standards used, the goal is to provide elementary through high school students the opportunity to study dance.

Many dance programs are embedded in public education. Some public school systems offer dance classes during the school day as part of their fine arts or physical education curriculum. Other public schools have after-school programs that focus on dance and other art forms. In performing arts high schools or arts magnet schools, students intensely focus on dance as a core subject. Dance programs in public education vary a great deal from state to state and district to district and can be a valuable component of elementary, middle, or high school curricula.

An undergraduate degree in dance or a related area is a prerequisite for teaching in the public education sector. Many states require teachers to be state certified to work in a public education setting. Addi-

Engaging WITH Dance

Emily Enloe (K–12 Public Dance Educator)

As a public school dance teacher, you must become a holistic teacher—approaching the technical, mental, and emotional aspects of dance. You must be open to every dance experience, big or small, that comes your way. Each has a valuable piece of information for you and will help to shape your own personal philosophy on teaching and dance. This also includes making as many teacher observations and practice opportunities as possible throughout your college career. Not only can you gain insight into the best (and sometimes worst) teaching practices, but this is a chance to make real, meaningful connections with other seasoned dance educators in your area. They can become your allies and biggest advocates, but you must make good first impressions. It is

also important to practice your time management skills, which will become valuable when you plan and execute future lesson plans. Have a calendar handy, and record every event, assignment, or other important date. However, if you are using a paper calendar, be sure to write in pencil; things will change, and flexibility is vital, especially as a public school teacher. As a first- or second-year college student, it is also important to open yourself up to other experiences and friends outside of your dance department. Attend functions or meetings with other education, theater, and music students. These are the people you will work with in the school system, and learning how to collaborate with them now will make the process easier as well as more exciting when you have your own classroom.

tionally, some states encourage their dance educators to obtain graduate degrees in education. Dance educators have a deep understanding of dance, a solid comprehension of educational and learning theories, and the ability to use their expertise in both areas to actively engage students in the learning process. An excellent dance educator not only teaches students dance but also empowers students as lifelong learners, helping them to become curious and knowledgeable about dance in diverse ways.

Preprofessional Conservatories

Some performing arts organizations and dance companies have schools that provide intense training to preprofessional students. Most of these types of schools are conservatories. In a **conservatory,** students primarily focus on the physical and artistic aspects of a specific dance genre. The goal is to be a specialist in a given dance genre or style. Some preprofessional conservatory programs are attached to well-known dance companies, such as the Ailey/ Professional Performing Arts School. Others are embedded into high schools, such as the University of North Carolina School of the Arts' High School Program. In preprofessional conservatories students receive concentrated training aimed at a professional career in dance performance.

Frequently, dance educators in company-affiliated preprofessional conservatories are former company dancers. This gives them a rich professional perspective of the dance genre they teach. Not all dance educators in preprofessional conservatories have degrees in dance or teaching certifications, but they do possess a great depth of professional experience. Many take advantage of professional development opportunities offered by national dance organizations so that they can continue to advance their expertise as dance educators. Dance educators in preprofessional conservatories, like dance educators in other settings, need a nuanced understanding of the dance genres they teach along with fundamental proficiencies in teaching and choreography.

Community and Recreational Centers

People also participate in dance through programs offered by community and recreational centers. Some dance companies and performing arts organizations have community outreach programs besides their preprofessional conservatories. Parks and recreation programs and municipal continuing education programs offer low-cost dance courses as a means for participants to meet other people or to get some exercise while learning about dance. Many national service organizations, such as the Boys & Girls Clubs of America, also offer dance courses to their local communities. Teaching dance in a community or recreational center is a great way to introduce dance as an art form to a wide range of people.

Dance teachers in community and recreational centers frequently have an undergraduate degree in dance or a related area. Many start as volunteer teachers or apprentices while in college so that they can gain proficiency in facilitation. Working as a dance educator in a community or recreational center requires the ability to facilitate creative movement activities as well as the capacity to teach theatrical, social, ritual, or ceremonial dance genres. The dance classes offered by community and recreational centers are diverse, ranging from creatively focused classes for youth to social dance genres for adults. Additionally, the aptitude to work with multiple ability levels is especially helpful, because many students in these classes may be new to dance.

Postsecondary Education

Postsecondary education refers to learning that happens after high school in a college, university, or collegiate-level institution that awards academic degrees or professional certificates. Dance has been a part of postsecondary education for almost 100 years. Today, dance can be academically pursued as a major or minor area of focus in approximately 665 postsecondary institutions. The dance genres and academic intents of these programs are vast, but all respect dance as a valid area of academic inquiry.

In postsecondary settings, most educators have graduate degrees in dance or a related area. Depending on the type of postsecondary institution, dance educators may be required to contribute to the ongoing evolution of dance through innovative scholarly research—such as publishing an article on teaching effectiveness or writing a book about an important dancer or choreographer—and creative research, such as choreographing a dance for a professional dance company or developing new technologies for incorporating media in dance. Postsecondary dance educators usually have professional experience along with their academic qualifications. Dance educators in postsecondary education have a specific area of expertise as well as a very broad understanding of dance as a discipline. Excellent verbal and written communication skills are a necessity. The abilities

Jenna Kosowski (Postsecondary Dance Educator)

My position requires that I teach five dance courses (a mixture of technique and lecture-based classes) and choreograph or perform a work each semester. Organization and time management are two skills I find necessary for managing the responsibilities of this position. Remaining prepared and ahead of schedule allows me to develop effective lesson plans for each class (also requiring time and patience). However, the ability to remain flexible once in the classroom or studio is just as important. I often use my intuition to gauge students' interests and abilities in order to keep them engaged and adapt my plan if necessary. Teaching dance is never fixed or static; rather, it

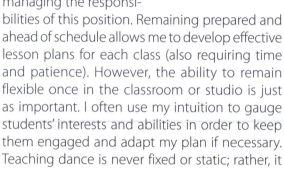

requires constant negotiation between the teacher and the student.

I find that teaching dance is like teaching a language—movements are like words filled with information and meaning. Depending on what I am teaching (which varies each semester), students are being exposed to a range of movement histories, different sets of rules and ideas, and are essentially conversing via dance. As the facilitator of the dialogue, I am able to witness students coming together to share in an experience. I seek to create an environment that is infused with a sense of curiosity, risk taking, mind–body awareness, and pride in one's abilities. It is exciting to teach dance!

© Perrine Photography LLC.

to critically and creatively think and to collaborate with others are fundamental. Being able to effectively teach a variety of class types, such as studio and lecture courses, is highly valuable and is viewed as an essential aspect of working as a dance educator in postsecondary education.

CONTEMPORARY TRENDS

It is an exciting time for dance education. In schools and society, there is an increased emphasis on creativity, which is central to dance. Advances in technology and media are forging new opportunities for dance education. Additionally, dance educators continue to frequently work with educators from other disciplines, both inside and outside of the arts, to devise inventive and comprehensive learning environments and activities for students. Familiarizing yourself with contemporary trends in dance education can help you identify how your own dance education connects to current practices within dance education and how your collegiate dance education relates to future careers in dance, dance education, and beyond.

21st-Century Skills

We are all part of a global community that values innovation. This means that today's students need to obtain specific learning and innovation skills and subject-specific knowledge. A framework for 21st-century learning provides a foundation for achieving this innovation by focusing on critical thinking, communication, collaboration, and creativity (Partnership for 21st Century Skills 2011). These 4 Cs, as they are called, are fully embedded in dance performing, dance making, and dance learning. In the dance classroom, dance educators address these competencies in numerous ways. Asking students to create dances and then reflect on their creative processes helps them become aware of how they are creative. Students gain valuable critical-thinking skills through evaluating dance works. Working as a team on a project, sharing peer feedback, and discussing dance are ways to promote collaboration. Communication skills are developed through peer teaching or presenting learning activities to others. The 4 Cs can be an organic part of dance learning when dance educators include 21st-century skills in their teaching.

Interdisciplinary Dance Teaching and Learning

In addition to the distinct disciplines within the arts, art is also created in between the specific arts areas. **Interdisciplinary art** combines two or more different art forms or media. In arts education, interdisciplinary work encourages students to find and create relevant links and discover new ways to unite divergent ideas within the arts. It also creates opportunities for students to discover new areas in artistic media that may more completely express their ideas. Dance educators may find themselves collaborating with other arts educators to offer special classes or full courses that focus on interdisciplinary work. Inside or outside of the classroom, dance educators may work with other arts educators to create student-centered interdisciplinary arts experiences focused on collaboration and discussion. By working across disciplines, an educator helps bring dance to more students and provides an integrated appreciation of the arts. Interdisciplinary work not only enhances student learning, it provides a glimpse into how interdisciplinary dance works are created in the professional dance field.

Integrated Curricula

Dance and other arts can be integrated across scholastic curricula to help students learn more about a given subject area outside of the arts. For example, a dance educator may help math students learn about geometry through prompting them to make different shapes with their bodies and to explore spatial relationships. In some cases, schools may have a dance educator dedicated to working across the curriculum. There are also organizations that facilitate placement of teaching artists in schools to work in an integrated way. This approach mirrors practices used by choreographers and dance performers who collaborate with people in other arts and fields to create new work. Integrated curricula help provide students with new understandings through dance. Additionally, integrated curricula illustrate how all areas of learning are interconnected and how looking for new connections between areas can lead to new areas to investigate through dance.

Media and Technology

In today's society, media and technology are everywhere. People have access to all types of information via the Internet, can share videos with friends and family in real time with their mobile devices, and can connect to people with shared interests around the globe through social networking sites. These methods all provide new opportunities for dance education. Online discussion forums about dance allow people to share their thoughts about dance, which can lead to a deeper understanding and new areas for personal inquiry. People can view archived and real-time dance performances and events through a variety of websites. Online learning permits people to fit in their class time around their daily lives instead of the other way around, which makes it easier to balance school with work or family obligations. Additionally, online dance courses make certain aspects of dance education available to a greater population. It is important that dance educators continue to capitalize on the advantages of media and technology in and beyond their classrooms so that dance education continues to evolve.

YOUR GROWTH IN DANCE EDUCATION

As you study dance on campus, your dance knowledge will increase in multiple ways. Besides engaging in a variety of artistic and cultural experiences in dance, you will engage in a variety of educational experiences, too. Each educational opportunity you take part in as a student, instructor, or peer tutor is a chance for you to reflect on how dance learning occurs. While on campus, it is also advantageous for you to seek and create ways to learn more about dance teaching and learning. Doing so will not only better prepare you to teach professionally, it will provide a broader understanding of the educational nature of dance.

Developing as a Dance Educator

If you are interested in becoming a dance educator or a teaching artist, you should create situations to practice teaching. Some opportunities may be present within your daily dance classes or within your dance program. When you are asked to share peer responses within your choreography or creative classes, you can view that as a chance to practice articulating your observations, which is an important teaching skill. Or, perhaps you can develop a series of classes or participatory experiences related to your creative process to share with a local campus or com-

Engaging WITH Dance

Leah Cox (Teaching Artist and Performing Arts Organization Dance Educator)

When I entered college, I wanted to become a dancer. As I progressed through college, my experience with my dance professors made me realize that I ultimately wanted to be a teacher and to be involved in dance education. Studying dance in college made me realize the complexity inherent to the field and the importance of dance's place in higher education. It also made me realize the importance of having well-educated teachers and administrators sensitive to the unique needs that dance has as a field of study. Pedagogy is as important as the content we teach. Well-structured administrations are crucial to the success of any enterprise.

My role as education director at New York Live Arts requires me to straddle the duties of developing and administering educational programs as well as teach in the programs I develop. I work with a wide range of people, from young students to professionals, artists to administrators, and teachers both experienced and new. My job is challenging, exciting, and created by me, for me. It is reflective of what I learned from my teachers in college: that options for engaging in the dance world go far beyond dancing in a company, and that I have the power and responsibility to define my future and, consequently, the future of dance.

The field of dance is constantly changing. This continual movement challenges me to continue learning and growing. My own movement and curiosity within the field of dance guarantees that it will continue to change and be reflective of those of us who actively engage in it.

© Paul B. Goode

munity organization. It may be possible to teach in a private studio or student teach with a K–12 dance educator. Your faculty can help connect you and your interests to your community and to the larger dance education field. The more experience you have sharing your dance knowledge in an educationally meaningful way, the more you will enhance your dance education.

Students who are curious about dance and arts curriculum development or arts education advocacy should proactively pursue activities related to curriculum development and advocacy while on campus. You may find apprenticeships with local arts agencies or volunteer work to engage in on campus. A simple way to practice advocating for dance education is by explaining the value of dance and arts education to anyone who will listen. This is an easy but important step in developing skills related to advocacy. Or, you can tailor class assignments and projects toward curricular issues related to the course's content. For example, if you need to complete a final project for your dance history class, you might design a curriculum that introduces the history of ballet to elementary school students. In a

dance teaching methods course, you might experiment with how teaching rhythm in dance relates to mathematics. There are numerous opportunities to acquire aptitudes related to advocacy and arts curriculum development while studying dance on campus—if you seek them.

All students should strive to teach and learn dance in a variety of settings. Nearly all dancers will teach at some point in their careers, even if they are not primarily interested in dance education. The ability to teach a dance class in a variety of genres is a valuable asset for a dance performer. Choreographers regularly teach movement to others. A broad teaching and learning background better prepares you to succeed in all areas of dance.

Relating to Contemporary Trends

As a student, you are already participating in contemporary trends in dance education. At times, some students view the teaching and learning that happens on campus to be separate from the teaching they hope to engage in after graduation. If you can start to see how the teaching methods and learning experiences you take part in on campus can be used in different contexts, you will be well prepared to succeed as a dance educator and to advance the field of dance education.

It is likely that you have already experienced dance learning focused on critical thinking, communication, collaboration, and creativity; or enrolled in an online dance course; or participated in an integrated curriculum or interdisciplinary art class. To become more mindful of how these trends affect your learning, you might examine how contemporary trends in dance education can promote a larger understanding of the artistic and cultural components of dance. There may be examples of this within your own program. For example, if you are required to make your own music or sound for a choreography project, that requires you to work interdisciplinarily. Co-creating and co-presenting a multimedia research project about the cultural contexts of a dance genre actively address creativity, collaboration, critical thinking, and communication.

You can also create tremendous opportunities to articulate, process, and practice newly gained information about dance education and dance learning. Outside of the classroom, you may start a blog about your experiences teaching dance in a private studio and how that relates to studying dance on campus. By identifying how learning theories, embodiment, or current trends influence your own dance teaching, you can start to realize how different approaches to dance education work in relationship to your own teaching. Or, you could work with a student outside of dance to find new ways to integrate dance education with other disciplines. Both of these examples can provide a means for you to synthesize and apply new knowledge while also engaging in lively discussion or collaboration, which can help you clarify your thoughts. The more you can unpack how and what you are learning while you are studying dance on campus, the more aware you will become of the comprehensive nature of dance education and how to prepare for a career as a dance educator.

SUMMARY

Dance education is fundamental to advancing dance. People can gain a fuller awareness of themselves and life skills through learning to move in an expressive manner, creatively engaging with dance, and appreciating the history and culture of different dance genres. Many students want to share their excitement about dance through teaching others. No matter what dance genre or aspects of dance interest

you, becoming a successful dance educator requires knowledge of what dance teaches people besides movement coordination, the intentions of various dance education sectors, the relationship between dance education careers, and recognition of current trends within dance education and the professional dance world. As you study dance on campus, seek opportunities to educate others about dance in as many ways as you can imagine. Doing so will deepen your own understanding of dance while also promoting the value of dance education to others.

REVIEW QUESTIONS

1. Briefly define or describe the following: constructivism, embodied and somatic learning, multiple intelligences, and life skills. How do each of these relate to dance education? How do they contribute to a comprehensive understanding of dance?

2. Briefly describe the responsibilities of each of the following careers: dance educator, teaching artist, arts curriculum specialist, and arts education advocate. What aptitudes are needed in each of these careers? How can you gain these skills while studying dance on campus?

3. What are the similarities between different sectors of dance education? What makes each sector unique? Select the sector that best relates to your future goals, and explain how this sector reflects your values as a dancer.

4. What competencies do all successful dance educators share? What skills do dance educators need to have in each of the sectors?

5. Provide a one-sentence summary of each of the following contemporary trends: 21st-century skills, interdisciplinary teaching and learning, integrated curricula, and media and technology. Then, discuss how these trends work together to create a comprehensive understanding of dance.

GLOSSARY

arts curriculum specialist—A person who develops and assesses the effectiveness of arts curricula for schools or other organizations.

arts education advocate—A person who encourages public policy makers to include arts education in schools through demonstrating the scholastic benefits of student engagement in the arts and the importance of arts in the larger society.

conservatory—A learning institution where students primarily focus on the physical and artistic aspects of a specific dance genre.

constructivism—An educational approach that requires students to build their own knowledge while gaining specific skills and information about a subject. Constructivist approaches embrace problem solving, structuring learning around primary concepts, seeking and valuing students' unique points of view, adapting lesson plans to address students' current understanding, and assessing student learning in the context of teaching.

curriculum—The total courses or lessons that a student completes within a given area of study, such as dance.

dance educator—A person who teaches dance to others in a way that values the comprehensive nature of dance.

embodiment—The philosophical assertion that the mind and ways of thinking are largely influenced by the existence of the human body.

interdisciplinary art—Art work that combines two or more different art forms or media.

lesson plans—Outlines for a daily class with a clear learning intention.

pedagogical knowledge—The *how* and *why* of teaching and learning.

postsecondary education—Learning that happens after high school in a college, university, or collegiate-level institution that awards academic degrees or professional certificates.

somatic practices—Movement modalities that aim to fully integrate the body and mind to increase movement awareness and expressivity.

standards-based curriculum—A curricular plan that outlines academic baselines for what students should know and demonstrate by a specific point within a given discipline.

teaching artist—A working professional artist who also has skills as an educator, and creates learning experiences centered on the arts for a variety of people.

BIBLIOGRAPHY

Arts Education Partnership. (2012). Mission/overview. www.aep-arts.org/about-aep/missionoverview.

Association of Teaching Artists. (2012). What is a teaching artist? www.teachingartists.com/whatisaTeachingArtists.htm.

Brooks, J., & Brooks, M. (2000). *In search of understanding: The case for constructivist classrooms.* Alexandria, VA: Association for Supervision and Curriculum Development.

Consortium of National Arts Education Associations. (2002). Authentic connections: Interdisciplinary work in the arts. www.arteducators.org/research/InterArt.pdf.

Gardner, H. (2006). *Multiple intelligences: New horizons.* New York: Basic Books.

Hagood, T. (2000). *A history of dance in American higher education: Dance and the American university.* Lewiston, NY: Mellen Press.

Kassing, G., & Jay, D.M. (2003). *Dance teaching methods and curriculum design.* Champaign, IL: Human Kinetics.

Matthews, J.C. (1998). Somatic knowing and education. *Educational Forum*, 62(3), 236-242.

McCutchen, B.P. (2006). *Teaching dance as art in education.* Champaign, IL: Human Kinetics.

McDonald, R.R., Hargreaves, D., & Miell, D. 2002. *Musical identities.* New York: Oxford University Press.

National Dance Association. (2010). Statistics on dance education and careers in dance. https://web.archive.org/web/20130701124729/http://www.aahperd.org/nda/issues/upload/NDA-2010-Statistics.pdf.

National Dance Education Organization. (2012). About dance education in the United States. www.ndeo.org/content.aspx?page_id=22&club_id=893257&module_id=56441.

Partnership for 21st Century Skills. (2011). Overview. www.p21.org/overview.

Schupp, K. (2012). Thinking like a dancer. *Theatre, Dance and Performance Training*, 3(1), 131-133.

Sellers-Young, B. (1998). Somatic processes: Convergence of theory and practice. *Theatre Topics*, 8(2), 173-187.

SHAPE America. (2014). National Dance Standards. www.shapeamerica.org/standards/dance.

Solomon R. Guggenheim Foundation. (2012). Learning through art. www.guggenheim.org/new-york/education/school-educator-programs/learning-through-art/about.

Weiss, G., & Haber, H.F. (1999). *Perspectives on embodiment: The intersections of nature and culture.* New York: Routledge.

Dance as a Multifaceted Discipline

After reading this chapter, you will be able to do the following:

- Compare diverse areas of dance artistry.
- Identify and evaluate the role of dance in community arts.
- Examine the goals in dance and ability.
- Distinguish between scientific, somatic, and therapeutic areas in dance.
- Differentiate between dance journalism and dance scholarship.
- Formulate new ways to expand your dance experiences.

Dance continuously pushes into new territories. Ideas about where dance can occur, who can dance, and what dance can teach people are always evolving. The photograph depicts a flash mob. In a flash mob, participants dance in unexpected places, may not necessarily be trained dancers, and bring dance to larger audiences in surprising ways. As with flash mobs, many areas of dance aim to create fresh ways for people to participate in and learn from dance.

Chapter 8 outlines some of the multifaceted areas of dance. As your understanding of dance intensifies through studying dance on campus, you will begin to see new opportunities for dance in unexpected places through engaging with dance in new artistic, social, scientific, and scholarly contexts. This chapter introduces established and emerging areas of dance performance. You will learn about the role of dance in community arts and about contemporary practices in differently abled dance. Different scientific, somatic, and therapeutic modalities in dance as well as the role of journalism and scholarship in dance are introduced. Various dance areas are presented so that you are better able to create opportunities for yourself inside and outside of dance, both on campus and beyond.

The dancers in the photograph are enjoying the physicality of dance movement. They are working as a community through performing together; and they are challenging notions about the purpose of dance, where dance can happen, and who can dance. The dance areas discussed in this chapter promote a larger understanding of dance by expanding ideas about the dancing body, where dance takes place, and reasons for dancing. This widening of ideas advances dance as a discipline. As part of the next generation of dancers, you will actively contribute to dance's evolution. Studying dance on campus gives you a solid foundation to build from and the ability to creatively solve problems, leaving you poised to push dance into new territories of your own.

DANCE AND OTHER ARTS

Dance evolves because dance artists and educators continuously question expectations about the arts. This evolution continues today as dancers explore cutting-edge physical, digital, and virtual places for dance performance and work between disciplines to develop new realms for dance such as site dance, video dance, digital performance, and interdisciplinary work. Although the roots of these realms were present more than 50 years ago, they are currently advancing at a rapid pace. Understanding these expanding realms of dance introduces you to some ways that dance is constantly widening its reach.

Site Dance

Although dance performance onstage or in theatrical settings has an extensive history, dance occurs in many other places. Dance works that are specifically created for a nontheatrical space are categorized as **site dance.** In site dance, the physical space itself is an essential part of the choreography. This means that a choreographer may research and compositionally reference the historical, cultural, or social relevance of a place; the dance work may be influenced by the architectural and aesthetic qualities of the place; or both.

Site dance works often create fresh impressions of familiar places for viewers. For a site dance work to be successful, choreographers and dance performers must fully commit to the uniqueness of their selected sites. Audience members may have the freedom to view the dance work from different perspectives and to enter and exit the performance as they please. Therefore, choreographers have to consider all the angles from which the dance could be viewed. Additionally, making site dance works challenges choreographers to carefully consider the context of their selected places. This promotes larger thinking about the content or choreographic intent for a dance work. Site dance expands notions about where and when dance can occur, the role and perspective of audience members, ideas about crafting movement, and the purpose of dance works. Site dance not only broadens expectations about dance, it challenges you to critically consider all the places where you make dance—including the theater—and extends your dance experiences.

Video Dance

From movie musicals to news stories about dancers to television shows devoted to dance, people are comfortable viewing dance on screens. Unlike the formats that frequently utilize video footage of live performances or rehearsals, video dance works are made specifically for the screen. **Video dance** explores how the relationship between the screen, the camera, and dance movement creates images that could not be achieved through viewing a live performance.

Successful video dance works create unusual perspectives on dance movement. In video dance, the viewpoint of the camera directs the audience's

• • • Site dance expands notions about where and when dance can occur.

focus in a specific way. Close-ups provide access to details that may get lost in live performance, and unexpected camera angles can frame movement in ways that are not possible onstage. Editing effects, such as slow motion and fast motion, reversals, and repetition, permit choreographers to manipulate movement into surprising, and perhaps humanly impossible, sequences. Because the performance will always be exactly the same, no matter when the video dance work is viewed, video dance work confronts the fleeting nature of dance. Video dance works can be narrative, abstract, or experimental and can be shown in dance concerts, film festivals, and online. Where dance can take place, the temporal aspects of dance, and notions about movement sequencing are widened through video dance. The skills you learn through creating video dance works are applicable to all aspects of your dance practice and will catalyze your growth as an artist.

Dance and Digital Performance

In contemporary society, digital technology shapes the way we interact with each other. Dance performance, too, has been impacted by digital technology. Works that use media technologies as a central element in their creation and performance are referred to as **digital performances.** Digital performance works can take place in live and virtual spaces, and they can use technologies ranging from video projection to motion capture and everything in between.

In many ways, digital performance amplifies the experience of the moving body in space. Dance art-

ists are prompted to consider how their movement choices shape the aural and visual components of a work when creating digital performance. In an interactive dance work, the dance performers' movements may trigger changes in the music or the speed of video projections. Motion capture technology can be used in live performance to draw shapes in the performance space through projections or to create animated dance works. Dance, visual projections, and music combine in multimedia works to create sensory-rich experiences, and telematic systems bring dancers and audience members from different locations together to share dance in real time. Digital performance both challenges and reinforces the role of the live body in dance performance. The comprehensive nature of creating and performing digital performance works multiplies your compositional and performance sensibilities, which will positively influence all areas of your dance practice.

Interdisciplinary and Transdisciplinary Work

All academic disciplines are inherently connected, and dance artists frequently collaborate with other artists and scholars to enhance their dance works or to address larger societal problems. Interdisciplinary art and transdisciplinary work actively investigate areas of overlap between distinct disciplines. Interdisciplinary art work combines two or more different art forms, as opposed to a more traditional approach that draws from one specific artistic discipline. **Transdisciplinary research** aims to examine and address complex societal problems, such as public health or migration, through recognizing the complexity of an issue, acknowledging the diverse perceptions of the problem, connecting abstract and case-specific knowledge, and developing outcomes and practices that advance what is seen to be the common good. For example, a choreographer may work with scientists to create a community dance project about sustainability to both bring awareness to the issue and to discuss potential solutions. When working transdisciplinarily, dance artists work with experts from a variety of fields, inside and outside of the arts. Dance artists can work collaboratively or combine diverse personal talents when creating interdisciplinary or transdisciplinary works of art.

Some interdisciplinary and transdisciplinary works clearly have dance as the artistic nucleus, whereas others are more movement influenced. Interdisciplinary and transdisciplinary works challenge dancers and audiences to consider three important questions. First, can you categorize a movement-based interdisciplinary or transdisciplinary work as dance? Second, how do dancers, choreographers, and audience members determine the boundaries of dance and other artistic disciplines? Finally, is it necessary to recognize artistic disciplines as distinct, or is it better to look at all the arts as permeable and interrelated? Interdisciplinary and transdisciplinary works make dancers question their personal definitions of dance and other artistic disciplines in a way that can lead to broader notions about what dance can encompass.

DANCE AND COMMUNITY ARTS PRACTICES

Strong bonds are developed between people who dance together. Because dance has an embedded sense of community, it makes sense that many dancers engage in community arts practices and promote social justice. Community arts practices embrace all dance genres as a way to increase access to dance and to encourage personal empowerment through dance. Working with community arts practices helps you better understand the transformative power of dance, and it expands your ideas about what is possible through dance.

Community Dance Projects

Dance has tremendous potential to empower groups of people through working toward a common creative goal, because it is an artistic, cultural, and educational experience. Community dance practices facilitate the expression of a diverse group of people or a specific community through creating and sharing dance movement. They extend access to dance while challenging both participants and facilitators as dance artists.

Community dance projects tend to focus more on the process of creating a work and less on the experience of performing. They are communally created, meaning that although there is usually a facilitator who leads the creative process, the final work represents contributions from all participants. Diversity (in terms of dance genres and demographics) is embraced, because the goal of most community dance projects is increased access to dance. The participants in community dance projects are not professional dancers, and frequently they have little previous experience with dance in a formal context. Senior citizen centers, youth organizations, and rehabilitation facilities are some of the places where community dance projects engage a larger population in dance. Community dance projects can be stand-alone projects or be connected to a larger choreographic or transdisciplinary work, and they expand expectations about who has access to dance, the role of dance in society, and notions about making and sharing dance works. This is a vibrant and rapidly growing branch of dance. When you take advantage of opportunities to work in community arts practices on campus, you will gain valuable skills that will enhance your dance knowledge as a future artist and educator.

Social Justice

Dance has a long history of confronting social injustices. Some dance genres and forms have emerged as a means to cope with or confront oppression, and social themes are frequently used as choreographic content. Today, many dance artists and educators actively use dance as a means to promote equality among people.

Dance intersects with social justice in many ways. Community dance projects may engage vulnerable populations, such as prisoners, political refugees, or at-risk youth, in dance as a means to develop self-esteem and to safely confront emotionally complex and disturbing life events. Dance ethnologists and dance anthropologists might work to preserve dance genres that are threatened by changing political situations. Dance performance has long been used as a means of social commentary as seen in Kurt Jooss's *The Green Table* and Pearl Primus's *Strange Fruit*. Dance artists may work transdisciplinarily with others to implement positive changes in their

Engaging WITH Dance

Sarah Levitt (Community Dance Practitioner and Dance Performer)

When I ask participants to step out of their comfort zones and into a creative process that may be unfamiliar to them, I need to be prepared to take risks as well, and get out of the theater and into the community. In Dance Exchange's two-and-a-half-week residency in Syracuse, New York, in 2012, we were commissioned by Syracuse University to work with faculty, students, and members of the surrounding community to develop a performance work. We'd been in rehearsal for a week when we were invited to attend a monthly gathering of ukulele players called SyraUke. My colleagues and I—none of us musicians—thought we were just going to watch them play, but by the end of the afternoon, we were playing and singing along as snow fell out-side the window, and we formed the kinds of bonds that only happen when you are making music together. This moment, not officially part of our residency, completely changed my relationship with community art making: I realized I could and would be as changed by the work as our participants if I brought not just my artistic skills but my whole self to a place. Since this residency, I've bought my own ukulele, music and song are frequently integrated into our workshops, and the company has written original songs that we'll perform in an upcoming stage work. We can't always anticipate the lasting effects of our work in communities, and I never could have guessed that such a short time in a place could so shift our ways of working.

Photo courtesy of Noelle Bohaty.

local communities. Working in dance and social justice situates dance, and dance artists, as agents of positive social change. Through linking your dance practice with social justice issues, you learn more about yourself as an artist and citizen while widening beliefs about the importance of dance in society.

DANCE AND ABILITY

From pushing the boundaries of physicality to altering the physical presence of the body in digital performance works, questioning the role of the body leads to innovative dance practices. The same is true for ability. Many areas of dance now embrace differently abled dancers. **Differently abled dance** refers to classes, dance companies, choreographic projects, or community dance projects that include participants with and without disabilities. Working in this setting pushes you to consider methods that promote inclusivity while nurturing empathy and creative problem solving in teaching, making, and performing dance. Considering issues related to dance and ability expands ideas about who can dance, how dance is taught, and the range of physicality present in dance.

Dance and Ability in Dance Education

Dance teaches more than physical coordination and artistic expression. Through dancing and learning to dance, the whole person can be educated and awakened. This happens regardless of a person's physical capabilities, which is why differently abled dance has such tremendous potential in educational and community settings.

There are private studios, performing arts community programs, teacher training programs, and community dance projects dedicated to differently abled dance. Differently abled dancers have a strong and long-standing presence in contact improvisation. Because contact improvisation focuses on sensation and collaboration without the use of a set movement vocabulary, there is an organic opportunity for dancers of all abilities to dance together. Outside of contact improvisation, differently abled dance classes can range from teaching creative movement and improvisation to social and theatrical dance genres. The goal of differently abled dance classes, like that of all dance classes, is to help participants achieve their highest creative and artistic potential while encouraging interaction through kinesthetic experiences. Working as an educator in differently abled dance education settings will challenge you to verbally and physically explain movement in diverse ways, to reconsider what is the most important aspect of a dance class, and to find innovative methods to facilitate dance learning. This growth informs your educational development in all dance genres.

Dance and Ability in Dance Performance

Differently abled dance performance addresses an array of choreographic intentions and exists across dance genres. As in all areas of dance performance, choreographers and dance performers in differently abled dance strive to make and perform works that are innovative and expressive through valuing the vast possibilities of human movement and interaction.

Around the world, there are differently abled dance companies as well as choreographers who primarily work in this setting. Usually, differently abled dance companies have a dual mission. By focusing on both professional performance and educational programs, differently abled dance companies are able to bring the power of dance to different populations. The creation and performance of differently abled dance works tend to rely on collaboration among dance performers and on finding a common physical expression among

dance performers. Because of the range of abilities in differently abled dance companies, the movement vocabulary organically embraces a wide range of physicality and movement qualities. Differently abled dance performance directly expands expectations about the body and movement in dance. After working with differently abled dance performance, dance performers and choreographers may find that their own movement vocabularies become more varied as a result of exposure to new ways of working and moving. Creating and performing in a differently abled dance setting can enhance your ability to embody extensive movement qualities and to think much more broadly as a creative artist.

DANCE AND BODIES

The expressive ability of the moving body is central to dance. In dance, there are people who work to better understand dance movement from scientific and somatic perspectives so that dancers can move more safely and with greater attention to internal sensation. Additionally, there are dance practitioners who use the physical and creative aspects of dance in therapeutic settings with nondancers and in health care. Dance scientists, somatic practitioners, and dance therapists explain the causes and effects of dance movement. Learning about dance science, somatic practices, and dance therapy while on campus provides insight into your own movement habits while also elaborating your comprehension of the simultaneous complexity and simplicity of expressive movement.

AXIS Dance Company 2012. Dancers: Joel Brown & Sebastian Grubb. In choreography by Amy Seiwert. Photo by David DeSilva.

• • • Choreographers and dance performers in differently abled dance strive to make and perform works that are innovative and expressive through valuing the vast possibilities of human movement and interaction.

Dance Science

Most dancers are naturally cognizant of how their bodies feel and how they create movement. At the same time, the physical demands of dance can sometimes test dancers' awareness of their bodies and unintentionally lead to injuries and unhealthy situations. The more dancers recognize how their bodies work on a physiological level, the more attuned they can become to safe and efficient movement. Dance science and dance scientists educate dancers about how their bodies work while dancing.

Dance science, sometimes referred to as dance medicine, addresses how scientific principles, primarily related to kinesiology, anatomy and wellness, apply to dancers and dance movement. **Dance scientists** are trained in anatomy, kinesiology, biomechanics, and motor learning, and can include physical therapists, nutritionists, and physicians who specialize in the prevention and treatment of dance-related injuries and health concerns. Dance scientists can work independently or can be affiliated with dance companies, postsecondary educational institutions, research centers, or hospitals. **Kinesiology** is the anatomical study of movement and addresses the physiological, mechanical, and psychological components of movement. Dance scientists advance knowledge of kinesiology and health in dance movement so that dancers can dance more dynamically with more longevity. While studying dance on campus, you will have many opportunities to learn about how your body creates movement from a kinesiological perspective. This knowledge will deepen your own understanding and may lead to new areas of inquiry about dance movement.

Somatic Practices

Learning to dance requires an awareness of internal sensations as well as an aesthetic alertness to how the movement is externally perceived. At times, dancers can become too concerned with how the movement looks on the outside. The feedback dancers receive from a mirror, teacher, or peers can

---

Engaging WITH Dance

Colleen Cully (Somatic Practitioner)

When I started my undergraduate education in dance it was not clear how my learning might translate into a career; I simply knew I wanted to share the benefits of dance with the larger world. A year out of college I started Move Into Greatness, Inc., a small business through which I do exactly that. Several choices I made early on were essential to making Move Into Greatness possible, especially becoming a certified Laban Movement Analyst (LMA), which allowed me to stay broad in my skills, while patiently carving out work related to my unique interests, and participating in small service- and education-oriented businesses.

Becoming certified in the Laban Movement Analysis/Bartenieff Fundamentals material nurtured sophisticated observation, analysis and coaching skills, which allowed me to understand movement diversely enough to bring its value to many different settings. My particular interests are

community dance and the body in the workplace, but developing work in these fields takes time. Both are part of my business, but I also work in other contexts, including fitness and dance education, which support me financially and keep my skills fresh.

Coaching and teaching are only part of my day-to-day experience; tackling the tasks involved with running a small business are the other part. Multiple work and internship experiences introduced me to what it means to run a small business and made owning a small business a viable option. Through behind-the-scenes work I learned about partnerships, marketing and outreach, scheduling, and financial flow that make small businesses function and I was able to implement similar processes for Move Into Greatness. Over time and with careful decision making, Move Into Greatness has been shaped by my needs and interests and ultimately has grown to work for me.

Lauren Bigalow, Photography Editor, The Cornell Daily Sun.`

override their internal awareness of movement. Somatic practices help dancers bring more internal attention to their dancing so that they can move more authentically, efficiently, and expressively. By teaching dancers to listen to and honor internal sensations while moving, somatic practices assist dancers in taking ownership of their dancing and dance learning.

Although somatic practices are not dance genres but rather methods of sensing and self-evaluating movement, they are used extensively in all areas of dance and across all dance genres. All somatic practices aim to strengthen the connection between the mind and body and to cultivate a focused internal awareness of the moving body. There are a variety of somatic practices, including Alexander Technique, Authentic Movement, Bartenieff Fundamentals, Feldenkrais Method, Ideokinesis, and Laban Movement Analysis, among others. **Somatic practitioners** are certified to teach a specific somatic practice and may work independently in educational settings, dance therapy contexts, or in health care. Somatic practices allow your perception of dance to expand by sharpening your internal sensitivity to movement.

Dance Therapy

Dancers are keenly aware of how their emotional states connect to how they move on a given day. Some dancers use movement as a way to work through or express emotional issues that they may not feel comfortable talking about. Because expressive movement is the cornerstone of dance, it is easy to see the therapeutic potential of dance.

Dance therapy, also called *dance movement therapy,* uses dance movement in a psychotherapeutic way to help patients integrate emotionally, behaviorally, cognitively, and physically. Through valuing the interconnected nature of the body, mind, and spirit, **dance therapists** use movement to help people work through psychological problems. Because dance therapy requires a solid comprehension of how the mind, body, and spirit are intertwined, becoming a dance therapist requires licensure that occurs at the graduate level. Dance therapy uses both group and individual sessions that are focused on the creative and somatic aspects of dance movement, and they emphasize the process of creating dance movement more than performance aspects. Rehabilitation centers, medical facilities, educational settings, nursing homes, day-care centers, and private practices are a few of the places where

dance therapy can take place. By prioritizing the interconnections between the body, mind, and spirit that are present in dance movement, dance therapists help people to psychologically heal through movement. Plus, it teaches dancers to progressively think about the significance of dance movement inside and outside of dance.

Dance and Health Care

Dance increases physical awareness and well-being, teaches participants about themselves and others, and can make people feel better physically, emotionally, and mentally. Because dancing benefits participants in numerous ways, it makes sense that health care professions are introducing dance to promote and nurture healing processes.

The arts can be used for therapeutic, educational, and expressive purposes in health care. Creatively interacting with the arts has been shown to reduce stress and the perception of pain in patients (Society for the Arts in Health Care 2012). Participating in the arts can increase the overall care of patients and increase patient adherence to treatment. Additionally, engaging in arts provides a safe place for patients and caregivers to process difficult experiences with illnesses. Research in the field of dance and health care continues to demonstrate that creatively participating in the arts increases overall well-being. In particular, dance has been shown to have a positive impact on patients who have diseases that affect movement, such as Parkinson's disease and fibromyalgia (Rollins, Sonke, Cohen, Boles, & Li 2009). The potential for dance in health care continues to grow and reminds everyone of the benefits of expressive movement. Dance and health care also encourage wider thinking about the role and place of dance in society.

DANCE AND WRITING

Physically participating in dance is a great way to learn about dance; however, information is also transmitted through reading and writing about dance. Like other areas of dance, dance writing requires creativity and an extensive knowledge of dance. Criticism, journalism, and scholarship are means for deepening and sharing what is known about dance. Writing about dance provides an opportunity to connect divergent thoughts, engage in lively debates about dance, and evaluate dance practices. Although the primary way to learn dance movement is through physical practice, reading and

Engaging WITH Dance

Alyssa Schoeneman (Dance Writer)

Dance writers educate the public about the professional dance world that exists beyond the mainstream media. They shine light on the field's successes and failures, its important initiatives and areas of need, and the people who make it all possible. Ideally, dance writers arm readers with the tools they need to consume and support an ever-evolving art form.

So, how is a dance writer made?

Although most college dance programs offer composition courses, a devoted dance writer can expect to do a lot of individual research. While in school, a dance writer should strive to see as much dance as possible—both live and on film. Dance video libraries often exist on campus as well as online.

A Twitter account is useful in keeping abreast of dance-related news. Dance writers often follow Twitter accounts representing dance companies, dance media groups, dance writers, and dance educators. By tuning into these sources, dance writers can access the most up-to-date information about their topics of interest.

To develop skills as writer-reporters, aspiring dance writers should get involved with their college newspapers or other local news organizations. Young dance writers can use these news media outlets to gain experience in working on deadlines and in working with editors.

Dance writers encounter professional dance artists and art administrators on a personal level—a rare and exciting opportunity for dance enthusiasts everywhere!

Photo courtesy of Ian Noble.

writing about dance is fundamental to an expansive understanding of the art form.

Dance Criticism and Journalism

In our everyday lives, we consult newspapers, magazines, and websites to find information. In these sources, journalism and criticism give us factually based data (such as weather forecasts), expert evaluations (such as restaurant reviews), and in-depth examinations of people and events (such as a feature articles on celebrities). Criticism and journalism are also present in dance, and inform people about dance in their communities and around the world.

Dance journalism includes writing, reporting, or editing about dance, or photographing dance for a general audience. **Dance journalists** are the people who find and then produce information about dance, dancers, or dance events, and then share it with a larger audience. **Dance criticism** refers to describing and evaluating dance works and performances. The individuals who specialize in the written evaluation and appreciation of dance are **dance critics.** Some dance journalists and dance critics may specialize in one dance genre but many cover a wide range of dance genres and interests. Dance publications, major and local news agencies, and a variety of websites and blogs employ dance critics and dance journalists. Regardless of where dance critics and dance journalists publish their work, they report various aspects of dance to the general public. As they boost the general public's awareness of dance, they also help dancers stay up-to-date on current happenings and trends in the dance world.

Dance Scholarship

Many thoughts are cognitively, intuitively, and physically processed while dancing or observing dance. This information is valuable but fleeting, and it is therefore impossible to retain it all at times. Dance research is one way to process, develop, and contextualize those thoughts and what happens in dance so that our understanding of dance goes beyond the physical experience.

Dance scholarship, or dance research, strives to increase the recognition of dance as an intellectual discipline grounded in artistic, cultural, scientific, and educational practices. **Dance scholars** are individuals who investigate, develop new knowledge, publish, and speak about dance through a dance research lens. Dance ethnographers and dance anthropologists are dance scholars, as are dance historians, philosophers of dance, and others. All areas and genres of dance are present in dance scholarship. Most dance scholars are affiliated with postsecondary educational institutions, but some work independently. Several have been involved with the physical practice of dance, either as a students or professionals, so they have a deep physical knowledge of dance movement. Dance scholarship bolsters your intellectual comprehension of dance in numerous ways. As you engage with dance scholarship, your intellectual understanding of dance intensifies, which in turn enhances your competency as a dance artist and dance educator.

EMBRACING DANCE AS A MULTIFACETED DISCIPLINE

By studying dance on campus, you are actively expanding your dance knowledge. As you learn more about dance and about yourself as a dancer, you will discover new possibilities for yourself and for the field of dance. It is important that you proactively create opportunities to connect your dance studies to emerging ideas and practices, inside and outside of dance. This will not only widen your dance education but will better prepare you to proactively contribute to the evolution of dance as a multifaceted discipline in a variety of ways and contexts.

Personal Expansion

Dance evolves because dance professionals embrace new challenges throughout their careers. Take advantage of your time studying dance on campus to test your understanding of dance in dance and beyond. Opportunities for collaborating with your fellow arts students or creating site dances may already be present in your dance curriculum. Or, there may be a chance to enroll in a class focused on video dance. These are valuable occasions to challenge yourself as a dance student in unfamiliar territories. At the same time, you should proactively step out of your comfort zone. It would be advantageous to collaborate with students outside of dance, to experiment with dance and digital media, or to work on a transdisciplinary project. The broader your art making and performing experiences are while studying on campus, the more possibilities you have for finding your personal niche in dance.

Maybe you are interested in bringing dance to different communities and populations. If so, you should take advantage of circumstances that bring you into contact with diverse communities. Some campuses have specific courses that address community arts practices. Fully investing in these courses

Tim Trumble

• • • By studying dance on campus, you are actively expanding your dance knowledge.

will give you opportunities to learn valuable facilitation skills that are applicable to all areas of dance while also preparing you to work in community settings. You may find it constructive to enroll in a course or workshop about dance and ability. These will expand your thinking about choreography and dance teaching and give you skills to work in the differently abled dance field. The more information you can digest about working with diverse populations, the better prepared you are for a potential dance career.

There are numerous resources on campus if you are curious about dance science, dance somatics, dance therapy, or dance and health care. It is likely that you will learn about kinesiology and somatics, both directly and indirectly, in your dance curriculum. Look for chances to apply this information in your coursework. When writing self-assessment papers or giving peer feedback, you can practice using anatomical and somatic language. This connects scientific and somatic knowledge of dance to your own personal experience of moving. Additionally, students who are excited about these fields would benefit from enrolling in kinesiology, psychology, or health and wellness classes. Volunteer experiences can also supplement your dance education in these disciplines.

Dance writing will be present in your curriculum. The more you can value writing as an opportunity to synthesize, reflect on, and share your dance learning, the more beneficial it will be to your dance education. Students who are passionate about dance writing should consider taking creative writing or research methods classes. Extracurricular activities, such as writing for the campus newspaper or contributing to a dance blog, can provide valuable real-life writing experiences. If you are interested in dance writing, the best way to grow is to practice, making it essential to find opportunities related to dance writing while studying dance on campus.

Regardless of what area of dance you are most passionate about, it is essential that you are cognizant of how dance is reaching into new territories. Understanding the breadth of dance practices encourages you to find new connections inside and outside of dance. This helps to deepen your comprehension of dance and contributes to the evolution of dance.

New Areas for Expansion

Dance advances because dance professionals continuously question accepted ideas about dance. As you study dance on campus and engage in critical and creative thinking about dance, you are actively contributing to dance's expansion. Often students think that the sole purpose of studying dance on campus is to gain skills to enter the professional field. While this is very important, it is equally imperative that you be prepared to shape and respond to the future progression of dance as a discipline.

You can contribute to broadening notions about dance in many ways while on campus. You may start by reflecting on how your own awareness of dance has increased since you started studying dance on campus. Noticing how your own perception of dance has perhaps changed a great deal in a short amount of time demonstrates how much potential there is for dance in the world. Perhaps you perform with dancers from your local private studio or high school, teach youth dance classes, or are involved in a community organization that would benefit from learning about emerging practices in dance. Sharing your accumulating ideas about dance can help you think in new ways about dance.

As you look to the future, think very broadly about what you can do with dance and what dance can do for the world. Hopefully, there is an area where your answers to these questions intersect. Keeping an open mind about dance and unfamiliar dance experiences is critical to finding this area of intersection. Staying open might lead to you finding a component of dance you are very passionate about but had no idea that it existed before studying dance on campus. Staying open and finding or creating personally relevant and innovative areas of dance let your own knowledge, skills, and abilities expand while actively contributing to dance's ongoing evolution.

SUMMARY

Dance continues to mature in all areas of the discipline. This expansion brings dance to more people and widens the purposes of dance in society. It also deepens appreciation for the knowledge inherent in dance. Studying dance on campus gives you not only a fundamental understanding of the current professional field of dance but also the ability to advance the artistic, cultural, and educational practices of dance. It is up to you, as a member of the next generation of dance professionals, to proactively shape the expansion of dance into areas that are relevant to you and society. The more opportunities you can find and create to familiarize yourself with expanding dance practices, the more prepared you will be to enter the professional field of dance and to move dance forward.

REVIEW QUESTIONS

1. Compare site dance, video dance, digital performance, and interdisciplinary and transdisciplinary work. How are they interrelated? How are they distinct?

2. Outline the goals of community arts practices. How do they relate to dance as an artistic, cultural, and educational practice? How do community arts practices expand ideas about dance?

3. Describe the ways in which dance can promote social justice. How can working with dance and social justice align with the goals of community arts practices?

4. What are the goals of differently abled dance? Differently abled dance education? How does differently abled dance connect to artistic, cultural, and educational dance practices?

5. What are the differences between dance science, somatic practices, dance therapy, and dance and health care? What are the similarities? How do these disciplines advance artistic, cultural, and educational dance practices?

6. What are the goals of dance journalism and dance criticism? What are the goals of dance scholarship? How does each area contribute to a wider and deeper understanding of dance?

7. Outline three ways you can expand your dance experiences and knowledge this semester. How do these pertain to ideas presented in this chapter? How do they relate to your previous dance experiences and future dance goals?

GLOSSARY

dance criticism—The act of describing and evaluating dance works and performances.

dance critics—Professionals who specialize in the written evaluation and appreciation of dance.

dance journalism—An area of dance writing that includes writing, reporting, editing, or photographing about dance for a general audience.

dance journalists—Professionals who find and then produce information about dance, dancers, or dance events and then share it with a larger audience.

dance scholars—Professionals who investigate, develop new knowledge, publish, and speak about dance through a dance research lens.

dance scholarship—An area of dance that strives to increase the recognition of dance as an intellectual discipline grounded in artistic, cultural, and educational practices.

dance science—An area in dance that addresses how scientific principles, primarily related to kinesiology and health, apply to dancers and dance movement.

dance scientist—A general term that refers to practitioners who work in dance science, and can include physical therapists, nutritionists, and physicians who specialize in the treatment of dancers.

dance therapists—Professionals who use movement to help people work through psychological problems.

differently abled dance—Classes, dance companies, choreographic projects, or community dance projects that include participants with and without disabilities.

digital performance—Works that use media technologies as a central element in the creation and performance of works.

kinesiology—The anatomical study of movement, which addresses the physiological, mechanical, and psychological components of movement.

site dance—Dance works that are specifically created for a non-theatrical space.

somatic practitioners—Professionals who are certified to teach a specific somatic practice.

transdisciplinary art work—Work that draws on any art form or non-arts discipline as needed to investigate a given topic and develops new knowledge.

video dance—Works that explore how the relationship between the screen, the camera, and dance movement creates images that could not be achieved through viewing a live performance.

BIBLIOGRAPHY

Albright, A.C. (2001). Strategic abilities: Negotiating the disabled body in dance. In Dils, A., & Albright, A.C. (Eds.), *Moving history/dancing cultures: A dance history reader*. Middletown, CT: Wesleyan University Press.

American Dance Therapy Association. (2012). About dance/movement therapy. www.adta.org/Default.aspx?pageId=378213.

Axis Dance Company. (2012). About us. axisdance.org/about-us.

Byrnes, W. (2009). *Management and the arts*. Oxford, UK: Elsevier.

Candco Dance Company. (2012). About us. www.candoco.co.uk/about-us.

Congress on Research in Dance. (2012). About us. http://cordance.org/aboutus.

Dixon, S. (2007). *Digital Performance: A history of new media in theater, dance, performance art, and installation.* Cambridge, MA: MIT Press.

Dodds, S. (2001). *Dance on screen: Genres and media from Hollywood to experimental art.* New York: Palgrave.

Eddy, M. (2009). A brief history of somatic practices and dance: Historical development of the field of somatic education and its relationship to dance. *Journal of Dance and Somatic Practices,* 1(1): 5-27.

Foundation for Community Dance. (2012). About us. www.communitydance.org.uk/about-community-dance.html.

Heaphy, A. & Bansal, A. (2008). Arts in health care: Best practices. http://www.med.umich.edu/goa/NEA%20model%20program%20pg4.pdf.

Hirsch Hadorn, G., Hoffmann-Riem, H., Biber-Klemm, S., Grossenbacher-Mansuy, W., Joye, D., Pohl, C., Wiesmann, U., & Zemp, E. (Eds.) (2007). *Handbook of transdisciplinary research.* Bern, Switzerland: Springer.

International Association for Dance Medicine and Science. (2012). About IADMS. http://www.iadms.org/?page=A8.

Jackson. N., & Sharpio-Phim, T. (Eds.). (2008). *Dance, human rights, and social justice: Dignity in motion.* Lanham, MD: Scarecrow Press.

Joint Forces Dance Company. (2012). Dance ability international history. www.danceability.com/history.php.

Kloetzel, M., & Pavlik, C. (Eds.). (2011). *Site dance: Choreographers and the allure of alternative spaces.* Gainesville, FL: University Press of Florida.

Kuppers, P. (2007). *Community performance: An introduction.* New York: Routledge.

LeFevre, C. (2008). Let's take it outside. *Dance Magazine,* 82(4). http://www.dancemagazine.com/issues/April-2008/Lets-Take-it-Outside.

Lerman, L. (2011). *Hiking the horizontal: Field notes from a choreographer.* Middletown, CT: Wesleyan University Press.

Rollins, J., Sonke J., Cohen, R., Boles, A., & Li, J. (2009). State of the field report: Arts in health care/2009. http://thesah.org/doc/reports/State%20of%20the%20Field%20Report%2009.pdf.

Society for the Arts in Health Care. (2012). Arts and health. www.thesah.org/template/page.cfm?page_id=604.

Society of Dance History Scholars. (2012). Mission statement. http://sdhs.org/about.

9

Dance and Reflection

After completing this chapter, you will be able to do the following:

- Define reflection and the purposes of reflection.
- Discuss reflection processes.
- Evaluate the use of reflective practices in dance learning and dance professions.
- Develop your own reflective practice.

The ability to make informed and relevant decisions is essential to your dance education and future success in dance. Each dance experience you partake in, from working with your peers on a class project to your first professional opportunity, contributes to your learning. You build on current dance knowledge and gain a broader understanding of dance through each dance experience. The students in the photograph are taking a moment to reflect on their dance experiences so that they can gain a deeper awareness of dance and their learning process. Reflecting on your present dance experiences can help you assess your dance learning, identify emerging areas of interest and challenges, and create personal growth. This sensibility allows you to make educated choices about how to deepen your comprehension of dance and to pursue new opportunities.

Chapter 9 introduces you to the value of reflective practices in your dance education and beyond. As you study dance on campus and throughout your career, the ability to reflect on your work and progress can lead to continuous self-directed growth. In this chapter, you will learn the definition and purposes of reflection. Reflection processes, such as journal writing and group discussion, are presented. You will evaluate the use of reflection in your dance education and dance professions, and you will learn to develop your own method for reflection. Recognizing the role of reflection in dance can help you feel anchored while embracing unfamiliar dance experiences, and it can help you navigate your dance education and future career in a knowledgeable and personal way.

In the photograph the dancers are reflecting on what they have just accomplished in class. This reflective pause encourages students to recall and evaluate their participation while also revealing some of the choices they have made. Through reflection you can uncover worthwhile information about recently acquired content, methods of learning, and fresh areas for investigation. As the world of dance evolves, it is essential that you be able to reflect on and assess your dance understanding. Doing so ensures that your dance proficiency will constantly expand, which can assist you in pursuing a variety of dance opportunities in personally meaningful ways.

REFLECTIVE PRACTICES

In all areas of life, people learn through experience. You learn to ride a bike by actually riding a bike, to read through the process of reading, and to cook through preparing food. It is likely that you made mistakes, discovered things, and found individual strategies for success while learning each of these and other skills. Taking the time to reflect on your experiences provides insight into how you learn,

Engaging WITH Dance

Alexandra Mathews (Arts Administrator)

Sometimes I think if my college diploma listed self-reflection as my major, it would more accurately represent my undergraduate experience. That is the skill I feel I developed most when I attended the World Arts and Cultures department at UCLA, studying dance and choreography. Intimate class discussions, dance composition, and experimental performances demanded varying degrees of self-reflection. They emphasized a need for basic curiosity.

To be self-reflective does not require absolute certainty. It's a process toward deeper understanding, not a means to an end. As a postgraduate professional, I find that the foundations built at UCLA support my yoga, creative writing, and teaching practice. Not to mention my work as a program assistant for the Herb Alpert Award in the Arts as well as a managing director for another arts organization called Pentacle. Each practice shapes my own understanding of how I think and act; they allow me to notice thought patterns, habits, and tendencies. Without a specific sense of awareness, intention is lost. Without intention, what's the point? It doesn't feel good. If I self-reflect, I have an opportunity to sharpen my listening. If I listen, I hear what questions I have. If I ask, I am likely to minimize self-doubt and further cultivate a vision I deem valuable.

your evolving interests, and emerging areas for exploration. Engaging in reflection helps you to proactively scaffold your learning, inside and outside of dance.

Defining Reflection

Reflection refers to the practice of taking time to notice, carefully consider, and assess an experience. Reflection values asking questions about your experiences in order to come to a more complete realization and understanding of what you have learned through that experience. It can illuminate aspects of the experience that may have been overlooked in the moment, and if regularly practiced, reflection can help you realize how you learn. When you think about your thinking, fundamental assumptions behind your practice are revealed. Engaging in reflection promotes a deeper comprehension of your experiences, highlights what you know and how you came to know it, and exposes knowledge gaps. It provides valuable information about how to enhance future experiences to increase your understanding.

Imagine that you just completed a memorable dance performance. During the performance, you are so deeply invested in your dancing that the only things you notice are the sensations of dancing, the connections with other performers and the audience, and being fully present in the choreography. When the performance ends, you realize that this performance felt more special than previous dance performances, yet you are not sure why. You can learn a lot from a dance performance if you take the time to reflect on what you have learned through performing. You might take time to recall the performance from your viewpoint as a performer. Then you might ask yourself about what made the performance feel magical, how you prepared differently for this performance than previous performances, and what you discovered through performing. After answering your questions you can take time to review your observations and answers to find out how and why this performance was different from others, what you have learned, and what types of performances you are now ready to pursue.

Purpose of Reflection

The act of reflecting on an experience helps people learn in four distinct yet interrelated ways. First, it helps people identify what they already know. Reflection also helps people determine what they need to know to advance their understanding of a given topic. Making contextual sense of new information gained through experience is another way that reflection helps people learn. Finally, reflection can help people determine choices for advancing their learning. In this way, reflection is needed because it helps people to identify what they know and how their previous knowledge relates to learning more about a subject, to understand new experiences, and to build on recently gained abilities. Although reflection can always be beneficial to the learning process, reflecting on specific types of experiences can be especially beneficial. Reflecting on struggles can bring out what is working and is not, which creates an opportunity to thoughtfully evaluate a challenging situation. On the other hand, reflecting on an aha moment can help affirm what is exciting or fulfilling about an experience and shed light on what fuels a person's creativity. Because reflection is based on noticing, questioning, and appraising an experience, a great deal of valuable learning can be unearthed.

Reflection can be useful in the creative process. For example, imagine you are choreographing a dance for an upcoming student performance. About three weeks before the show, you suddenly feel very frustrated with one section of the choreography. No matter what you do, that section just isn't working. Reflecting on this struggle will help you find what is working and not working in your choreographic process and assist in determining areas that you need more information about, which can range from advice about choreographic tools to learning more about your choreographic subject matter. You may find that you were calling upon skills gained from a previous choreographic situation, such as choreographing a dance routine for children, without considering how that know-how applies to this specific context. Reflecting on difficult moments brings attention to your current choreographic process while also revealing ways for your choreographic process to advance. Hopefully, reflecting on your choreographic process will lead to many breakthrough moments, which can bring light to how your creativity is expanding.

Reflection Processes

Chances are that you already participate in reflection. There are many approaches, but the reflection process is always focused on examining a specific experience. Most reflective practices combine narrative descriptions and asking questions or discussing as a means for excavating relevant knowledge from an experience. Narrative descriptions, or telling your story of an experience, require you to notice and describe what happened. Discussing allows

Engaging WITH Dance

Tomoko Takedani Sater (Artistic Director and Choreographer)

I moved to New York City after completing my dance degree, hoping to further my dance career. After auditioning for several companies and not getting any callbacks, I started to think back on my experiences: *What happened or didn't happen, and why? What could I have done differently to change that experience?* Then, when I had a particularly satisfying class, I'd ask myself these questions: *What happened? What made it happen, and how? How did it make me feel? How was it perceived by others? Why did I do it that way?*

These internal investigations led me to the most fundamental and essential questions in my career: *Why do I dance?* and *What does dance mean to me?*

In my quest for answers to these questions, I cofounded a dance theater company with two

© Aruna Mall

of my very close friends, who asked themselves the very same questions. Our creative process always started with asking these questions: *Why do we want to create this work? What do we want to communicate through it?*

Then it hit me that it was exactly the same kind of exercise my dance professors had us do with journal assignments, which I absolutely hated. Back then, dancing to me was all about experiencing the *now,* and reflecting on that experience felt irrelevant. I wish I had listened to my dance professors and journaled better.

Just like dance, our lives consist of fleeting moments. Reflection is a way to make a lasting impression out of it.

you to build and articulate your thought process during and around the experience. Reflection can take place individually, such as through journaling, or collectively, such as through group discussions. Frequently, people engage in both individual and collective reflective processes, especially in subject areas that require a great deal of self-awareness and collaboration.

Young dance educators frequently participate in individual and collective reflection in order to make sense of their teaching and to refine their pedagogy. Newly hired high school dance educators might maintain teaching journals in which they recount their day-to-day teaching as well as engage in a written dialogue with themselves about the struggles and breakthroughs they observe in their teaching. This personal journal is a way for teachers to track their development as educators. From time to time, high school dance educators from a school district might get together, either formally or informally, to collectively reflect on what is working and not working in the district's dance curriculum and teaching methods. Because the dance educators have already

individually reflected on their own practices, the collective reflection will be much more valuable. In the case of dance education, both individual and collective reflection are needed, because teachers need to constantly assess their own teaching with an awareness of the evolving goals of their schools and districts.

When to Reflect

Although learning can usually be heightened through reflection, you might find that some experiences are more ripe for reflection than others. Reflecting on first-time experiences, such as starting college, can help you feel more grounded; it will reveal what you already know and the strengths you have to build on. Concluding experiences, such as finishing your first semester of college, are excellent check-in points for reflection. Reflecting on these moments provides an opportunity to survey changes in your learning, how much you have grown, and areas to improve on next semester. Discipline-specific milestones, such as completing your first college dance exam, are also important reflective moments, because these situations usually involve applying previously obtained knowledge to different contexts, and it is important to notice how you are using information in new ways. The opportunities for reflection are everywhere, and it is up to you to determine and create chances for reflection so that your learning and experiences continually expand.

Because reflection helps you make sense of an experience, it can be incredibly useful when encountering an unfamiliar culture. Imagine you are studying abroad in New Zealand, where you learn about the Maori, the indigenous people with a rich dance tradition. As part of your curriculum you enroll in a Maori dance class. The movement and music are both unusual to you, and at first you feel very lost in your dance class. After taking some time to reflect, you realize that you can use previously obtained skills, such as rhythmic acuity gained from tap dancing, isolation skills from urban dance forms, and the discipline that you use in all of your dance studies to approach this dance genre. At the same time, you might realize that it is okay to struggle with a dance genre and that you enjoy learning dances of diverse cultures. Taking the time to investigate where you are, what you need to know, how you are applying your knowledge, and how you can continuously scaffold your dance learning is essential in all areas of dance.

Routines for Reflection

Reflection is a great way to gain insight from your past experiences, to bring awareness to your current experiences, and to determine future areas of inquiry. However, reflection is only valuable if it is put into practice. How often, how much, and why reflection occurs vary from person to person and experience to experience. Reflection can occur daily or after significant events. The depth of reflection can span from simply observing your present experience to an in-depth analysis of past events. Some people may engage in reflection to identify habitual thinking patterns, while others might participate in group reflection to develop collective thinking about a specific issue. The range of reasons and methods for reflecting are as unique as the individuals who partake in reflective practices. The habit of creating time for reflection allows people to examine their experiences in a way that recognizes how their thinking and learning are constantly evolving.

Imagine a group of students enrolled in a campus dance class where the class content is exciting and new to all students. One student may decide to take 15 minutes after each class to write in her journal about that day's class. She records the discoveries and challenges of the class, and she reviews her journal writings about once a month to look for reoccurring challenges, things that are improving, and fresh

---

Engaging WITH Dance

Lindsay Chmielowiec (K–12 Dance Educator)

I have been a lifelong journal writer, but during my undergraduate years at Kent State University I was required to reflect on movement in a direct manner, using composition journals, imagery exercises, critiques, and student-teaching progress notes. That practice of reflection is now something I incorporate into my own dance teaching at Schenectady High School in New York State. I require my students to keep a dance journal, which then allows me to access their thoughts and experiences in ways they may not be comfortable sharing in class.

Each summer, I attend an annual dance teacher intensive that rejuvenates and re-focuses me for the coming year. Reflection with notes and concepts from the intensive helps me to incorporate the information I learn into my own instruction and teaching goals. In the eyes of education, reflection is documentation required for evidence of growth and professional development. Personally, however, it has prevented stagnancy in my creative movement process by archiving thoughts and ideas from a specific time and place.

Photo courtesy of Laura Naso.

ways of thinking. Another student calls his parents every week and describes his progress in the class. As his parents ask questions about the class, he is able to see how his thinking about dance is changing. There may also be a group of students who meet once a month to discuss what is working and not working in their approaches to class as a means to unpack their learning. Although these students are part of the same class, they have each found their own way to reflect on the class. Personalizing their reflective practices helps them to make sense of their experiences, which empowers them in their learning.

PURPOSE OF REFLECTION IN DANCE

While the practice of reflecting is incredibly valuable to everyone, it is especially useful in dance. Reflection values learning through experience and inquiry, both of which are central to all areas of dance. Because of this, it is important that you realize how reflection can empower you in your education while dancing on campus and help you expand your knowledge and practice of dance as a professional.

Dance and Reflection on Campus

Your time on campus will include several firsts, such as living away from home for the first time, studying an unfamiliar dance genre, traveling abroad, trying diverse choreographic methods, and many others. Each of these firsts is a learning opportunity for you. Some of these situations might make you feel uncertain at first, but most will lead to important discoveries and information that will contribute to your overall growth as a person and dancer. Taking the time to step back and observe your experiences can make you feel more grounded. Becoming aware of what you know and how you are using that expertise can make you feel more secure in a new situation, which in turn can help you become more open, and increase your ability to learn about yourself, a situation, and a given subject matter.

Because reflection is an important way for you to take account of your learning, you might find that several of your courses include elements of reflection. In a movement or technique class, you might be required to complete self-assessments in which you discuss your progress in relation to a specific technical or aesthetic principle. Identifying how you make decisions is an important part of comprehending your creative process, so many composition and improvisation classes require students to maintain journals as a way to notice choreographic choice making, tendencies, and how an idea becomes a dance. In contextual courses such as dance history, students are often expected to discuss how course content relates to their dance interests. In order to do this, students need to examine their thinking about various historical events and innovators to determine how they relate to their personal dance interests. Incorporating elements of reflection helps you understand how the large and expanding field of dance relates to your individual interests.

In addition to your in-class dance learning, you will likely participate in several out-of-class dance experiences while studying dance on campus. Although these experiences may not be directly related to a specific course, they provide excellent opportunities to learn how your coursework relates to the field of dance. Sometimes, it is easier to notice your growth outside of class, which makes reflecting on out-of-class performances especially valuable. If you are a member of a dance club on campus, you might reflect on how your development of technical and artistic proficiency is present in your dance club performances. Perhaps the dance studio you studied and taught at before starting college invites you to teach a guest class. Taking the time to notice how your teaching methods have changed since you last taught at your studio can help reveal how you are using recently learned pedagogical theories. Each new dance experience you participate in, both in class and outside of class, can contribute to significant learning if you take the time to reflect on each one. By figuring out what you know, what you need to know to advance, and how you are applying information can help you determine opportunities to advance your learning. To fully benefit from studying dance on campus, it is important that you engage in a reflective practice. Doing so allows you to navigate your changing ideas about dance in relationship to new dance experiences on campus.

Dance Professions and Reflection

Success in dance, regardless of what area of dance you pursue, depends on constant learning. The dance education you receive on campus will give you not only the skills to smoothly enter the field of dance but also the aptitudes to continuously learn more about yourself, dance, and potential opportunities in dance. Through thoughtfully reflecting and determining next steps, dance professionals can proactively shape their areas of expertise and successfully navigate rewarding career trajectories in dance.

Reflection is a part of many careers in dance. Choreographers need to engage in reflection so that they can honestly assess their choreographic processes, consider how their choreographic approaches work in different contexts, such as work for the stage versus site-specific choreography, and discover evolving choreographic interests and challenges. These discoveries can provide insight about how to approach a new dance work or to seek out diverse venues for presenting their choreography. Dance educators practice reflection to ensure that they are effective teachers. When they take the time to notice teaching tendencies, dance educators unearth their strengths and challenges as teachers. Reflection helps educators carefully consider approaches to build on their strengths in order to address their teaching challenges, potentially leading to original teaching methods and more comprehensive student learning. Somatic practitioners use reflection as a means to help their clients better sense the postural and emotional changes that can occur through strengthening the link between the mind and body. Once these changes are observed and recorded, the somatic practitioner and client are able to make informed decisions about how the somatic work will progress. Frequently, dance professionals' interests change as their careers progress. The ability to identify changing interests allows dancers to seek dance experiences in a directed way. For example, through consistent reflection, a dance performer might realize that he is becoming increasingly interested in dance science. The ability to recognize this interest might lead to taking anatomy classes at a community college while still working as a performer. Dance is a multifaceted discipline, and through active reflection, dance professionals are able to continuously learn more and follow their interests in a proactive way.

Additionally, reflection is important to dance because it inspires people to better know themselves. Dance is an expressive art form and, in many cases, it is a collective activity. In most areas of dance, professionals are expected to express their ideas through movement and words. Communication, whether it be portraying an idea through a dance or explaining an idea in a classroom, is a central component of most dance careers. Through reflecting, people's core values and fundamental assumptions are revealed. People learn how they process information and the experiences that are important to them. This self-knowledge is a pathway to expressivity and effective communication. Dance professionals can learn more about themselves through reflection, which can lead to a more personal engagement with dance.

DEVELOPING A PERSONAL REFLECTIVE PRACTICE

As you experience dance, both on campus and as a dance professional, it is important to pause and reflect on what you are learning about dance, yourself, and how dance relates to other interests. This ongoing assessment situates you as a lifelong learner

Engaging WITH Dance

Stephanie West (Pilates Instructor)

© Roger West

As a dance performance major at Kent State University, I was constantly "on" until a near-fatal car accident forced me "off" to the sidelines. With a broken back and pelvis, I could not participate in class, but I sat and took notes. It was there that I was almost forced into reflection. Watching the dancers and noting their anatomical vulnerabilities to injury eventually led me to a full-blown career as a Pilates teacher of teachers in New York and internationally. Without that time to reflect, I wouldn't have been able to find my niche in the movement world. Whatever country or city I'm in, I always remind the apprentices to take some time and work **on** their practice rather than always working **in** their practice. What they discover through this reflection might just spark an idea that will fuel the rest of their career.

of dance, which is essential to finding and creating new opportunities for yourself in dance. It also provides you with tools for navigating an expanding professional field. As you learn more about dance, you may find that your interests evolve and that you need more education about a certain area in order to move forward. At the same time, the professional field of dance is always expanding. Developing a personal reflective practice is a way for you to proactively respond to personal and professional changes while experiencing dance on campus and beyond.

You may already have ways of reflecting on your experiences. Many people keep journals where they write their observations, successes, and frustrations on a regular basis. Others need to talk through their days with a trusted companion. Maybe you find that you need to take a walk to clear your head, or that swimming or another rhythmic and repetitive physical activity helps you organize your thoughts. All of these means provide a way for you to pause and observe recent experiences, which is part of developing a reflective practice.

After you determine which method of reflection works most organically for you, the next step is to center your reflection on observation and inquiry. Starting with a nonjudgmental description of an experience provides a way to record your experience before questioning it. Asking yourself three simple questions can help you determine what you have learned from a given experience. A good place to start is to assess the positive aspects of the experience. Questions related to this might include *What worked, and why?* or *How and where was I successful?* Next, it is important to notice any challenges that emerged. At this point, you might ask the question *What did not work, and why?* or *When and how did challenges emerge?* The last question you ask yourself should provide a link to future experiences. Questions such as *What did I learn from this experience? What might I do differently next time?*, or *What questions are still lingering?* help you determine what experiences or information are needed for personal growth. When you pause to observe and question an experience, you are able to reveal what you already know and do well, what you need to learn next, and how you make sense of newly gained knowledge, and you are able to determine where to go next.

Of course reflection is only valuable if it is practiced. This means that you need to create a habit of reflection. For most people, setting up a daily or weekly routine works best. Perhaps you can set aside 20 minutes a day to collect your thoughts. Or, you can make sure to set aside time after significant experiences, such as your first time teaching a dance class or completing a dance film, to reflect on what you have learned. While you study dance on campus, formal opportunities for reflection will likely be built into your classes. It is important, however, that you create your own habit of reflection. Individualizing your reflective practice and making it a part of your normal routine will ensure that you reflect on your dance experiences as a young professional.

Perhaps the most important aspect of reflection is acting on what you have learned through the process of reflection. For example, imagine that through reflecting on the coordination of a student dance performance you discover that you really enjoy the organizational aspects of this type of work but that you lack expertise in this area. The next step would be to find opportunities to learn more about arts administration so that future experiences coordinating dance performances continue to expand your knowledge base. Engaging in reflective practice puts you in the driver's seat of your dance education and career. Therefore, it is important that you develop a reflective practice while studying dance on campus so that you are successful in your studies as well as throughout your career.

SUMMARY

Taking time to reflect on an experience is a great way to assess and shape your current understanding of dance. The act of reflecting on experiences helps you make sense of what you know, how you are using that knowledge, what additional information you still need to learn, and which new areas for investigation might be useful to you. Engaging in reflection is a way to constantly learn more about yourself and dance, so it can deepen and expand your comprehension of dance both while studying dance on campus and as a professional. As you learn more about dance, reflection can give you the necessary skills to navigate changing personal interests and changes in the professional field by situating yourself as a lifelong learner of dance.

REVIEW QUESTIONS

1. Define reflection. What can be learned though reflection, and how does it relate to dance?

2. What are the purposes of observation, narrative descriptions, asking questions, and discussing in reflection? Describe how observation and questioning work in individual and collective reflection.

3. How and when should reflection take place?

4. Why is reflection useful when studying dance on campus? Why is reflection valuable in dance professions?

5. What are the benefits of establishing a personal reflective practice?

GLOSSARY

reflection—The practice of taking time to notice, carefully consider, and assess an experience.

BIBLIOGRAPHY

Amulya, J. (2011). What is reflective practice? www.communityscience.com/images/file/What%20is%20Reflective%20Practice.pdf.

Dewey, J. (1933). *How we think*. New York: Heath.

Raelin, J. (2002). "I don't have time to think!" versus the art of reflective practice. *Reflections: A Journal of Writing, Service Learning and Community Literacy,* 4(1), 66-79.

Schon, D. (1983). *The reflective practitioner: How professionals think in action*. New York: Basic Books.

UK Centre for Legal Education. (2010). Introduction to developing reflective practice. www.ukcle.ac.uk/resources/personal-development-planning/introduction.

PART three

Dance on Campus

*T*echnique and Movement Courses

After completing this chapter, you will be able to do the following:

- Understand the types of technique and movement courses offered at your campus.
- Assess the approaches used in technique and movement courses.
- Distinguish the types and importance of feedback in technique and movement courses.
- Discuss opportunities for continuing your technique and movement education off campus.
- Create and articulate your personal approach to your technique and movement courses.

One of the more familiar ways to study dance on campus is through an exciting variety of technique and movement courses. Like the students in the photograph, during your time on campus you will enroll in an array of technique and movement courses, some of which are requirements for your degree program and some of which are electives. Although your technique and movement courses will share some similarities with your previous dance experiences, some differences exist, too. Knowing and understanding the expectations of college-level technique and movement courses will help you prepare to grow as a dancer in each class you take.

Chapter 10 discusses the expectations of college-level technique and movement courses. In this chapter you will learn about the types of technique and movement courses that may be offered at your campus. So that you can best comprehend your role as a student in these classes, you will assess the approaches used in college-level technique and movement courses. The chapter examines the importance of feedback in technique and movement courses to help you be proactive in your dance learning. Because your dance education may continue off campus, options for broadening your technical and movement education off campus are discussed. Finally, you will create and articulate your personal approach to your technique and movement courses on campus to ensure that you are getting the most out of them.

Your technique and movement courses create opportunities for you to refine your dance ability through learning new movement, honing your technical skills, finding anatomical and somatic connections, cultivating artistry, and expanding your knowledge about a dance genre or movement form. Technique and movement classes are comprehensive learning experiences grounded in physical practice. The students in the photographs know this, which allows them to deeply invest in their dance learning. You are more able to be self-responsible and proactive in your dance learning if you understand the various approaches used in your technique and movement courses. Recognizing how the expectations of college-level technique and movement courses are related to, but perhaps different from, your previous dance experiences is a significant step in the evolution of your study of dance on campus and beyond.

TYPES OF TECHNIQUE AND MOVEMENT COURSES

Typically, when students imagine studying dance on campus, they picture themselves in technique and movement classes. Whether in a high school, private studio, or recreational setting, taking these types of classes is what initially draws many students to dance. As you continue your dance education on campus, you will continue taking technique and movement courses. Some technique and movement courses will be familiar to you, and some will introduce you to unfamiliar dance genres, somatic approaches, and ways of training. It is likely that you will encounter technique courses, somatic movement education courses, and additional movement forms while studying dance on campus. These courses provide a tremendous opportunity to learn new movement techniques, dance genres, ideas about movement, and methods of expressing your ideas through movement. Learning the distinct and overlapping purposes of these classes gives you a glimpse of how much you can learn about dance and movement during your time on campus.

Technique Courses

Your technique courses will be dance-genre specific and will address the movement techniques, stylistic concerns of major eras and contributors, and contextual elements of a given genre. Although the majority of class time will be focused on the physical practice and artistic expression of a dance genre, you should also expect to implicitly and explicitly learn more about the philosophical, cultural, and historical aspects of the dance genres you study through these courses. For example, you may enroll in a ballet course in which you learn one specific style of ballet, such as the Vaganova technique or Cecchetti method, or a general overview of ballet styles. An urban movement course could primarily focus on urban dance forms, such as locking and house dancing, but also address the role of music and DJs in the performance of these dance forms. A Latin dance course may include a unit on the cultural evolution of samba to demonstrate how Brazilian samba differs from more stylized ballroom samba seen in the media. Depending on your degree program, your technique courses may be predetermined or you may have some choice

Courtesy of Kristmar Muldrow/The Daily Gamecock

• • • Although the majority of class time will be focused on the physical practice and artistic expression of a dance genre, you will also learn more about the philosophical, cultural, and historical aspects of these genres.

in the technique courses you select. However, it is likely that you will enroll in technique courses regularly while studying dance on campus.

Somatic Movement Education Courses

Besides technique courses, your degree program may offer or require a variety of somatic movement education courses. **Somatic movement education courses** focus on developing awareness of the human body in movement. In these courses, students are led through a variety of experiences that deepen their understanding of how they individually move. Somatic movement education courses are not specific to a dance genre, or even dance, but they offer immense amounts of insight and information about how the body moves. Your campus may offer a considerable diversity of types of somatic movement education courses. Various somatic practices, such as Alexander Technique, Feldenkrais Method, or Laban Movement Analysis, fall into this category of courses. These modalities strengthen the link between the mind and body and aid in the establishment of efficient movement and greater expressivity. Courses such as conditioning for dancers and Pilates can also be considered somatic movement education courses, and they provide information about how to best train the body to meet the physical demands of

being a dancer while strengthening the connection between the mind and body. Somatic movement education courses can be incredibly valuable both for receiving a comprehensive dance education and for physically and mentally preparing yourself for a career in dance. Many students benefit from taking these classes in tandem with their technique courses or, if recovering from an injury, in place of a technique course. Regardless of the reason for enrolling in a somatic movement education course, you will gain knowledge about your body and movement that will enhance your study of dance on campus and your future career.

Additional Movement Forms

Some campuses also offer additional movement forms through the dance program that are not dance courses but feature the moving body as a central element. For example, you may find that your campus offers capoeira, tai chi, or aikido courses. Although these forms are not dance genres and they are not explicitly focused on improving your embodiment of dance movement, there are several advantages to enrolling in these types of courses. For starters, they will introduce you to distinct types of movement coordination that may assist your execution of specific dance genres. For example, capoeira frequently involves inversions and supporting the body's weight through the arms, which could assist students who study dance genres that emphasize floor work, such as modern dance. Because these classes are not specific to dance, some students find it incredibly refreshing to experience movement in a new context, which can lead to more comfort and range of motion in other classes. For example, aikido organically incorporates endurance, ease, and flexibility, so the benefits of studying aikido will likely show up in your dancing. Some movement forms, such as yoga, can reduce stress, which is an asset while studying dance on campus. The coordination of movement and breath in tai chi can help you relax, which may make you better equipped to juggle the various obligations you may have as a student. Studying diverse movement forms such as these can enhance your understanding of dance through introducing you to unique ways of moving.

Areas of Overlap

In each of your technique, somatic movement education, or other movement form courses, you may find traces of the others. For example, your modern dance class may include exercises from Alexander Technique to help you find greater ease and verticality. A Laban Movement Analysis class might draw from different types of courses, such as West African dance practices and tai chi, to demonstrate how effort is expressed in various movements. The anatomical language used to explain movement in an aikido class may be similar to the language used in your technique and dance science courses. Because each type of class contributes to a comprehensive, embodied understanding of dance movement, it makes sense that some overlap will exist. It is advantageous to recognize how these courses explicitly and implicitly work together. Doing so links your dance knowledge from one dance course and one dance genre to the next so that your dance learning is constantly building from experience to experience.

APPROACHES TO TECHNIQUE AND MOVEMENT COURSES

Your previous experiences with technique and movement classes prepared you well to continue your dance education in these types of classes while studying dance on campus. While some elements of these courses will be similar to your previous experiences, you will also experience many new challenges. In college technique and movement courses,

you are expected to be more self-responsible for and proactively invested in your learning. In all parts of your campus education, but especially in your dance courses, it is your responsibility to fully absorb information presented and then apply it to your dancing. You are expected to show a sincere interest in both the content and approaches used in your dance courses and to be fully engaged in the process of learning about dance. This means attending and fully participating with an open mind in all classes, reviewing material outside of class time, doing your homework, and asking for assistance as needed. Essentially, you want to implement the same behaviors for success that you use in all of your coursework to your dance studies. Doing so will ensure that you are getting the most out of each individual dance class and your campus dance education.

Some of the learning goals may also be very different from your previous experiences in technique and movement courses. In campus technique and movement courses, students are expected to work independently and to be comfortable learning through group or collaborative experiences. Somatic approaches to learning dance are commonly used, and out-of-class assignments, such as completing readings, watching videos, and writing papers, are frequently required. Many learning goals, such as those dealing with dynamic alignment or personal artistry, are long term and take more than one semester to master. All of these components provide a comprehensive understanding of dance movement and bridge the work in your technique and movement courses to other courses such as choreography, dance kinesiology, and music for dancers. You will still experience full-bodied movement and the joy of dancing in these classes, but the goals of the courses can be much larger than that. Becoming cognizant of how college-level technique and movement courses progress can illustrate the continuous advancement of your dancing and dance education.

Self-Responsibility and Teamwork

In all of your college courses, you are expected to be self-responsible and proactive in your education. The same is true in your technique and movement courses. Because one of the goals of a college dance education is to develop lifelong learning skills, many dance professors structure their technique and movement courses so that students develop not only proficiency in dance but also the facilities needed to continue learning about dance

Engaging WITH Dance

Katherine McGaha (Middle Tennessee State University)

© evanedianestoner

Entering dance studies at the collegiate level can provoke many emotions, such as nervousness, excitement, anxiousness, or eagerness. Studying dance in a university setting allows you to better understand yourself and others as movers. Regardless of your prior training, collegiate dance can be intimidating; however, that intimidation will develop into encouragement, permitting you to grow in various ways. Achieving success through a collegiate dance program starts in technique class. Here are my top five ways to succeed in technique classes:

1. Attend dance class! Even if you're tired from late-night studying, your body and mind need to become acquainted with dancing extensively, under whatever circumstance but especially if you are planning to dance professionally.

2. Properly warm up your body. If you need to arrive to class 15 to 30 minutes early, do so. Knowing what your body needs and catering to those needs is crucial to a long life of dancing.

3. Exercise classroom etiquette. Even though this may seem elementary, you would be surprised as to how often it still occurs. Don't chew gum in class. Don't talk to other dancers on the side (unless the class allows for verbal communication). Don't be late to class. Always say *thank you* to your teachers. Turn your phone off. In an audition setting, the people holding the audition are not only watching you dance; they are also watching how you act while not dancing. Are you paying attention, or are you disengaging and checking out from what is happening?

4. Try not to compare yourself to other dancers. (This one is hard.) Focus on yourself and what you need to improve. If feedback is given to someone else, definitely take that into account, but relate it to your individual practice.

5. Enjoy yourself. Remember that dancing is fun. Whether you are doing a tendu exercise or an end-of-class combination, always be dancing to fullest ability.

after college. This self-responsibility for learning may be promoted through using peer feedback and self-reflection along with teacher feedback; asking students to incorporate their own choreography in dance exams; the use of questions and discussion in the classroom; in-class journaling; and other methods. Each of these elements encourages you to pause, self-assess, and observe your learning process, which all relate to fostering reflection and self-responsibility as a dance student. In addition to self-responsibility, many college professors emphasize the importance of learning and working as a group. You may experience this through class exercises focused on developing sensitivity to other dancers in the space, and through improvising as a group to explore technical concepts, peer feedback, and group discussions. Because most dance careers involve working with others toward a common goal,

such as performing in a dance company or teaching in a public school system, it is important that building a sense of community be part of your technique and movement courses.

Somatic Approaches

For many students, the use of somatic approaches in their technique and movement courses is new. If your previous dance experiences have emphasized the external perception of your movement, through relying on the mirror to know if something looks correct, primarily worrying about how movement looks and what the audience will think, or relying on your teacher for external feedback, switching to somatic approaches may take some time to get used to. Strengthening your internal perception of movement through somatic approaches may feel foreign at first, but it can be incredibly beneficial. Somatic approaches are used in technique and movement classes so that students can better feel their movement from the inside. When you develop the skills to internally assess your movement based on how it feels instead of how it looks, you will be more self-responsible in your dance learning. Furthermore, the incorporation of somatic approaches can reduce the possibility of injuries by encouraging a dynamic alignment of the body and efficient movement and increase the expressivity and qualitative range of dancers.

Your technique and movement courses may draw on specific somatic exercises or images to help you sense a specific skeletal relationship, such as utilizing Bartenieff Fundamentals so that you can feel how contralateral movement (the diagonal coordination of the upper and lower limbs) exists in the body. Some classes might include the incorporation of general somatic concepts including breath, postural and movement efficiency, movement initiation and sequencing, connectivity in the body and to the ground, and sensing the environment and other dancers. These ideas may exist as stand-alone experiences at the beginning of a class, or your professor may draw attention to them as you are executing full-bodied movement. The incorporation of somatic approaches in your technique and movement courses does not negate the role of external feedback, such as information from your professor, peer observations, or visual feedback from the mirror; rather, it aims to empower you in your dancing through developing a fuller and more accurate awareness of how you move.

Long-Term and Short-Term Goals

Depending on your previous dance experiences, you may be used to learning choreography, such as combinations and routines, in your technique and movement classes. In these situations, one of the major goals of the class can be to learn and perfect choreography for a performance situation, and sometimes you can master it in a short amount of time. In your college technique and movement courses, it is unlikely that you will focus on learning choreography for a performance in class. The majority of class time will be spent learning genre-specific movement vocabulary, refining movement coordination, advancing aesthetic specificity, and enhancing artistic expression through movement, each of which are long-term goals. For example, in an introductory modern dance technique course, weeks may be spent examining the role of the pelvis in relationship to

alignment, movement vocabulary, and aesthetics. Even though a considerable amount of class time might be dedicated to this topic, it may take students a whole semester or even longer to consistently sense the balance and weight of the pelvis in movement, because this kinesthesia requires a shift in awareness and a rebalancing of muscles. At the same time, many college dance instructors break down a large goal into several smaller, short-term goals so that you can notice how your dancing is evolving. Continuing with the previous example, you may spend 5 weeks total examining the role of the pelvis, but each week may have a distinct focus. You may start by bringing attention to the location and shape of the pelvis in the body, then move on to finding a dynamic balance of the pelvis, to discovering how the thigh joints work and sensing the sacrum in movement, to finally sensing weight in the pelvis. Having short-term goals allows you to focus on one thing at a time, and to bring attention to small changes and accomplishments in your dancing. Regardless of the dance genres you study, you will find that each technique and movement course combines long- and short-term learning goals so that you are dually aware of how your dancing is improving as well as how it can continue to mature.

Out-of-Class Assignments

Some technique and movement courses require out-of-class work so that students achieve a fuller comprehension of the dance genres or movement forms they are studying. These assignments can include reflective self-assessment papers, research projects, posting responses to an online discussion board about videos, and reading articles and book chapters and addressing them in class. Each of these activities has a clear educational purpose and should be taken just as seriously as the work you do in class. Out-of-class assignments help you learn more about your own progress in class, explore the stylistic range of a dance genre or movement form, and expand your knowledge of the technical and choreographic history and trends of a dance genre or movement form. All of this information can make you a better dancer if you apply it to your physical practice. Many students are surprised at first that their technique and movement courses require out-of-class assignments, but as they see how this information broadens their understanding of the dance genres and movement forms they study, they realize the importance of these assignments. Additionally, many professors expect students to review, rehearse, and reflect on class material between classes. It is to your advantage to set aside time between classes to mentally review class material, rehearse key movement phrases, and reflect on your approach to class. Each out-of-class experience, whether it is a formal assignment or a review between classes, makes you more prepared for each individual class, which creates greater potential for growth throughout the course.

FEEDBACK IN TECHNIQUE AND MOVEMENT COURSES

The use of feedback challenges you to move beyond your habits into new modes of thinking and moving. Therefore, it is a critical part of the learning process in technique and movement courses. Your dancing will improve through receiving, applying, and offering constructive criticism and objective observations. In your technique and movement courses, feedback will come from multiple sources. Along with receiving feedback from your professors, at times in class you may give and receive feedback with your peers or be asked to comment on your own improvement. Regardless of the source, all observations and constructive criticism have the potential to improve your dancing if you are able to hear the feedback without judgment, consider how it relates to your improvement, and then take steps to apply the information. Comprehending the importance of feedback in your technique and movement courses is critical to your ongoing growth as a dancer.

Teacher Feedback

In addition to creating and teaching movement sequences in your technique and movement courses, your professors will also offer you feedback about your dancing. As your professors observe your dancing on a daily or weekly basis, they are able to offer strategies for improvement. If you keep this in mind, you will be better able to hear and apply your professors' feedback to your dancing. Remember, your teachers are here to guide your growth as a dancer, and one of the main ways they do so is by giving students feedback on their progress.

Your professors will use several types of feedback in your technique and movement courses. Some of the feedback will be general, such as *Good work everyone*, while some will be more specific, such as *Your use of a circular sensation in your plié is really changing how you shift your weight*. There will also be a balance between feedback that addresses the whole group and feedback that addresses students individually. Tactile aid (the use of respectful touch to help students embody anatomical connections and coordination) is frequently used in these classes. Questions may be used as feedback. For example, after observing how students use their arms in a dance phrase, a professor might ask students *How can you best sense a dynamic connection between the scapula and fingertips while moving your arms?* so that students can investigate and find their own answers. Besides in-class feedback, you will also

• • • At times in class you may give and receive feedback with your peers.

© Karen Schupp

receive teacher feedback on your out-of-class assignments or in formal and informal meetings with your professors. Each type of feedback has a specific purpose and is valuable to your dance education. Many students listen to and consider all feedback offered in class, even if it is directly offered to someone else, as a means of constantly gathering information about movement. The more you can become comfortable with each type of feedback and taking responsibility to apply it, the more empowered you can be in your technique and movement courses.

Peer Feedback

Giving and receiving peer feedback in your technique and movement courses may be an unfamiliar component in your dance learning. Peer feedback refers to respectfully exchanging feedback with a classmate. It may happen formally in your classes. For example, your professor may assign partners to "pair and share" feedback and observations throughout a given class or after a specific exercise. You can also exchange peer feedback informally inside and outside of class. You may ask a peer for assistance learning a dance phrase, or you might have a spontaneous group discussion over coffee about how your alignment is changing as a result of a specific class. Whenever you engage in peer feedback, be sure to take it seriously and be respectful.

Many professors incorporate peer feedback into their technique and movement courses because it is incredibly constructive in your dance learning.

Observing another dancer and then explaining your observations and offering specific feedback for improvement help you to synthesize and communicate your current understanding of dance. Watching a peer successfully perform a movement that you are struggling with can help you see various pathways to improvement. Additionally, research suggests that learning and observing a peer's mistakes with movement is sometimes more effective than observing an expert's demonstration, because when you observe how a peer fixes movement in the moment more information is taken in than when you watch a teacher's near-perfect execution (Enghauser 2003). Sharing feedback with your peers also promotes communication and critical-thinking skills, which will be valuable throughout your dance education and career. Of course, you also learn a lot about your dancing through receiving peer feedback. In a large technique or movement course, working with a partner can be a means to gather individual feedback, to collaboratively learn, and to create a sense of community. Acknowledging the purpose and benefits of participating in peer feedback will increase your growth in technique and movement courses.

Self-Feedback

Throughout your dance education and in your dance career, the ability to self-assess and reflect on your dancing and dance learning is what keeps you growing as a dancer. There will be times after you graduate where you are taking a technique class,

• • • Increasing your ability to self-assess and reflect on your dancing is essential to attaining a full dance education and to preparing yourself for your future career.

learning choreography, or improvising with limited outside feedback. Therefore, increasing your ability to self-assess and reflect on your dancing so that you can develop and apply strategies for improvement is essential to both attaining a full dance education and preparing you for your future career.

As you are dancing, you are likely making small or large adjustments to your movement based on your immediate experience. For example, if you feel yourself falling out of a plank freeze in your breaking class, you will probably make some changes in your body to prevent you from falling. Or, after completing an adagio phrase in a ballet class you might quickly assess what was working and what needs more attention so that when you repeat the phrase you can bring your attention to the moments that are most challenging. Both of these scenarios likely happen in a very fleeting way, therefore your professors may build in class activities to bring attention to this process and cultivate habits for self-assessment and reflection. Some professors may assign reflective self-assessment papers that align with dance exams so that students can take time to assess their current understanding. Other professors may include in-class journaling and discussion so that students can have the chance to immediately process their approaches to class material and to consider new approaches. As a student, you can also participate in self-assessment by reflecting on your process outside of class, monitoring your progress, and asking specific questions in class. Doing so will ensure that you are tailoring your dance learning to your specific dance needs. Formally and informally developing methods to observe yourself and strategize improvement makes you more proactive in your dance learning, engages you in the learning process, and nurtures skills needed for a lifetime of learning in dance.

TECHNIQUE AND MOVEMENT COURSES OFF CAMPUS

While studying dance on campus, some students also seek off-campus opportunities to partake in technique and movement courses. You may find places in your local community to take class or you might be interested in summer and winter intensive programs. If you decide to take technique and movement classes off campus, it is important to integrate the knowledge from these classes with the courses you take on campus. It helps you stay on track in your campus technique and movement courses

while also providing you with a wider grasp of dance movement, more information about a specific aspect of dance movement, or both, depending on your interests.

Your Local Community

Your local community may provide several ways for you to participate in technique and movement classes off campus. If your campus is in a large urban area, you may have access to an established professional dance community with dance studios where local professional dancers take drop-in classes on a regular basis. Taking classes in this setting is a great opportunity to relate what you are learning on campus to the professional field and connect with your local professional dance community. There may be community centers focused on urban arts or specific cultures that regularly bring in guest teachers or performers to teach classes in a specific dance genre that interests you. On campus or locally, you may find yoga and Pilates studios, martial arts schools, or fitness centers that have somatic movement education courses that are not offered in your dance department. These classes can positively supplement the technique and movement courses required for your degree program. Some students continue to study and teach at their hometown dance studios. Doing so keeps you connected to family and friends and gives you a chance to implement and share some of the dance knowledge you are learning on campus. Although your study of dance on campus may be quite rigorous, it can be beneficial to regularly or occasionally take classes off campus and approach them as an integrated part of your dance education.

Festivals, Intensives, and Certification Programs

Studying dance on campus is an essential step in bridging your current dance experiences to your future dance goals. In addition to the expertise you will gain studying dance on campus each semester, it can also be pragmatic to take advantage of festivals, intensives, and certification programs during your semester breaks. Festivals and intensives provide in-depth dance experiences over the span of a few weeks. Most dance festivals—such as ImPulseTanz in Vienna, Juste Debout in Paris, the Bates Dance Festival in Lewiston, Maine, and the American Dance Festival in Durham, North Carolina—feature a variety of teachers and artists. Intensives are usually focused on a specific technique or choreographer's style of moving and creating, such as the Saratoga Summer Dance Intensive, which focuses on ballet, and the Taylor School Summer Intensive, which focuses on Paul Taylor's modern dance technique. For intensives and festivals, you can expect to dance all day, and to enroll in technique and movement classes as well as repertory or creative classes. Certification programs are geared toward professional credentialing in a specific movement form, such as Pilates or yoga, or a somatic practice, such as Laban Movement Analysis or Feldenkrais Method. Festivals, intensives, and certification programs are also great ways for you to continue your dance education over the summer and winter breaks and to test out locales where you might move after graduation. They also allow you to personalize your dance education by spanning your campus dance education to your emerging interests.

YOUR APPROACH TO TECHNIQUE AND MOVEMENT COURSES

Now that you have an awareness of what to expect in your college-level technique and movement courses, you can outline steps to increase your learning in these classes. Because many students are already comfortable with some aspects of their technique and movement courses, these courses can be important opportunities to open up to new methods of investigating and learning movement, and to diverse dance and movement genres. Examining your current approach to these classes and finding ways to broaden your study of movement are key components of studying dance on campus.

As you become more comfortable balancing the requirements of your degree program and being a college student, you may find that you have time and energy to invest in an unfamiliar dance genre or movement form. It can be helpful to balance breadth and depth in your dance education. Some students may desire expertise in a specific dance genre, while others seek an overview of many different dance genres and movement forms, while still others want some specificity and breadth in their dance education. These options are all valid for studying dance. Depending on what you are looking for, you may find it beneficial to enroll in elective technique or movement courses on campus or to look into off-campus options. If your current professional aspiration is to have a career performing modern dance, it would be valuable to enroll in a summer program in a larger urban area so that you can gain exposure to current choreographers as well as sample what it is like to live in a big city. Perhaps you are interested in opening your own dance studio that offers a range of styles. In this scenario, it would be smart to develop your technique in the genres you plan to offer at your studio, meaning you may need to enroll in supplemental or elective dance classes on and off campus. Students who are interested in dance science or dance therapy may find it beneficial to enroll in courses focused on somatic practices and dance training even if they are not required for their degree program. There are numerous ways to expand your dance education while studying dance on campus so that you are actively connecting your current understanding of dance to your professional aspirations. Your professors are incredibly knowledgeable about various resources, festivals, and classes that would benefit your individual growth, so don't be afraid to ask for help.

In your technique and movement courses, you are probably discovering that you respond more favorably to certain approaches and types of feedback than others. It is likely that early on in your campus dance studies, you will feel more comfortable with the approaches and feedback that relate most closely to your previous experiences. This is good to realize, because it indicates which approaches and types of feedback you can bring more attention to in your dance learning process. For example, if you are nervous about giving peer feedback, try to keep in mind that exchanging peer feedback is a learning activity for both you and the receiver. If your previous dance training has focused on short-term goals (e.g., learning a routine for competition), and long-term goals (e.g., finding a dynamic sense of alignment) are tricky for you, you may find it helpful to subdivide the long-term goal into several milestones. Students who are in the habit of setting aside time before or after class to physically review class material can use those time management skills to designate time to complete class readings and written assignments. Every element of your technique and movement courses, from the physical material, to the artistic explorations, to the various approaches used in class, to the different roles and types of feedback, to out-of-class assignments, play a key role in your comprehension and embodiment in these classes. Establishing a holistic approach that honors the various types of content, the diversity of approaches and feedback, and your role in the learning process allows you to acquire a rich comprehension of dance and movement through these courses.

SUMMARY

Developing awareness of what is expected and what occurs in campus technique and movement courses provides you with a strong foundation for success. When you identify the types of technique and movement courses your campus offers; understand why certain approaches are used; comprehend the multiple roles of feedback; and learn about, take advantage of, and continue your technique and movement education off campus, you discover ways in which you can be more proactive in your dance education during your time on campus. Your campus dance education will offer you a tremendous amount of information about dance, but it is your responsibility to take advantage of new knowledge, opportunities, and ways of learning. Doing so deepens your personal investment in your dance education and growth beyond campus, and it can help you gain the competencies needed to succeed while dancing on campus and as a young professional.

REVIEW QUESTIONS

1. How do technique and movement courses, including technique courses, somatic movement education courses, and courses in additional movement forms, contribute to a comprehensive dance education? What is uniquely valuable about each type of course, and how do they complement each other?

2. Compare the approaches used in technique and movement courses. Which approaches do you think are most beneficial to your dance learning, and why?

3. Why are so many types of feedback used in technique and movement courses? How does each type of feedback enhance your develop-

ment in dance? How does each of type of feedback develop skills needed for success in your future career?

4. What are the benefits of taking technique and movement classes in your local community, attending an intensive or festival, or completing a certification program while studying dance on campus?

5. How does developing a proactive and comprehensive approach to your technique and movement classes increase your learning while studying dance on campus? How does a proactive and comprehensive approach to technique and movement classes relate to success in your future career?

GLOSSARY

somatic movement education courses— Courses that focus on developing awareness of the human body in movement.

BIBLIOGRAPHY

Brodie, J., & Lobel, E. (2004). Integrating fundamental principles underlying somatic practices into the dance technique class. *Journal of Dance Education,* 4(3), 80-87.

Enghauser, R. (2003). Motor learning and the dance technique class: Science, tradition, and pedagogy. *Journal of Dance Education,* 3(3), 87-95.

International Somatic Movement Education and Therapy Association. (2013). Home. www.ismeta.org/home.html.

Schupp, K. (2010). Bridging the gap: Helping students from competitive dance backgrounds become successful dance majors. *Journal of Dance Education,* 10(1), 25-28.

CHAPTER • • • • **11** • • •

Creative, Compositional, and Performance Courses

LEARNING OUTCOMES

After completing this chapter, you will be able to do the following:

- Comprehend the various types of creative, compositional, and performance courses offered at your campus.
- Evaluate the diverse approaches used in your creative, compositional, and performance courses.
- Examine the roles and types of feedback in your creative, compositional, and performance courses.
- Identify ways to continue your artistic development off campus.
- Formulate and explain your personal approach to creative, compositional, and performance courses and opportunities.

Many students are drawn to the expressive elements of dance. Whether you desire to express ideas through movement as a choreographer, performer, or both, the potential to communicate your ideas through movement is likely a large part of your dance interests. The students in the photograph are learning about the role of creativity, compositional craft, and various performance methods as well as their own creative processes in their creative, composition, and performance classes. Just like the students in the photograph, you will learn more about your creative process, dancemaking, and dance performance through courses and additional artistic opportunities while studying dance on campus. Familiarizing yourself with the goals of creative, compositional, and performance courses can help you feel more secure in your dance learning so that you can continuously challenge yourself as a dance artist.

Chapter 11 focuses on the expectations of creative, compositional, and performance courses that you may enroll in on campus. For starters, you will learn about the various types and goals of creative, compositional, and performance courses offered on your campus. Because these courses promote exploration and personal artistic growth, you will evaluate the diverse approaches used in classes so that you are best prepared to push yourself as an artist. Feedback is essential to understanding your own ways of creating and performing as well as to revising and evaluating your compositional work and performance. Therefore, this chapter examines the roles and types of feedback you may encounter. You will discover ways to continue your artistic development off campus. Finally, you will formulate and explain your personal approach to these classes so that you can be proactive in your development as an artist while studying dance on campus and beyond.

The acts of making and performing dances may be a large part of your campus dance education. The students in the photograph are actively involved in the process of creating a dance. Perhaps they are collaboratively creating a structured improvisation, or maybe one student is choreographing a dance for her peers to perform. Comprehending the expectations of your creative, compositional, and performance courses can lead to greater development as a dance artist. Learning about the types of creative, compositional, and performance courses available to you, the various approaches used in class, the importance of feedback, and chances for off-campus development prepares you to fully dive into this aspect of your campus dance education.

TYPES OF CREATIVE, COMPOSITIONAL, AND PERFORMANCE COURSES

For many students, the ability to express themselves through dance leads to a deep and personal investment in this art form. You may have already created dances for younger students at your local dance studio, created and performed solos for high school class projects, or developed confidence as an improviser. Now that you are studying dance on campus, you will have opportunities (both inside and outside of your degree program) to learn more about how to translate an idea into movement. You will learn more about your own creative process in dance, improvisational approaches, compositional tools and methods, and theories and practices of performance. Your previous experiences in improvisation, dancemaking, and performance provide you with a strong artistic foundation to build on in your creative, compositional, and performance courses. Comprehending the unique and common goals of these courses bridges your current understanding of dance with new artistic challenges, and it allows you to envision a larger range of artistic possibilities in your dance education and future career.

Creative Courses

Creativity is deeply embedded in all aspects of dance; therefore, you may find courses that generally focus on the role of creativity in dance. **Creativity** refers to the experience of making something new of recognized value such as a dance, a painting, or a new scientific approach by giving it form. A person's **creative process** includes all the steps and cognitive approaches a person uses to exercise his or her creativity. One of the key goals in creative courses is to bring students' awareness to their creative processes while also expanding their ideas about what is creatively possible in dance.

These courses help students realize their individual creativity by emphasizing discovery, exploration, and outside-the-box thinking. For example, your degree program may require a creative process class in which you unearth what interests you about dance movement and how you make choices in dance. A creative practices class may address broad approaches to making dances or how various aspects of creativity in dance, such as improvisation, composition, and production design, intersect. Some campuses offer creative movement courses

● ● ● In creative courses students find a wider range of possibilities in dance movement and more options for creating work.

so that students see the creative and expressive potential in everyday movements, such as sitting and walking, that they may not initially consider to be dance. In essence, in these courses students find a wider range of possibilities in dance movement and options for creating work along with a deeper awareness of how each student is uniquely creative. This leads to a larger movement and design palate to select from in performance and dancemaking, which is important to your overall artistic growth and dance education.

Composition Courses

In dance, **composition** refers to the process of dancemaking as well as the structural elements of a dance work. Therefore, composition courses focus on the hows and whys of dancemaking. Regardless of the type of composition course you take, it will likely include elements related to finding ideas to explore and express through dance; various methods for structuring your ideas; a great deal of practical experience articulating your ideas through movement and explaining your compositional approach; as well as evaluating and revising your work. **Improvisation** (the act of making spontaneous yet informed decisions while dancing) is likely to be introduced as both a compositional tool as well as a performance method in this family of courses. Compositional courses are practice-based classes, which means you learn how to create dances through creating and performing improvisations and making dances.

Composition courses cover a large range of interrelated topics, and the course content can be specific or general. For example, your degree program may require a course in improvisational structures that introduces the exploration of movement through various improvisational frameworks. A contact improvisation course, on the other hand, addresses a specific approach to improvisation. You may enroll in a course in approaches to dance composition, which introduces you to the manipulation of basic compositional elements such as time, space, energy, and relationship, or in a course in dance and media composition, which examines the use of media in the creation and performance of dance works. Some courses may spiral throughout your dance curriculum, meaning you may take introductory improvisation in year 1, then advanced improvisation in year 3. Depending on your degree program and personal interests, you will find that there is a range of breadth and depth in each of your compositional courses, and that each aims to deepen your understanding of how and why you make dances so that your work is unique to your interests and artistic voice.

Performance Courses

Performance courses are geared toward developing students' performance skills through providing performance opportunities, advancing students' understanding of dance performance, or both. **Performance skills** include the wide range of aptitudes needed to successfully perform dance, such as stage presence, embodying a character or intention, group awareness, and musicality, to name a few. Many degree programs have formal performance requirements built into their dance curricula so that students can cultivate performance skills. Your campus may have a campus dance company, a repertory ensemble, or a performance group organized around a specific dance genre or cultural category of dance. In each of these courses, students can expect to learn dances created by their faculty, visiting guest choreographers, or by their peers for public performance, and they can expect to increase their proficiency as performers.

Other degree programs may offer more specific courses in and outside the field of dance or additional performance opportunities. For example, some degree programs may require a course in performance methods, in which students learn strategies for embodying a wide range of performance intents and movement styles; or an introduction to acting course, in which students learn how various acting methodologies can be useful in dance performance. Still other campuses may have several informal performance events for students that provide great learning experiences, although they are not official courses. Participating in dance performances gives you the chance to constantly evolve as an expressive artist, and it can challenge you to move beyond your comfort zone as a performer. Working with faculty and guest artists provides a great opportunity for consistent feedback on your performance abilities, which over time refines knowledge of your dance performance—a tool that is beneficial to many careers in professional dance.

Areas of Overlap

Creativity, composition, and performance do not exist in isolation. For example, innovation is highly valuable in choreography, and that comes from being able to find creative ways to present an idea. Performers need to grasp how a work is compositionally structured to fully sense and communicate the progression of a work to an audience. Because dancemaking and performance are large components of dance, it is advantageous for all dance professionals to know how creativity, composition, and performance work together. Therefore, it is very likely that you will find overlapping ideas among your creative, compositional, and performance courses.

Your composition class may frequently focus on how your creative process is evolving so that you perceive how your ways of working are changing and how that development is reflected in your work.

When working as a performer with a guest choreographer, you may be asked to contribute movement to the development of a work. The content and format of these courses work in tandem to help you learn the various ways in which ideas become dance works and the various phases of and roles in that process. The more you can realize how these classes provide a very broad and interlinked understanding of creativity, composition, and performance in dance, the more your dance artistry will advance while studying dance on campus.

APPROACHES TO CREATIVE, COMPOSITIONAL, AND PERFORMANCE COURSES

Whether or not you realize it, you probably already have knowledge about making and performing dances. Perhaps as a young child you made up dances to your favorite songs to share with your family. Maybe your previous technique and movement courses required you to perform combinations and phrases in class for your peers. Or, maybe you have had more formal exposure to making and performing dance works. Regardless of your previous experiences, the approaches used, both to teach creativity in relationship to composition and performance and to teach the philosophies behind the creation and performance of dance introduced in class, are likely to challenge your current understanding.

In your campus creative, compositional, and performance courses, you will focus on the roles of process and product in the development of work. You will be required to complete both small studies and larger-scale projects for class. So that you are well prepared to work in a variety of ways after graduation, you will learn to work both independently and collaboratively. Out-of-class assignments will be incorporated to help you reflect on your learning process, to expose you to new ways of working, and to give you a broader picture of what is happening in dance. Each of these approaches pushes your creativity, dancemaking, and performing so that your artistry is constantly expanding. Recognizing how the approaches are different from, although perhaps related to, your previous experiences allows you to see how each of these classes contribute to your overall dance education.

Process and Product

Process and product are directly linked to each other, and it is questionable if one can exist without the

Engaging WITH Dance

Isabella Ingels (University of Michigan)

Growing up I studied at a primarily ballet-based studio. However, for college I went to a modern-based program. I struggled for my first few semesters because I was so caught up in what everyone else was doing and how amazing everyone else looked. I lost my own creative voice while I was mentally comparing myself to everyone else in the room. But that finally changed once I embraced my own unique qualities of movement. Once I realized that I too had something to offer to the room and I too could inspire others, I opened up so much more and I was able to discover so many more movement possibilities in my own body, such as leading movement with an elbow through space or using the back of my head as an initiation point. Therefore my best advice for you is to realize that you have your own voice, and that voice does not necessarily need to be the same as everyone else's.

Photo by Christine Calleja. Courtesy of Isabella Ingels.

other in the making and sharing of a dance. **Process** refers to the methods used to create a work, and **product** refers to the actual work itself. At various times in your campus dance education, your professors will probably ask you to focus on one element more than on the other. Early on in your campus dance education, your creative process and improvisation professors may offer you reflective prompts in class so that you can discover how you are making choices while you are moving. The choices you make reflect your process because they demonstrate how you are moving from idea to idea. Your first dance composition class may primarily address the processes of making dance, such as generating movement, structuring movement, evaluating and revising, so that you can better articulate and understand how you make dances. At the end of a course or at the end of your campus dance education, more attention may be brought to the product (the choreography) or to evaluating and sharing what you actually made. Your degree program may require a public performance of a self-created work, or your composition class may require you to present a 3-minute solo for your final exam. In both of these examples, the product is emphasized because it is what is shared, discussed, and evaluated.

Process and product coexist, and many dance professionals find that they are either equally invested in both phases simultaneously or that depending on where they are in the development of a work, one phase might be emphasized more than the other. You may find that you are much more comfortable with one or the other. For example, frequently students from competitive dance backgrounds are initially much more focused on the product of their dancemaking because it mirrors their previous experiences. Students who studied improvisation as a large part of their high school dance education may be more comfortable in the process phase. It is critical to your dance education as well as your growth as a creative artist to comprehend how process and product work together. The more you can embrace both as equally valuable and rewarding, the more complete your knowledge of making and performing dance will be.

Studies and Projects

In your technique and movement courses, you are likely familiar with the idea that some dance phrases are only taught and performed once as a way of introducing an idea, and others are repeated and expanded over a series of classes so that you can gain a more comprehensive understanding of the movement. A similar approach is used in creative, compositional, and performance courses. In these courses, you will be required to create and perform both studies and projects. **Studies** usually explore a specific aspect addressed in class and tend to be shorter in duration. **Projects,** on the other hand, are more comprehensive in nature and require you to synthesize several ideas presented in class. They tend to be longer in duration and take longer to develop than studies. Both are valuable to your dance education.

Your dance composition class may require you to create a 1-minute study that explores various elements of time so that you can discover the effects of tempo and rhythm on movement. You may be required to show this in class, then make some quick revisions, and show again at the end of class. Then, for your midterm, you may be required to create a 5-minute project about a topic of your choice that demonstrates how you can manipulate time, space, energy, shape, and relationship to convey your ideas. Perhaps you work on this project over a period of a few weeks so that it has time to develop before you share it in class. As you can see, studies provide a space for you to experiment with one or two specific concepts, whereas projects allow for a more comprehensive exploration of ideas.

Some students are more comfortable creating and sharing studies, and some students are more comfortable creating and sharing projects. Studies can be challenging because they are narrowly focused. This careful examination encourages you to find as many solutions as possible to a specific prompt. Doing so can help you move past your current tendencies as an artist. The comprehensive nature of projects can be intimidating, but dividing the project into smaller steps, or even smaller studies, can make a project feel more manageable. Plus, with this approach, you can better see how new information gained from creating and sharing studies leads to a complete understanding of dancemaking and performing. Recognizing the value and interconnected nature of studies and projects can reveal how you are maturing as a dance artist by increasing your awareness of how ideas scaffold in your creative development.

Working Independently and Collaboratively

The study of dance, as well as most dance careers, requires the ability to work independently and collaboratively. Your creative, compositional, and performance courses develop the skills to do both. In the professional field, various choreographic and performance practices are used. In some cases, the choreographer is viewed as the author of a work, and the performers are viewed as interpreters. On the other end of the spectrum, some dancers collaboratively and democratically create and perform works. To make sure that you have a complete understanding of how dances can be made and performed, your creative, compositional, and performance courses will introduce you to a range of approaches. At times, you may be assigned to work with other students on a collaborative project. In your improvisation class, you might be required to create an improvisational score for your classmates to implement and perform. In your performance courses, there will be

Engaging WITH Dance

Therese Ronco (Goucher College)

Creative, compositional, and performance courses are great opportunities to explore movements and movement qualities that are not addressed in technique classes. Exploring new movements can be challenging if you are only used to trying to master the traditions that have been passed down or to training your body for a specific dance genre. It scares some students; they freeze up and don't know what to do. Some students may resort to what they know and have been taught instead of taking artistic risks and finding new movement. But, that's why these classes are vital to your dance education; in order for your dance knowledge and skills to keep thriving and evolving in a dynamic and interdisciplinary way, you need to take full advantage of these classes. Composition classes and improvisation classes can help you generate unique movement that is special to your mind, body, and spirit. These movements are often charged with an intriguing energy that accompanies the act of creation. I find both improvisation classes and composition classes to be magical and raw. They teach me something new about myself and about the practice of dance every time I go to class or complete an assignment for one. They are a chance to let go, flow, and find the natural essences of your movement that have not yet been explored and need uncovering.

times when you learn work that has already been performed by other dancers, which will require you to act as an interpreter of the dance work, or you may work with a choreographer who asks dancers to creatively contribute to the choreography. Each one of these scenarios increases your proficiency to work independently and collaboratively, and better prepares you for a future in dance.

As a student in these classes, it is important to remember that each of these approaches is valid and that at times they can coexist within one study or project. Some students are naturally comfortable working collaboratively, whereas other students prefer to work as the sole author of a work, and still others find a great deal of empowerment through interpreting work as a performer. The professional field has room for all of these options. While you study dance on campus, you should make sure that you fully invest in each creative, choreographic, and performance assignment or opportunity, and that you expose yourself to a wide spectrum of ways of making and performing work. It is okay to have a preferred way of working, but gaining comfort in a variety of choreographic and performance approaches broadens your dance education and creates more chances for you to grow as an artist on campus and as a young professional.

Out-of-Class Assignments

Out-of-class assignments are frequently assigned in creative, compositional, and performance courses. These assignments can include journal writing, reading book chapters or articles and writing responses, writing reflective papers about your creative process, doing research assignments about major choreographers and performers, exchanging peer feedback through an online discussion board, or writing critiques of various dance performances. Because you process and exchange a tremendous amount of information while creating and performing dance, these assignments help you better identify and articulate your experiences while also providing a wider contextual understanding of the various methods, theories, and innovators referenced in class. Therefore, these assignments are an incredibly useful way to track what you are learning, how you are applying that information, and how your personal approaches relate to the larger field of dance. Out-of-class assignments are vital to learning how dances are made and performed, and they should be taken just as seriously as the various studies, projects, and performances required in these classes.

At first, some students may find it difficult to articulate their creative processes and their experiences performing, or to explain the link between the compositional structures and thematic content of a work. Just like anything else, it may take time to develop these skills. It is likely that your assignments in these classes will progress from small to large so that you have the time to develop these abilities. If your creative, compositional, and performance courses require or suggest that you maintain a daily or weekly journal about your artistic approaches, be sure to do it, even if the journal is not collected or graded. Students who consistently set aside a small amount of time each day or week to reflect on their creative process are usually better able to articulate their approaches, which leads to greater artistry. Take advantage of in-class peer feedback exchanges so that you can strengthen your ability to articulate what you perceive in choreography. It is a small step you can take toward more comprehensive discussions of works. Each required assignment contributes to your maturity as a dance artist and to the competencies that are essential to your dance education and future successes.

FEEDBACK IN CREATIVE, COMPOSITIONAL, AND PERFORMANCE COURSES

In your creative, compositional, and performance courses, your professors will design learning experiences that lead you to create and perform dances in new and more comprehensive ways. Because the goals of these courses relate to developing students' personal voices as creative artists, it is rare that all students arrive at the same choreographic or performative outcome to a given prompt. Therefore, feedback can revolve around objective observation, asking questions, and encouraging new approaches. Instead of telling you how to "fix" your dances, professors and your peers will instead offer objective observations so that you can better determine how your dance reads to others, questions to encourage new thinking, and suggestions about new approaches so that you can move beyond your habitual ways of making and performing dances. There will be times, especially if you are used to the teacher providing feedback about what is correct and incorrect, when this process of figuring out what is best for you but still relates to the given prompts can be challenging. Keep in mind that great growth can come from feeling challenged, objectively listening, reflecting on and applying feedback, and proactively asking questions. That is why it is important to understand the types of feedback used in your creative, compositional, and performance courses.

Many creative, compositional, and performance courses establish a method of exchanging feedback early in the semester. This ensures that feedback is traded in a respectful manner, that students presenting work know what to expect, and that students providing feedback know both what to look for while watching work and how to thoughtfully articulate those observations. The process of giving and receiving feedback sharpens your skills as a choreographer and performer because it strengthens your critical eye, which assists you in determining how your own choreographic and performance choices may be interpreted by others.

The majority of feedback exchanged in class aims to promote a better understanding of students' creative processes as well as the work they are creating. Some courses may draw on Liz Lerman's Critical Response Process. This is a means for artists to exchange peer feedback in a way that promotes questioning and thoughtful reflection. This process has four phases: affirming the work of the artist; time for the artist to ask observers questions about the work; time for the observers to ask neutral questions about the work to the artist; and the exchange of opinions, if the artist wishes to hear them (Lerman & Borstel 2003). Other courses may follow an adaptation of Larry Lavender's (1996) ORDER approach. ORDER

stands for **o**bservation, **r**eflection, **d**iscussion, **e**valuation, and **r**ecommendations for revisions. The Fieldwork method is also commonly used as a jumping-off point for giving feedback. In this approach, artists present their work without explaining it beforehand, and then feedback is focused on articulating what observers see in the work before offering noncorrective and nonsuggestive feedback to the artist (Dance Theatre Coalition 2013; The Field 2013). Each of these methods empowers artists by positioning them in a place where they can seek and apply the feedback they need and learn how the work reads to others, while also bringing attention to the processes of reflection, evaluation, and revision, which strengthens the artists' and observers' abilities to critically analyze work.

Like in your technique and movement courses, feedback will come from your teachers, peers, and yourself. All feedback can be potentially valuable to your artistic development. Therefore, understanding the role of feedback is central to your growth as an emerging artist.

Teacher Feedback

In these courses, your professors may situate themselves as facilitators of your creative development. This means that instead of providing prescriptive feedback, they will frequently offer suggestions, ask you questions about your process and your work, and give you space to figure things out on your own.

Peter Bailley / Knox College

• • • Your professor will facilitate feedback sessions by helping students stay on track when giving feedback, assisting students in formulating questions and articulating their observations, and supporting students as they make sense of the feedback they are receiving.

The purpose for this is to allow your artistic voice to develop in a way that is individual to you and not overly shaped by the teacher's personal perspectives on dancemaking and performing. In most classes, your professor will also facilitate feedback sessions by helping students stay on track when giving feedback, assisting students in formulating questions and articulating their observations, and supporting students as they make sense of the feedback they are receiving. In more introductory courses, the professor may refrain from giving feedback at first so that students can develop comfort improvising and taking creative risks. In more advanced classes, professors may offer stronger opinions on students' work, especially if it will be publicly performed, so that students are aware of the impact their work has on an audience. In addition to in-class feedback, your professors may provide written, more comprehensive feedback on larger projects or be available to discuss your artistic development outside of class during office hours. Throughout your creative, compositional, and performance classes, your professors will use their expertise as artists and educators to offer you specific yet open-ended feedback about your process and work so that your ways of making and performing work are always expanding in an informed way.

Peer Feedback

You probably already participate in peer feedback outside of your creative, compositional, and performance courses. In rehearsals with your peers, you might have conversations about what aspects of the dance you find exciting. After your improvisation class, you may discuss what you observed with your peers as you walk to your next class. After an outstanding dance performance, you and your friends may talk about how and why the choreography and performance moved you. Many students are already comfortable exchanging informal conversational feedback about dance, yet for some students, exchanging peer feedback in a more formal way in creative, compositional, and performance courses can initially be intimidating. Some students find it difficult to put their gut reactions to dance into words. Others worry that their observations about a work are "incorrect" or that the artist will be upset about their observations. It is important to realize that these are valid concerns, and that learning to quickly, accurately, and respectfully talk about the work of others is an important part of your dance education. This process develops your critical eye so that you can better determine what is working and what is not in your own work as well as the work of others. Furthermore, it strengthens your communication and critical-thinking skills, which are essential for your ongoing development in dance. Keep in mind that your professors have carefully designed feedback methods to enhance these aptitudes, and that all opinions and observations are valid and helpful if respectfully presented.

Self-Feedback

Along with feedback from your professors and peers, you will receive constant feedback from yourself about your approaches to making and performing work. Whether or not you are aware of it, you make several decisions in the processes of improvising, creating, and performing dance. Improvisation develops the ability to make informed, intuitive choices in response to your own preferences as well as what is occurring in the space around you. When you are choreographing a dance, you are constantly assessing your choices to determine where to go next. Dance performers make small, and sometimes large, adjustments to their performances to adapt to different performance situations. All of these choices are in response to feedback you get in the moment. To bring your attention to this process, you may be required to keep a journal or to write reflective self-assessments throughout the semester. You learn more about your own ways of making and performing work through these assignments. Once you acknowledge your approaches, it is easier to identify areas that need to be addressed or new areas for exploration. Furthermore, in these classes, it is ultimately up to you to process and make sense of the feedback your teachers and peers provide. The more you can articulate your strengths and challenges as an artist, your goals for a given work, and what you hope to learn, the more proactive choices you can make about how to apply teacher and peer feedback. In these courses, it is important to reflect on your ongoing development so that you are empowered as a dance artist and so that your artistic voice is consistently evolving in a personally unique and relevant way.

ADDITIONAL CREATIVE, COMPOSITIONAL, AND PERFORMANCE OPPORTUNITIES

Besides enrolling in creative, compositional, and performance courses on campus, some students seek additional opportunities to develop their artistry as creative artists, choreographers, and performers. There may be the potential to collaborate with students from other disciplines in the creation and performance of a work. Your local dance community may host a variety of shared festival performances where you can show your work, or maybe you can work and perform with a local professional dance company. There are also regional, national, and international workshops and festivals specifically related to improvisation, dancemaking, and performance. You will find numerous occasions to continue your artistic growth outside of your degree program's requirements—if you look for them.

Out-of-Department and Noncredit Opportunities

There are likely opportunities on campus to practice and refine your artistry. In many degree programs, students are encouraged to create and present dances outside of their required coursework. Some of these are credited and some are not, but they are all very valuable to achieving a well-rounded dance education. For example, some degree programs have student dance concerts where all the selected works are created, performed, and produced by students. If you are interested in choreographing and performing work, these concerts provide a means for you to implement the aptitudes you are developing in creative, compositional, and performance courses in a collaborative setting. At times, your faculty members may create work and ask for students to be involved as performers. This is a great way to work more closely with a faculty member and to get detailed feedback about your performance ability. Outside of your degree program, there may be ways to create and share work with students from other departments. You might find a music composition student who is interested in creating music for dance, or a theater student who needs a choreographer and performers for a staged reading. Taking advantage of the opportunities on campus can deepen and expand your artistry and contribute to a vibrant, artistic campus community.

Your Local Community

You might be surprised by how many chances there are to artistically engage in your local community, regardless of its size. Larger urban areas with active artistic communities might have local dance companies, which at times include college students as either company members or apprentices. Many regional areas have dance festivals that feature the works of several choreographers. This can be a fantastic way to share your work as a choreographer or performer off campus. Dance studios are always looking for new choreographers, museums and galleries frequently welcome dance events, and site dance can happen anywhere. Each of these opportunities requires you to be proactive and to follow through on your commitment. In other words, you need to seek them out and see them through to completion. Consider your emerging artistic interests, take an inventory of your local community, and then contact the people or organizations that are interesting to you. The process of creating and following through on opportunities in your local community allows you to challenge yourself as an artist while also strengthening your leadership, collaboration, initiation, and follow-through skills. If you are interested in an artistic career as a young professional, these aptitudes are essential to your success. The more you can develop them alongside artistic proficiency while studying dance on campus, the better prepared you will be as a young dance professional.

Festivals and Workshops

Participating in festivals and workshops is an important step in pursuing your emerging dance interests while also connecting your campus dance education to the professional field. As such, festivals and workshops about improvisation, composition, and performance can help students learn more about their specific interests. For example, there are festivals that generally focus on improvisation, such as the Seattle Festival of Dance Improvisation, as well as improvisation workshops that address specific approaches, such as Nina Martin's Ensemble Thinking or Earthdance's contact improvisation workshops. In the area of composition, some workshops revolve around a specific choreographer's or company's way of working, such as Dance Exchange's Summer Institute. Composition and performance are often important elements of larger dance festivals, too. Students who are interested in learning how to perform the movement of a specific choreographer should look into repertory workshops, such as those held by large dance companies during the summer and winter. Finding and enrolling in a workshop focused on improvisation, composition, or performance is a productive way to use of your semester breaks while also applying what you have learned on campus to a professional or preprofessional setting.

Creative, Compositional, and Performance Courses ••• **133**

Engaging WITH Dance

Marcia Custer (Kent State University)

Getting connected to your campus and local community is so important. Not only is it great to become familiar with your surroundings, but through getting involved with people and organizations outside of your department you may be able to achieve goals that can't be accomplished through school. One year ago, I met with a local gallery owner. We talked about the need for more performance in the community, and he allowed me to host performance art evenings in which local dancers, artists, and musicians could showcase their work in town. Through this experience, I have learned how to organize, promote, and run a successful event. I have learned that I have a flair for networking, and I hope to use these skills when I start my own company some day!

Working with other groups on campus, outside of your dance department, can also be a great way to expand your resources and find opportunities to collaborate with other artists. I found this to be true when I began working with an alternative theater group that was looking to host more performance events. We worked together to promote a works-in-progress event where dancers, actors, musicians, and directors could all test out their own work on the stage before turning it into a full-fledged student production. Some students who attended began discussing possible collaborations (e.g., dancers spoke with student directors about choreographic possibilities), while other students became inspired and are now asking to perform at the next works-in-progress event. I have learned that in creating these opportunities for informal performances, we as a club are also creating a supportive community and culture among all of the performing artists in the school. We have had many requests to host another one next semester, and we hope to host a feedback session following it to continue to expose new work and discussions to all of the disciplines!

© Meg Billy

YOUR APPROACH TO CREATIVE, COMPOSITIONAL, AND PERFORMANCE COURSES

Your creative, compositional, and performance courses form a main component of your campus dance education. Through these courses you discover and cultivate your unique artistic voice by embracing new ways of making and performing work; sharpening your critical eye; and learning about various philosophies, innovators, and artistic contexts. For your artistry to truly develop, you need to be proactive in your approach to these classes so that your creative, compositional, and performance knowledge expands in a personally relevant yet widely contextualized way.

Your campus dance education will likely require coursework in creative, compositional, and performance areas. As you learn more about the vastness of the field of dance, you may find it beneficial to take additional coursework or to pursue additional opportunities to ensure that you are getting a good balance of specificity and breadth in these areas. Students who are interested in dance education need a broad understanding of composition and performance so that they can cultivate this knowledge in future students. Choreographers need compositional expertise, but they also need a clear comprehension of performance skills. Conversely, dance performers are better able to contribute to the artistic development of a work if they have an awareness of choreographic processes. Dance and movement therapists frequently use improvisation and creative activities in their work, so a deep knowledge of the creative process is essential in this field. Your coursework and additional opportunities in these areas create a foundation for success in numerous dance careers. Throughout your time studying dance on campus, consider taking advantage of elective coursework, seeking additional occasions to create and perform work on and off campus, and enrolling in summer workshops so that you are well prepared as a young dance professional.

In your creative, compositional, and performance courses, remember that every experience, whether it is making work, performing in a peer's choreographic study, exchanging in-class feedback, or completing out-of-class assignments, contributes to a complete understanding of the artistic process in dance. Many students will have approaches and types of feedback that they are more comfortable using. Some students may feel more comfortable performing someone else's work, whereas others are confident in exchanging peer feedback, and others feel more able to express themselves through written assignments. It is okay to have a comfort zone, but expanding that personal comfort zone is an important part of your dance education. If you are hesitant about sharing in-class feedback, you may benefit from writing your observations down before sharing them until you get used to quickly articulating your thoughts. Students who are initially uncomfortable with improvisation because it is more subjective than their previous dance experiences can keep in mind that many students have felt this way, and that their professors are available to assist them through this transition. If writing papers about choreography or performance is perplexing, you might start by listing objective observations, such as what the movement looked like, the music used, any themes you observed, and so on, and connecting them to your interpretation of the work before formally completing your assignment. Remember, your professors are here to mentor your artistic growth and can suggest ways for you to gain comfort and proficiency in all aspects of your creative, compositional, and performance courses.

SUMMARY

Understanding the creative, compositional, and performance aspects of dance is central to a complete campus dance education. The more you realize the importance and roles of the types of creative, compositional, and performance courses of your degree program; the diverse approaches utilized to provide a holistic comprehension of the artistic process in

dance; feedback in these courses; and opportunities to increase your competencies in these areas outside of your degree program, the more empowered you can be in your campus dance education. Coursework in these areas provides you with content knowledge as well as critical-thinking, communication, leadership, and collaboration skills that are central to all areas of dance. Being proactive in your approach to learning about the creative, compositional, and performance aspects of dance allows you to gain a complete dance education, encourages your artistic voice to blossom, and better prepares you for success as a dance professional.

REVIEW QUESTIONS

1. How do creative, compositional, and performance courses relate to each other? To a comprehensive dance education? To a variety of dance careers?

2. Describe the various approaches used in your creative, compositional, and performance courses. What is the purpose of each approach, and how does each approach challenge you?

3. What is the role of feedback in creative, compositional, and performance courses in your dance education? How does exchanging feedback with your teacher and peers, as well as processing feedback from yourself, contribute to your artistic growth?

4. How can out-of-department and off-campus opportunities in composition and performance strengthen your dance education? Consider what content and skills you may learn through these activities and how that relates to your emerging dance interests.

5. Why is it important to your dance education and overall artistic growth to be proactive in your approach to creative, compositional, and performance courses?

GLOSSARY

composition—The process of dancemaking as well as the structural elements of a dance work.

creative process—A process that includes all the steps and cognitive approaches a person uses to exercise his or her creativity.

creativity—The experience of creating something new of recognized value, such as a dance, a painting, or a new scientific approach by giving it form.

improvisation—The act of making spontaneous yet informed decisions while dancing.

performance skills—The wide range of aptitudes needed to successfully perform dance.

process—The methods used to create a dance work.

product—The actual dance work that results from a rehearsal process.

projects—Comprehensive creative assignments that require the synthesis of several ideas presented in class. They tend to be longer in duration and take longer to develop than studies.

studies—Creative assignments that explore a specific aspect addressed in class and that tend to be relatively short.

BIBLIOGRAPHY

Butterworth, J. (2004). Teaching choreography in higher education: A process continuum model. *Research in Dance Education*, 5(1), 45-67.

Dance Theatre Coalition. (2013). About fieldwork. www.dancetheatrecoalition.org/Fieldwork.html.

Lavender, L. (1996). *Dancers talking dance: Critical evaluation in the choreography class*. Champaign, IL: Human Kinetics.

Lerman, L., & Borstel, J. (2003). *Liz Lerman's critical response process: A method for getting useful feedback on anything you make, from dance to dessert*. Takoma Park, MD: Dance Exchange.

Schupp, K. (2010). Bridging the gap: Helping students from competitive dance backgrounds become successful dance majors. *Journal of Dance Education*, 10(1), 25-28.

The Field. (2013). Fieldwork workshops. www.thefield.org/t-workshops_fieldwork.aspx.

12

Contextual Courses

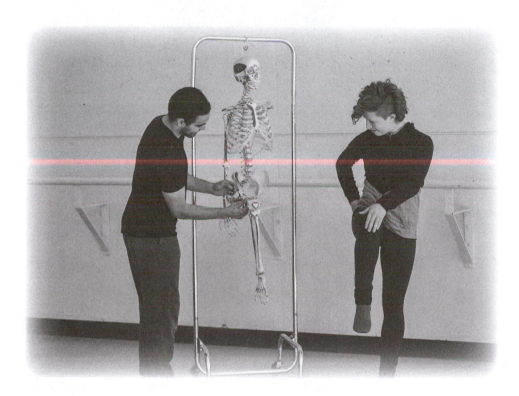

LEARNING OUTCOMES

After completing this chapter, you will be able to do the following:

- Recognize the various roles and types of contextual courses offered on your campus.
- Compare the various approaches used in your contextual courses.
- Evaluate the roles and types of feedback in your contextual courses.
- Recognize opportunities for expanding your contextual knowledge outside of your degree program.
- Design and articulate your personal approach to contextual courses.

As you are coming to learn, the academic study of dance encourages you to find a comprehensive understanding of dance. In addition to learning about diverse dance genres and ways of performing and making work inside the dance studio, your campus dance education will also include contextual coursework. In the photograph, students are learning about dance wellness. Other contextual elements of dance are theories about dance, the histories of dance genres, the relationship between music and dance, and production and design elements. This information works in tandem with what you learn in your technique and movement courses and creative, compositional, and performance courses. Contextual knowledge contributes to an extensive understanding of dance, which is essential to a complete campus dance education.

Chapter 12 introduces you contextual courses. You will learn about the array of contextual courses your campus offers as well as their distinct roles in your dance curriculum. Because studying the contextual elements of dance is often an unfamiliar area for students, you will learn about the distinct approaches used in these courses so that you are well prepared for success. Feedback is an important part of the learning process in contextual courses, so you will evaluate the roles and types of feedback used in these courses, allowing you to be a proactive student. You will learn about additional opportunities for expanding your contextual knowledge, and you will design and articulate your personal approach to these courses. Each of these components prepares you to learn as much as possible about dance through your contextual coursework so that you are continuously developing a comprehensive and solid grasp of dance.

As you can see, contextual courses expand your dance knowledge in new and exciting ways. In each of these classes, students discover connections between the execution of dance and the theoretical, historical, cultural, educational, and scientific aspects of this art form. The students in the photograph are learning to think about dance from some these of contextual perspectives, which in turn builds their overall understanding and embodiment of dance. Like these students, you will have the chance to widen your thinking about dance through contextual coursework. The knowledge you gain in these courses is essential to your success as a young professional, regardless of your dance interests, because it ensures that you will achieve a complete dance education. Keeping an open mind in these courses, recognizing the roles and types of contextual courses in your curriculum, understanding the approaches and types of feedback used, and finding ways to increase your contextual knowledge off campus allow you to fully invest in your study of dance on campus.

TYPES OF CONTEXTUAL COURSES

For many students, learning about the contextual elements of dance leads to a broader understanding of dance from multiple, interrelated perspectives. **Context** refers to the surrounding circumstances and facts of a given situation, event, or approach. Whether or not you realize it, you may already have contextual knowledge about dance. Perhaps your high school dance class required projects about specific choreographers, which enhanced your historical awareness of a dance genre. Maybe your dance studio held or attended workshops that discussed different teaching approaches or injury prevention. Many local communities hold events that celebrate the food, arts, and customs of cultural groups, which can provide contextual knowledge about a specific culture. Contextual knowledge is embedded in the physicality of dance, but often it goes unnoticed unless careful examination takes place. This careful examination takes place in your contextual courses.

Historical and Theoretical Contexts

Learning the historical and theoretical perspectives of dance makes you aware of how dance genres developed and how those historical and theoretical underpinnings are reflected in the movement of the dance genre, in a choreographer's choices, or in the purpose for a dance event. Your degree program will likely include courses that address the history and theory of dance. For example, many campuses offer dance history courses that cover the evolution of Western theatrical dance genres. Depending on the focus of your degree program, you may find more specialized courses in which you examine various theories about dance. **Theory** refers to a group of ideas intended to explain specific events or facts. Courses in dance theory subjects such as philosophy of dance, traditions in ballet and modern dance, or African and diasporic aesthetics in American dance address the influences, values, aesthetics, and approaches of choreographers or dance genres. Each of these courses is a place for you to broaden your comprehension of dance and to consider how your personal study of dance fits into that larger

Engaging WITH Dance

Molly Howel (University of Southern Mississippi)

When studying dance at the college level, most students don't realize that they are now studying dance as an academic discipline. It is no longer just about having fun or hanging out with friends after school; it's now hard work—and not just the kind that makes you sweat. Studying dance in college means dance history courses. Many don't really take these classes seriously, but they are integral to learning about dance and becoming a well-rounded dance educator or performer. For example, I had a conversation with a few of my friends in which Twyla Tharp was brought up. Many of my friends in this discussion had no idea who she was and how much she has affected the dance world. Dancers should know about innovators in dance history regardless of their style, because these innovators have influenced what we are learning today. Also, in technique class if a professor decides that we should take time to focus on, say, Graham technique, then we should know who Martha Graham was and how influential her work was and still is today. Knowing our history makes us dance literate, and besides, how can we really ever move forward if we don't know how we got started in the first place? Knowing what came before can only inspire us to be pioneers of our time, to make our mark on history.

understanding. Historical and theoretical contextual courses help you discover the evolution of dance so that your own embodiment and knowledge of dance can be richer and more informed.

Cultural Contexts

All dance genres reflect the cultures they emerged from and exist in, so increasing your knowledge of the cultural aspects of dance is a critical component of your dance education. Cultural contextual courses investigate how dance reflects culture by providing a variety of lenses through which to examine the connections between dance and cultural values. For example, you may enroll in a course in dance and global contexts that introduces a range of dance genres found across the world as well as various ethnographical and anthropological approaches to studying dance. Some coursework in this area may be more specific, such as a dance ethnography course that solely focuses on ethnographic methods used in researching dance, or a dances of Southeast Asia course that focuses on the dance genres of this particular part of the world. Regardless of the cultural contextual courses your degree program offers, your discernment of how cultural values are reflected in the making, performing, and teaching of dance will greatly increase while studying dance on campus.

Artistic Contexts

In your creative, compositional, and performance courses you address making and performing dances, and in your technique and movement courses you learn about the technical and artistic execution of various dance genres. Your degree program will also include artistic contextual courses, in which you will learn more about the artist elements of dance. These courses explore the theories and skills needed to complete your artistic visions. For example, courses such as music for the dancer or rhythmic theory for dance address musicality in dance, which is necessary to fully embody a range of dance genres and styles. Because music plays a large role in many dance genres, a comprehensive understanding of musicality, which includes the ability to hear and respond to various rhythmic pulses, the ability to explain the relationship between music and movement to others, and an awareness of various types of music, is central to your success in all areas of dance. Courses in dance production develop knowledge of technical theater, such as backstage work, light and sound board operation, and introductory stage management skills, in relationship to dance. Some campuses may offer courses in design for dance lighting or design for dance costuming, which introduce students to basic lighting or costume design and construction principles. As the use of media in dance becomes more popular, many campuses are offering courses in dance and media, in which students learn how to incorporate various elements of media, such as interactive technologies and video projections, into their creative work. The competencies gained in these courses are applicable, either directly or indirectly, to all careers in dance, and they contribute to your overall artistic growth.

Wellness Contexts

Dance is a physically demanding activity that also has many health benefits, which is why dancers must have a solid understanding of the body. Therefore, many degree programs offer courses related to dance and wellness. These contextual courses address the science of movement and dance. Many campuses offer courses in dance kinesiology or experiential anatomy for dance, in which students learn how the body's muscular and skeletal systems function during movement as well as the roles of the cardiovascular and respiratory systems. Other courses may be more specific, such as dance nutrition, which outlines nutritional theories in relationship to dance and health, or courses that link dance and psychology, in which students learn about the psychological components of dance. These courses aim to empower students through providing a great deal of knowledge about how their bodies and minds function in the context of dance, and they contribute to healthy dance movement. This knowledge allows you to dance in a more scientifically informed way, which enhances your embodiment of dance movement.

Learning Contexts

Regardless of what areas of dance currently interest you, it is very likely that you will teach dance or that you will need the skills for teaching dance in your professional career. Therefore, coursework focused on the learning contexts of dance are frequently offered on campus. These courses promote the educative nature of dance, effective teaching practices, and various pedagogical theories of teaching dance. Many campuses offer a course in dance pedagogy or teaching methods that provides an overview of contemporary pedagogical approaches for use in a variety of teaching scenarios. Some courses may be more narrowly focused. For example, you may encounter a course in children's dance that

introduces student-centered approaches to teaching dance to children in diverse educational settings, emphasizing creativity. Students specifically interested in becoming state-certified K–12 dance educators will also likely enroll in pedagogy courses, either in the department of dance or in the department of education, that explain educational theories and teaching methodologies that can be applied to dance. All of these courses reveal the depth of what you can learn through dance, and they provide you with the skills and capacity for becoming an effective dance teacher.

Areas of Overlap

The historical, theoretical, cultural, artistic, wellness, and learning contexts of dance are deeply interwoven with each other. For example, it is difficult to discuss the history of a dance genre without acknowledging the cultural components of that genre, or to separate the physiological demands and the artistic aims of a dance genre. Therefore, some overlapping content in your contextual courses is highly likely. Acknowledging this overlap cultivates an integrated contextual knowledge of dance. The more you perceive how these areas are interwoven, the more you can investigate how the contextual knowledge of dance supports the physical and artistic aspects of dance—and vice versa. Your contextual coursework ensures that you are able to examine, talk about, and participate in dance from a multitude of informed perspectives, which can provide an excellent framework for your success as a professional.

APPROACHES TO CONTEXTUAL COURSES

For many students, contextual courses are exciting places to learn more about elements of dance that are new to them. Because these classes introduce a wide range of topics, including dance history, dance production, and dance science to name a few, several different approaches are used to help students see how the knowledge gained in their contextual courses relates to their current dance interests. Your contextual classes will draw from a wide array of resources both in and outside of class; and lectures, presentations, and group discussions are commonly incorporated. It is likely that you will be required to demonstrate your understanding through both practical and creative experiences so that you have the opportunity to apply newly obtained contextual knowledge. As with many of your other courses,

Tim Trumble

• • • Contextual courses are exciting places to learn more about elements of dance that are new to you.

some of your learning experiences will take place online and you will complete written assignments. Comprehending the methods and formats of contextual courses makes you better able to excel in these classes and promotes a well-rounded understanding of dance from multiple perspectives.

Class Resources

Contextual courses contribute to a holistic awareness of dance. Because contextual courses are multifarious, they draw from a variety of resources. Textbooks, book chapters, and articles are used to give an overview of a course's topic and to help students learn more about specific aspects. For example, a course titled introduction to dance in world cultures may use reading materials to introduce key definitions, fundamental facts and theories, and divergent viewpoints about a topic. Using media, including in-class video viewing, watching video clips online, and listening to audio tracks, provides tangible examples, enabling you to see the practical application of contextual information. In your dance production class, you may learn about the various parts of lighting instruments so that you can hang and focus lights during your crew work on an upcoming dance event. In several contextual courses, you may interact with primary sources and objects, such as the actual instruments used to create music for a specific dance or a human skeleton in your dance kinesiology course, so that you gain a more firsthand experience in the topic you are studying. This variety of resources gives you multiple entry points to learn-

ing about a topic and ways to recognize the practical application of contextual information.

At first, you may be surprised by the amount of reading that some of your contextual courses require. However, it is important to remember that the knowledge you acquire through assigned readings establishes an essential foundation for your dance education, both in your contextual courses and in your dance curriculum. The same is true for assigned videos, audio tracks, and interacting with primary sources and objects. Taking the time to learn about history, theory, and application of contextual knowledge allows you to engage with dance in an informed and knowledgeable way.

Lectures, Presentations, and Discussions

Just as technique and movement courses, and creative, compositional, and performance courses have a somewhat regular way of structuring in-class time, so do contextual courses. Lectures and presentations, both from your professor and guest experts, as well as discussions are commonly incorporated in many types of contextual courses. Lectures and presentations are great ways to introduce new material and expand on information gathered from course resources. Perhaps your professor of teaching methods will give a short lecture on classroom management skills to familiarize students with best practices, or your professor of dance history will invite a former dancer from the Merce Cunningham Dance

Company to talk about her experiences performing this historic repertory of dances. Class discussions encourage students to articulate how their own experiences relate to new contextual perspectives, to learn from other students in the class, and to constantly synthesize and assess their learning. For example, maybe after learning about preventing ankle injuries in dance kinesiology, your class will discuss personal injuries experienced and consider how those injuries could have been prevented. Most contextual courses include lectures, presentations, and discussions on a regular basis. Doing so ensures that you are consistently scaffolding new information as well as considering how this new knowledge relates to your emerging dance interests.

In your contextual courses, you will benefit from implementing the same note-taking skills you use in your general education courses. Doing so will help you stay engaged with each lecture or presentation as well as be better prepared to participate in class discussions and complete out-of-class assignments. When a class discussion takes place, be sure to actively contribute through providing thoughtful and informed commentary and relevant questions while respectfully acknowledging your peers' contributions. When you fully engage in lectures, presentations, and class discussions, you can take a proactive role in your dance education.

Practical and Creative Experiences

Along with readings, video viewing, lectures, and discussions, your contextual courses will include practical and creative experiences. These experiences may take place quickly in class as a way to succinctly demonstrate how a given concept can be applied to the physical aspects of dance, or they can be more comprehensive. An introduction to dance course may include a series of introductory dance classes in a variety of dance genres to familiarize students with some of the embodied components of the dances they are studying. Courses in dance production and technical theater require students to complete numerous practical experiences, such as "teching" (working backstage as a member of the technical crew) a performance, designing and creating costumes, or perhaps calling cues for a dance work, so that they have a better sense of how these elements work in the creation and performance of dance. Courses in dance pedagogy and teaching methods might have students create and implement lesson plans, and courses in dance wellness may require stu-

dents to assess their own dancing and movement in relation to newly introduced anatomical principles. Smaller experiences may include quickly standing up and "trying on" the essential movements of a given dance genre or choreographer, or using body percussion to embody various rhythmic counterpoints in a course in music for dancers. Each of these experiences directly links the theoretical and the practical.

Many students enjoy the practical and creative experiences that are embedded into their contextual courses, because they clearly demonstrate how newly gained contextual knowledge relates to aspects of dance that are perhaps more familiar. Therefore, these experiences are great opportunities to reflect on how your dance knowledge is increasing and to consider how diverse aspects of dance, such as the theoretical, historical, practical, artistic, and physical knowledge of dance, work together in all areas of dance.

Online Experiences

You are probably already comfortable using the Internet and various online platforms to find information and to learn from others. The Internet and online experiences will also be a part of your campus dance education, and they may be a large part of your contextual coursework. In fact, some contextual courses may take place entirely online, meaning that instead of meeting for class in a physical classroom, you access class content and experiences through a course website. Other contextual courses may be hybrid courses. In a **hybrid course,** part of your learning will take place in a face-to-face setting, and part of it will take place online. For example, if a hybrid course meets twice a week, on one day the class will take place in a classroom, and on the other day it will take place online. Still other contextual courses will heavily rely on the Internet and your online learning platform to disseminate course materials, such as readings and videos, links to course-relevant websites, and discussion boards. Regardless of the type of contextual courses you take, it is likely that you will partake in some online experiences.

Key to successfully participating in online platforms are time management and distraction avoidance. The Internet is convenient and allows a great deal of access to content otherwise difficult to attain, such as up-to-date video clips of recent dance events. Yet, it is also tempting to procrastinate when it comes to completing online experiences because you can access the Internet at any time, or to become distracted by a plethora of Internet-related activities such as social networking. Keep in mind that

• • • It is tempting to procrastinate while working on online experiences.

although your online experiences may be virtual and not require face-to-face communication with your professor and peers, they still form a valuable component of your dance education. Completing online contextual coursework and online experiences can give you more access to dance—if you take full advantage of each online activity.

Written Assignments

Although most of your dance courses will require some writing assignments, your contextual courses may require more written work than your other courses. This is because the written assignments in these courses create opportunities for you to synthesize and demonstrate your learning, and your professor can provide valuable feedback on your progress. Written assignments in these courses vary greatly. In a dance criticism class, you may be assigned to write a position paper in which you defend a certain stance on a dance-related subject. Research papers about key historical figures are commonly assigned in dance history courses. An experiential anatomy course may assign self-assessment responses in which students are expected to first summarize what they have learned, then discuss its application to their habitual ways of moving. In dance education or dance and cultural context courses, analytical essays may be assigned in which students need to compare different theories introduced in class. Creative writing assignments, such as integrating historical information about a specific era and its dances into

a fictional short story, may also be used in these courses. You can expect to write reflective essays, analytical essays, research papers, and more in your contextual coursework.

Some students get excited about the prospect of writing about dance, whereas others are less keen on the idea. Even if at first you are nervous or less than enthusiastic about writing about dance, don't avoid doing it. The ability to articulate your thoughts in writing is critical to your dance education. First, the act of writing about newly acquired dance knowledge gives you the opportunity to demonstrate what you have learned and how that knowledge relates to your interests. It also develops written communication skills, which are essential to many areas of dance. The research opportunities embedded in these classes develop skills to critically evaluate and synthesize information from a variety of sources, which is valuable to all dance professions. In a nutshell, thoughtfully completing your written assignments is a way to deepen your dance knowledge and to practice communicating your understanding to others. Both knowledge and communication are critical to studying dance on campus and to your future dance endeavors.

FEEDBACK IN CONTEXTUAL COURSES

As in all areas of your campus dance education, feedback plays an important role in your contextual courses. Feedback in these courses can help you gauge your current learning, encourage you to think in new ways, and guide you to find new connections between diverse ideas or areas of interest. Feedback in your contextual courses will come from your teachers, peers, and yourself, and it may be in response to written assignments, creative and practical work, online experiences, or part of class discussions. Each type of feedback has the potential to expand your contextual knowledge of dance and strengthen your individual thinking about dance, as long as you are able to objectively hear it and thoughtfully apply it to your study of dance on campus.

Teacher Feedback

Besides selecting course resources; providing prompts for written assignments, class projects, and group discussions; and conveying information through lectures and presentations, professors of contextual courses guide learning through providing thoughtful feedback. Over the course of a semester, professors give feedback on assignments and in class activities so that learning is consistent and so that students can determine how their dance interests relate to contextual knowledge. The ability to hear and apply teacher feedback in contextual courses is vital to increasing your overall comprehension of dance. Therefore, realizing the ways your teacher may provide feedback can better prepare you for success.

In your contextual courses, your professors will provide feedback in many ways. On your written work, they will offer suggestions about how to improve your writing skills and provide comments on your expanding dance knowledge. Professors may use questions during class discussions as a way to guide you to think from multiple viewpoints, gain a broader perspective of dance, and challenge your critical thinking skills. Some professors may chime in on online discussions as a way to refocus students' learning. For practical and creative experiences, professors may offer suggestions about how to be more efficient or creative in the application of contextual knowledge. Many professors are also available to meet outside of class time to provide feedback on your approach to class, and to offer strategies for participating in class discussions and preparing assignments. Remember, your professors want to increase your understanding of dance and help you gain skills for a successful career in dance, and their feedback is tremendously valuable to achieving both.

Peer Feedback

Peer feedback is useful in contextual courses for many reasons. First, it helps students sharpen their verbal and written communication skills. It also makes students synthesize and assess their own dance learning, because they need to be secure in their knowledge of a topic before assisting others. Finally, exchanging peer feedback can foster a sense of community within the classroom, identify areas that need more development, and keep students engaged in a dynamic learning process. As students become more comfortable exchanging peer feedback, many find that they are better able to understand and apply contextual information.

Just as there are a variety of approaches used in your contextual courses, peer feedback can also take place in many different ways. You may be required to review a draft of a peer's assignment, and she to review yours so that you can assist each other in fully articulating your ideas. If your course includes online discussions, you may need to take turns, either individually or in groups, developing discussion questions and moderating online discussion forums. This responsibility gives you the opportunity to direct and focus your peers' learning on a specific area of interest. During class discussions, you may be encouraged to ask each other questions as a way of exchanging feedback and challenging each other's current awareness of dance. Remember to keep an open mind when receiving feedback, and be considerate when giving peer feedback. Creating an atmosphere of respect is critical to exchanging peer feedback. The incorporation of peer feedback creates a robust classroom experience, and it can assist you in clarifying your ideas about contextual knowledge.

Self-Feedback

In all areas of dance and throughout your dance education, self-feedback—the ability to objectively measure your current mastery of a topic, identify your achievements and challenges, and outline steps to further increase your knowledge and skills—greatly contributes to your advancement as a learner and dancer. Self-feedback is a large component of lifelong learning inside and outside of dance, which is why cultivating a habit of reflection is important in your contextual courses. Doing so allows you to be proactive in your acquisition of new contextual knowledge as well as to find relevant ways to apply this new knowledge to your personal dance interests.

Contextual courses provide many opportunities for self-feedback. For example, each time you revise a written assignment, you are making changes based on what you think is working and not working in your paper. As you take notes on class readings and jot down questions, you are indicating areas that you need more information about. In class discussions, you are actively linking new contextual knowledge to previous experiences, which requires you, on some level, to assess how your dance knowledge is evolving. Practical and creative experiences are often a place to connect contextual knowledge to other areas of interest, which causes you to consider how the application of this material is personally relevant to you. You may even have reflective or self-assessment assignments built into your contextual courses. Each of these instances provides a way for you to assess and challenge your current contextual understanding of dance, which allows you to be more proactive in your campus dance education.

ADDITIONAL OPPORTUNITIES TO EXPAND YOUR CONTEXTUAL KNOWLEDGE

While campus dance curricula afford numerous opportunities for students to expand their contextual knowledge of dance, some students may wish to acquire additional experience in specific areas related to their personal aspirations. Most campuses offer coursework in a variety of disciplines, so some students may find it intriguing to enroll in courses outside of dance as a way to further their comprehension of a dance area. Off campus, there are likely several ways to apply contextual knowledge of dance. Across the country and around the world, numerous professional organizations hold annual conferences and conventions where experts from specific disciplines share the latest research and practices. If a contextual aspect of dance piques your interest, there is likely a way to learn more about that area in addition to your required dance curriculum.

Related Disciplines on Campus

Studying dance on campus is exciting, not only because of how much you will learn through your dance curriculum but also because of the additional resources available to you on campus. Perhaps one of the most valuable campus resources is the ability to enroll in classes outside of dance in fields related to your personal dance interests. For example, if you are passionate about dance kinesiology, you can increase your comprehension of the body and movement by enrolling in an anatomy or exercise science course. Taking additional coursework in design and technical theater, either through the theater, art, or architecture departments, could give you new ideas about how to design and implement your dance production ideas. Many degree programs in dance education require additional coursework through

www.projectdance.com

• • • Contextual understanding of dance deepens through application.

the education department. If you are intrigued by the scientific, historical, or cultural contexts of dance, you may consider enrolling in a research methods course. Once you discover what excites you about the contextual components of dance, you will find that many ways to cultivate that interest are already present on campus.

Your Local Community

Contextual understanding of dance deepens through application. Therefore, creating and finding opportunities in your local community to practice what you are learning on campus is a great way to gain practical experience in areas that interest you. If you are especially inspired by what you are learning in your teaching methods course and how it applies to young children, you can offer to teach a class at a local dance studio or community center. Assisting with the behind-the-scenes work of a high school's dance performance is a great way to test out your emerging dance production skills. Perhaps after completing a course in dance ethnography, you are interested in the dance traditions of diverse cultural groups. You may find that a nearby community center or museum is focused on a cultural group, and you could volunteer there. Each of these opportunities expands your awareness, gives you practical experience, and better connects you to your field of interest. Taking the initiative to find and create chances to apply your contextual knowledge of dance off campus is a great way to build your dance education.

National and International Conferences

Many students new to studying dance on campus are surprised by the number of professional organizations that exist to promote the advancement of research, scholarship, and practice within the contextual areas of dance. Several of these organizations hold an annual national or international conference where members meet to take classes, hear research presentations, and network. Additionally, many organizations offer student membership and conference rates that are affordable. Becoming involved with one or more of these organizations as a student is a fantastic way to learn more about your specific areas of interest, meet leaders in each field, and stay up-to-date with current research and practice. If you are passionate about teaching dance, it would be beneficial to look into the National Dance Education Organization (NDEO) and SHAPE America (Society

of Health and Physical Educators). Organizations such as the Congress on Research in Dance (CORD) and the Society for Dance History Scholars (SDHS) promote the study of the historical, theoretical, and cultural aspects of dance, and they could be great resources if you are curious about those areas. The International Association for Dance Medicine and Science (IADMS) is a good resource for students invested in dance wellness, and the International Guild of Musicians in Dance is useful for students interested in the relationship between music and dance. In addition, many other professional organizations focus on a variety of dance interests and professions. Attending a national or international conference as a college dance student can spark new—or perhaps more specific—areas of interest, introduce you to working professionals from across the country and the world, and increase your awareness of your field of interest. If you have the opportunity to join a student chapter or a professional organization or attend a conference as a student, do it!

YOUR APPROACH TO CONTEXTUAL COURSES

Courses that enhance your awareness of the historical, theoretical, cultural, artistic, learning, and wellness contexts of dance will be a component of your campus dance education. Through these courses, you will learn how contextual aspects of dance, such as the historical development of a dance genre, are present in and support the physical aspects of dance. Because these courses contribute to a well-rounded and informed dance education, it is important that you proactively engage with your contextual coursework while studying dance on campus.

Although some contextual coursework will be required for your degree program, you may find that you want to pursue additional opportunities in your department, in other departments on campus, or beyond, related to your current dance interests. Regardless of what area of dance excites you, understanding the breadth of contextual information about dance is critical. Dance performers should have an awareness of the history and development of the dance genres they perform. This historical awareness allows them to relate more deeply to dances and movements from various eras and to visualize the evolution of their art form. Dance educators, especially in K–12 settings, are responsible for providing their students with a well-rounded dance education, which includes teaching the artistic, historical, and cultural components of dance as well as safely teaching dance movement. As such, contextual knowledge is essential to becoming an effective dance educator. Choreographers need to realize how production elements, such as lighting, costumes, sets, and music, contribute to conveying their ideas. Essentially, understanding how contextual information applies to various areas of dance provides a solid foundation for many dance careers. Taking the time to fully invest in these courses and in additional opportunities to expand your contextual knowledge while studying dance on campus is a critical step in preparing for a career in dance.

Every experience you have while studying dance on campus contributes to your overall dance education, including your work in contextual courses. Each paper you write, project you create, class presentation you share, and lecture you attend is a valuable educational experience. For some students, the idea of sitting still while studying dance is challenging at first. Because many students are drawn to the physicality of dance, taking time to pause and learn about the theories and nonmovement foundations of dance can be a very new experience. However, keep in mind that many of your contextual courses will include opportunities for you to actively apply your contextual knowledge to the physical components of dance so that you can seek links between all of your coursework. In your contextual coursework, you can use the same behaviors and aptitudes for success that guide all of your coursework. Doing so will better prepare you to excel in your contextual courses and contribute to a larger comprehension of dance while studying dance on campus and as a dance professional.

SUMMARY

Contextual courses form an essential component of a complete dance education, and the information gained through these courses is applicable to many areas and careers in dance. Therefore, recognizing the roles and types of contextual courses your campus offers, understanding the various approaches used to promote learning in these courses, evaluating the role of feedback, finding opportunities to expand your contextual knowledge, and articulating your own personal approach to these courses are important to your development in dance. Taking a proactive approach to your contextual coursework allows you to directly connect this knowledge to your emerging areas of interest while also helping you

achieve a wider awareness of what dance is and can be. This approach will enhance your understanding of dance both as a student on campus and as a dance professional.

REVIEW QUESTIONS

1. What are the purposes of contextual courses? How do they contribute to a complete understanding of dance? What can you learn from each type of contextual course?

2. Compare the distinct approaches used in contextual courses. What is valuable about each approach, and how do the approaches contribute to your overall learning?

3. Why is each type of feedback used in contextual courses important? How does each type of feedback contribute to your dance learning in contextual courses and beyond?

4. Why is it important to be a proactive student in your contextual courses?

GLOSSARY

context—The surrounding circumstances and facts of a given situation, event, or approach.

hybrid course—A course in which part of the learning takes place in a face-to-face setting and part of it takes place online.

theory—A group of ideas intended to explain specific events or facts.

BIBLIOGRAPHY

Anderson, J. (1992). *Ballet and modern dance: A concise history.* Princeton, NJ: Princeton Books.

Clippinger. K. (2007). *Dance anatomy and kinesiology.* Champaign, IL: Human Kinetics.

Hammersley, M., & Atkinson, P. (2007). *Ethnography: Principles in practice.* New York: Routledge.

Kealiinohomoku, J. (1983). An anthropologist looks at ballet as a form of ethnic dance. In Copeland, R., & Cohen, M. (eds.), *What is dance?* (pp. 533-549). New York: Oxford University Press.

McCutchen, B. (2006). *Teaching dance as art in education.* Champaign, IL: Human Kinetics.

13

Personalizing Your Campus Dance Education

LEARNING OUTCOMES

After completing this chapter, you will be able to do the following:

- Appraise the importance of individualized instructional opportunities in your degree program.
- Evaluate the role of working with your peers while studying dance on campus.
- Discuss practical tools and skills needed for professional success, such as resume and cover letter writing, interview and audition preparation, and networking.
- Outline preliminary steps to connect your campus dance education to your emerging professional aspirations.

Throughout your campus dance education, you can personalize your studies in many ways. In your courses you will have numerous chances to further investigate specific areas of interest and to make and perform work about topics that are especially relevant to you. Many dance curricula also include the option of individualized instruction, which permits for a more formal study of a topic, and encourage students to work with their peers outside of formal class settings. In the photograph, students are pursuing an opportunity for individualized instruction. In these situations, students accumulate knowledge and information in particular areas of dance and can create a strong bridge between their campus dance education and future enterprises in dance.

Chapter 13 addresses individualizing your campus dance education. You will start by appraising the importance of individualized instructional opportunities, such as independent studies, internships or apprenticeships, and scholarly and creative research experiences that are present in your dance curriculum. Because many dance careers and the study of dance are collaborative, you will evaluate the role of working with your peers on student-driven projects. Practical tools and skills needed for professional development and success are outlined, and you will establish preliminary steps for linking your study of dance on campus to your emerging professional goals. Fostering an awareness of these goals allows you to specialize in certain aspects of dance while also continuously embracing a wide understanding of dance.

Taking the initiative to engage in individualized or specialized learning situations while studying dance on campus allows you to learn more about what excites you in dance. When working one-on-one with a faculty member, gaining preprofessional exposure through an internship or apprenticeship, working on a student project, or assisting with creative or scholarly research, you can potentially achieve a deeper comprehension of a specific aspect of dance, just like the students in the photograph. These opportunities can connect your widening knowledge of dance to your unique passions in dance, which make them essential components of your campus dance education. Understanding what individualized instruction can do for your dance education, the importance of collaborating with your peers, and establishing tools and skills needed for professional development and success are foundational to your continuing education in dance on campus and beyond.

OPPORTUNITIES FOR INDIVIDUALIZED INSTRUCTION

Opportunities for individualized instruction will be present in your campus dance curriculum, although they may not be required components. Nonetheless, these opportunities afford you the chance to follow through on your dance interests; work more closely with a faculty member or professional organization; and practice leadership, collaboration, initiation, follow-through, advocacy, and creative and critical-thinking skills. These courses are frequently credited, meaning that you register for class credit even though you are working outside of a class setting. Many campuses offer independent studies, the possibilities of apprenticeships or internships, and scholarly and creative research experiences. Discerning the role of individualized instructional opportunities helps you realize how you can pursue your unique dance interests while studying dance on campus.

Independent Studies

The majority of your campus dance education will involve taking an array of courses with your peers, which is important because it establishes a broad and interconnected comprehension of dance. However, independent studies can also be beneficial to your growth in the field of dance. An **independent study,** sometimes also referred to as a *directed study,* is a form of learning in which a teacher and student mutually agree on a topic for the student to independently investigate under the faculty member's mentorship for an agreed-upon number of credits. Because independent studies can be more flexible in format than other types of courses, it is critical that students demonstrate immense maturity and responsibility.

Independent studies can take a variety of forms. For example, let's say that after taking your dance history course, you are especially intrigued by the postmodern movement of the 1960s and '70s. The following semester, you and your dance history professor may devise a course of study for you to independently learn about the major contributors, how dance is related to other arts, and the sociopolitical elements of the work created in this era for a three-credit independent study. You may meet with the professor biweekly to discuss what you are learning, and you may submit monthly assignments.

Engaging WITH Dance

Eric Chapman (Arizona State University)

My passion for arts legislation and administration led me to find my own route in education. Copyright policy especially intrigued me with its ambiguity, corruption, disregard by artists, and obvious neglect of dance. I formulated an independent study to tear it apart and understand it in relation to dance specifically. I began by researching the basics of what it is, why it is, and how it works. Gradually I worked to find understanding in the potential of copyright policy, how to raise awareness of its use among dancers, and how to make it more applicable to dance. The study was difficult, because few dancers and lawyers have taken on the task, leaving me to fend for myself. The true challenge before me now lies in conveying my information to dancers and artists. Jargon of the law and jargon of dance are worlds apart; finding connections will be the key to harmony.

© Alexandra Chapman

Or, after taking a course in urban dance forms, you want to learn more about the history and advancement of hip-hop culture so that you can integrate that information into your future teaching. Perhaps you can build an independent study based on reading important texts about hip-hop culture with your professor of urban dance forms. Independent studies can also occur in relation to creative work, teaching and pedagogy, and technique and movement courses. If you have an area that you are very passionate about investigating, it is highly likely that you and a faculty member can develop an independent study about this topic.

Apprenticeships and Internships

Practical learning is at the heart of dance education. In other words, dance education naturally calls upon the value of learning through doing. This concept is embedded in all areas of your dance education as you learn movement phrases in your technique and movement courses, attain expertise making and performing dances through composing and performing dances, and apply your advancing contextual knowledge to various aspects of dance. Apprenticeships and internships are means to gain preprofessional, practical experience outside of the classroom while still in college. Although the terms are often used interchangeably, they do have different meanings. An **apprenticeship** frequently refers to accruing proficiency in a specific skill or trade that

is directly related to the student's career goals. An **internship** can be more exploratory or broader than an apprenticeship but also helps students attain professional experience. Both are equally valuable, and they allow you to test the waters of a professional career in dance.

Apprenticeships and internships can take place off campus or on campus, and frequently you can obtain college credit for them. If a strong dance community exists near your campus, you may create or find an apprenticeship with a local dance company where you learn repertory, either witness or participate in various aspects of the creation of new work, and perhaps even perform with the company. Internships can take place in arts organizations (such as state arts commissions or performing arts venues), through community centers, or in other professional settings. If an apprenticeship or internship takes place off campus, usually a faculty member will be assigned to communicate with the hosting organization about your progress. Occasionally, there may be apprenticeships or internships on campus. If your degree program is very large, there may be a chance for you, as an upper division student, to apprentice the teaching of an introductory dance class. There may also be internships focused on certain campus events, such as the hosting of a large dance festival or the production of a dance event. When considering apprenticeships and internships, honor your interests, but remain open minded about how you can gain exposure in those areas. Doing so will help you proactively guide how your dance education can expand.

Scholarly and Creative Research Experiences

Scholarly and creative research is what advances dance as a discipline. Advances in dance science, new information about cultural aspects of dance, the expansion of effective dance pedagogies, innovative methods of creating work, and the evolution of technique are some examples of how scholarly and creative research allows dance to evolve. As part of the next generation of dance professionals, you will contribute to this evolution. One way to start contributing to the advancement of dance is to become involved in undergraduate research opportunities that are present on your campus, which usually involve working with a faculty member on his or her research projects. This is a growing trend on campuses, so it is likely that you will have a chance to contribute to creative or scholarly research while studying dance on campus.

As with independent studies, apprenticeships, and internships, the range of topics and formats of scholarly and creative research experiences varies from campus to campus and subject to subject. Perhaps you are enthusiastic about dance pedagogy, and a faculty member on your campus is writing a journal article about best practices for teaching dance. There

may be an opening to work with this faculty member, and your duties might include gathering background material or creating a database of the ways teachers address best practices. Maybe a faculty member is creating a work that will tour, and he or she would like to involve a student in the creative process or to assist in organizing rehearsal schedules and performance events. Most faculty members value involving students in their research, because they know that it is an incredible learning experience and a means to ensure that dance will continue to grow as a field. If you are aware of a project that is taking place on your campus, it is a good idea to be proactive. See how you can become involved so that you can deepen your understanding of a specific area of dance through engaging in scholarly or creative research.

COLLABORATING WITH YOUR PEERS

Another approach to integrating what you are learning in your coursework with your professional aspirations is to collaborate with your peers. Outside of your class requirements, you may find yourself creating and performing work with your peers. Some students find it helpful to establish study or review groups or to teach informal dance classes to each other. Many degree programs, colleges, and universities also have student government and extracurricu-

---

Engaging WITH Dance

Eric Chapman (Arizona State University)

© Alexandra Chapman

Through working with the concert and early music choirs at Arizona State University, opportunities I could have never fathomed fell into my lap. My dance works have been seen throughout Phoenix, Arizona, and by artists from around the world. For example, when a student pursuing his PhD in composition at Queens University in Ireland traveled abroad to the United States, we collaborated to make a work composed for violin, small vocal ensemble, and a dance trio. Based on my experiences, there are three main pieces of advice I would offer dancers and choreographers interested in collaborating with others outside of dance.

1. Don't limit yourself. Pursue dance with a burning passion, but know dance would not be where it is today if not for music, theater, and the visual arts. Use them.
2. Network! Don't be shy; walk up and say hi!
3. Be yourself. Have a unique voice, and send a unique message.

lar organizations in which you can foster leadership skills and meet people outside of your discipline. The students in your campus cohort are your future professional peers and collaborators. Therefore, taking advantage of and creating circumstances to work with your classmates outside of class settings can enhance your campus dance education.

Collaborating with your peers can be beneficial to your dance education because it provides an opportunity to test out what you are learning in your courses in a student-directed setting. Because your professors may not be involved in these projects, you will need to rely on your aptitudes for success as well as your evolving dance knowledge to accomplish your projects. You will use and mature your leadership, stewardship, collaboration, negotiation, and initiation skills in tandem with your dance knowledge in a fully integrated fashion when working with your peers. In this way, collaborating with your peers through making and performing work, teaching each other, and becoming involved in extracurricular activities provides a framework for bridging your campus dance education to your emerging dance aspirations.

Making and Performing Work

You will make and perform work with your peers through your creative, compositional, and performance courses. At times, you may find that a study or project from one of these courses really sparks your imagination and that you want to develop it further outside of class. Or, you may be inspired to create a new dance work that is not connected to a class assignment, for an upcoming student performance or off-campus event. Students who are excited about improvisation may want to set aside a time weekly outside of class to explore approaches to improvisation and see how they progress. At times you will find yourself collaborating with students from your academic cohort, but at times you might perform in an upper division student's capstone work or graduate student's thesis project. Students who see a future in performing arts administration or in having their own dance companies may take the initiative to organize and produce a student dance performance. If you have the desire to choreograph, perform, or be involved with dance performance, whether that is your primary career goal or part of a larger range of dance interests, collaborating with your peers in the making and performance of dance outside of your required coursework can be a valuable learning experience.

Teaching

No matter what area you pursue, teaching dance will probably be a part of your future in dance. In addition to the pedagogy courses and teaching activities built into the curriculum, you may want more practice teaching dance. To begin this added practice, you may volunteer to tutor your peers or lead study groups outside of class time. This is a good way to gain hands-on experience teaching in one-to-one or small-group settings, and it will increase your own comprehension of a given subject. Meeting with your peers and teaching each other dance classes in genres outside of what your curriculum offers can expand your awareness of dance and release stress while also increasing your confidence as a dance teacher. You could also teach dance to a variety of populations on campus, which would increase your comfort level in teaching dance to beginners. If teaching is your first priority in dance, seeking and creating teaching opportunities is an effective way to consistently evaluate, scaffold, and integrate your dance and teaching expertise. Even if you do not foresee a career in dance education, teaching others outside of your coursework encourages you to practice communication and interpersonal skills that are essential to all areas of dance and to your professional life in general. Refining your teaching abilities outside of your required coursework can assist you in assessing your progress in this area and in cultivating skills required for success in a variety of dance professions.

Extracurricular Opportunities

Besides the numerous courses and projects embedded in your dance curriculum to help you develop as a dance professional, extracurricular opportunities are also present on your campus, and some may be dance or arts focused. These opportunities might include a department-level student advisory board that is responsible for organizing student events and acting as a liaison between faculty and students; or a fine arts council organization that brings together students from across the arts to network, advocate for the importance of the arts on campus, and represent arts students in larger campus organizations. Outside of dance and the arts, you will find student government organizations as well as clubs organized around distinct social, political, cultural, and recreational interests. Becoming involved in extracurricular activities gives you the chance to meet people from outside of dance who could be future collaborators; practice your leadership, collaboration, initiation, and negotiation skills; and enhance your ability to effectively communicate about dance. All of these activities are valuable to your future successes in dance, regardless of what areas you choose to pursue. Finding time to get involved in extracurricular organizations rounds out your dance education and can increase your professional preparedness.

ACQUIRING PRACTICAL SKILLS AND TOOLS

As you advance in your campus dance education, you will have the chance to personalize your dance education through individualized instruction, collaborating with your peers, and seeking off-campus opportunities to expand your dance knowledge. It is likely that you will need to present resumes and cover letters, participate in interviews and auditions, and network to continue developing your dance knowledge after graduation. When you enter the professional field, these materials and tools are how you will present yourself to other dance professionals. Therefore, acquiring and constantly updating these skills while studying dance on campus can create a smooth transition into the professional realm.

Resumes and Cover Letters

Before meeting in person a potential employer, representatives from a dance program, or an internship advisor in person, you will often be required to submit a resume and cover letter. A **resume** is a one- or two-page paper or electronic document that provides a summary of your skills, education, and relevant experiences as well as your contact information. Essentially, a resume outlines your accomplishments and demonstrates that you are qualified for a specific job or opportunity. Although various resume formats exist, all resumes must include certain essential information. First, you need to list your contact information—your name, address, phone number, e-mail address, and website. Your resume should list the significant aspects of your dance education, such as main teachers, degree programs, and certifications. You should outline relevant experiences, which may include performances, presentations of works you choreographed, teaching, administrative work, and work experience. Because most resumes are only one page in length, it is best to tailor your resume to each particular opportunity so that you can highlight the most germane information. It is critical that your resume be absolutely free of typographical, grammatical, and spelling errors. Be sure

that your resume is easy to read and well organized. Remember, in some cases your resume will be the first thing a person knows about you, so you want to make a good impression. A sample resume is included to illustrate what a resume for someone currently studying dance might look like.

In some cases, you will present your resume at the start of an audition or interview, but sometimes you are required to send your resume ahead of time. In that case, it is a good idea to include a cover letter. A **cover letter** introduces you and your materials to the reader. Cover letters should be written using a proper business letter format and be impeccably organized and presented. A well-written cover letter has four parts. The *heading* includes your contact information, which is immediately followed by the date and the company contact information. Next comes the *introduction*, which should include a formal greeting. Then, address the reason you are writing, and provide a short overview of how your values and experiences align with those of the company. The *middle* of the cover letter is where you articulate why you are a good fit for this opportunity, so you should use a positive tone, demonstrate that you have the desired skills needed, and show how the organization will benefit from selecting you. Last is the *closing*, where you restate your main points and thank the readers for their consideration. Most cover letters are one page in length, so double-check that your cover letter is cohesive and concise and, like your resume, absolutely free of grammar, spelling, and typographical errors. A sample cover letter is included.

Resumes and cover letters can be submitted on hard copy or electronically, depending on what the organization requests. If submitting paper versions, be sure to use a high-quality, neutral-color paper. When submitting materials electronically, use a file format that can be read by a variety of computer types, such as a portable document format (PDF). Regardless of whether you submit your resume and cover letter electronically or on hard copy, use a 10-point or larger font and standard margins. All of these details make your materials easier to read, which contributes to a positive first impression. Remember, these documents are how you communicate your successes in dance, so you want them to accurately and completely represent who you are as an evolving dance professional.

Interviews and Auditions

After submitting your resume and cover letter, frequently the next step is to meet the prospective employer through an interview or an audition. An

Jane Smith

123 Main St. • Phoenix, AZ 85012 • 555-555-5555 • jane.smith@email.com • www.janesmith.com

EDUCATION

2012 – present	Bachelor of fine arts, dance major, Arizona State University, Tempe, AZ. Anticipated graduation 2016.
2008 – 2012	Fine arts major, dance program, University High School, Tempe, AZ. Graduated with honors in dance.
2005 – 2013	Miss Karen's School of Dance, Tempe, AZ. Jazz, tap, modern and contemporary dance, urban dance, and ballet.

PERFORMANCE EXPERIENCE

Year	Role	Production	Company	Location
2013	Dancer	*Dance Annual*	ASU	Tempe, AZ
2012	Sugar Plum Fairy	*The Nutcracker*	University High School	Tempe, AZ
2011	Chorus	*Annie*	University High School	Tempe, AZ

TEACHING EXPERIENCE

2010 – 2012	Miss Karen's School of Dance Assistant teacher for all levels of jazz, tap, and contemporary dance

WORK EXPERIENCE

2012 – present	ASU School of Dance, Student assistant in main office
2010 – 2012	Jones Restaurant, Tempe, AZ, Server

SPECIAL SKILLS

Tumbling
Ballet partnering and pointe work
Fluent in Spanish and French

REFERENCES

Available upon request.

● ● ● Sample resume.

Joe Smith
456 Main St.
Phoenix, AZ 85013
555-555-5555

April 24, 2013

Jennifer Roberts
Center for the Arts
789 1st St.
Phoenix, AZ 85013

Dear Ms. Roberts:

I am applying for the dance production internship advertised on your website. My relevant experiences both as a dance student and student assistant stage manager make me a strong candidate for this position.

My dance and dance production experiences are extensive. I have worked as a member of the department of dance's production team for the past three semesters. In this position, I have worked as a student assistant stage manager on four productions, as a sound and light board operator, and as a member of the deck crew. As a dance major, I am constantly learning more about how dances are performed and made, which informs my work on the production team. I am also the vice president of the dance department's student advisory board, a member of the Hip-Hop Dance Club, and a volunteer at the Boys and Girls Club. In my coursework, work on the production team, and extracurricular activities, I strive to demonstrate leadership and collaboration skills and to learn as much as possible. I am positive that I will bring the same drive and sense of responsibility to this internship.

My expertise in dance and production combined with my leadership, collaboration, initiation, and follow-through skills make me well suited for this position. I am available for an interview at your convenience, and I can be reached by telephone or e-mail. Thank you for your consideration.

Sincerely,

Joe Smith

• • • Sample cover letter.

interview is a conversation between two or more people, such as you and a representative of the organization, in which the interviewer asks questions to learn more about you and your qualifications. Interviews may be required to obtain certain jobs; receive internships or apprenticeships; or gain acceptance to schools, festivals, and workshops. Because interviews usually take place in person (although they can also take place over the phone or the Internet), it is critical that you be fully prepared so that you make a strong first impression. Before the interview, it is advantageous to research the organization and position you are applying for so that you can speak from an informed perspective. It is equally important to be prompt, professional, and courteous; to dress appropriately; and to know the format of the interview. While the interview is occurring, be honest and positive, and be sure to show your enthusiasm about the organization through asking thoughtful and informed questions. Common interview prompts may include questions about your experience and strengths, your knowledge of the organization, and your specific interests about the job for which you are applying, as well as a chance for you to ask the interviewer questions. Remember, interviews allow interviewers to get to know you and to visualize how you will fit into and succeed in their organization. Therefore, it is best to be prepared.

Auditions are similar to interviews in that they both provide a chance for you to interact, usually in person, with an organization. An **audition** is an opportunity to illustrate your performance abilities to an organization. Some auditions may require you to prepare material beforehand, while others teach you material that you need to quickly learn and perform, and some will require both. Although a wide variety of audition formats exists, you should keep certain things in mind when preparing for an audition. First, as with interviews, it is critical to do your research before the audition. This research includes knowing the dance genres, methods of making work, and performance expectations of the organization you are auditioning for as well as knowing the audition format. If possible, take a class offered by the organization before auditioning. Some auditions include a warm-up, but others do not, so it is always best to fully warm up before the start time. Because each organization will have different expectations about what a dancer should wear to an audition, be sure to look into this beforehand and then dress appropriately. Remember to eat before the audition and to bring water and a snack. Also, it is best to arrive early, have a positive and polite attitude, and be yourself. Auditions can be mentally, physically, and emotionally demanding, so it is beneficial to be prepared.

Like many things in life, expertise comes with practice. Successfully interviewing and auditioning are no different. It is a good idea to practice your interview and audition skills before the actual events. Perhaps you and a peer can have a mock interview with each other to increase your confidence, or your degree program may offer audition workshops to help you better navigate the process. Both interviews and auditions are chances for you to demonstrate your understanding of dance to others, which is why

• • • An audition is an opportunity to showcase your performance abilities to an organization.

you should practice interviewing and auditioning while studying dance on campus. Members of your campus dance faculty are also available to help you gain proficiency in these areas, so do not hesitate to ask them for advice.

Networking

Besides introducing yourself to others through resumes and cover letters and through participating in interviews and auditions, you will meet people and find opportunities through networking. **Networking** refers to building and maintaining a supportive framework among people with a common interest. As a campus dance student and future dance professional, having a network of people with similar or related interests is necessary to learn more about your professional field. For some, networking can be intimidating because it may seem awkward to introduce yourself to new people, or it may be uncomfortable to seek assistance from others. However, if you approach networking as a technique of making contacts, forging relationships, and learning more about your specific dance interests, it can be much more enjoyable and useful. You should also remember that you have something to offer to others, and that oftentimes, networking develops reciprocal relationships. It is never too early to start networking, and it is critical to keep track of your contacts as you meet new people. If a contact offers you advice, tells you about an event or opening, or offers you mentorship, be sure to say thank you. To facilitate networking, it may be helpful to create business cards that you can give to new contacts. Finally, because you never know who you will meet and when, it is always a good idea to be your best self in every situation, and that includes your campus activities. Your faculty, staff, and peers are already part of your networking community, so be mindful of this during your campus dance education.

In contemporary society, networking takes place not only in person but also through social media and the Internet. As a result, many dance professionals maintain websites to share their work with others. Websites can contain work samples, your resume, and other items that demonstrate what you do. If you decide to design a website, make it simple and well organized, prominently list your contact information, keep it current, and make it user friendly. Some dance professionals may opt to use a blog format, whereas others want an independent website. If you maintain an independent website, choose a simple domain name and register it with a reputable com-

pany. Along with websites, some dance professionals create fan pages on social media sites or use their personal social media accounts to let their contacts know what they are working on. Social media and websites may be the first way that potential employers inside and outside of dance learn about you and your expertise, so be sure to keep this in mind when updating your social media pages and websites. Regardless of how you establish your online presence, taking the time to be professional, which includes proofreading for spelling and grammar and selecting clear, appropriate images and media, can really pay off. Remember, cultivating and maintaining an online presence is another way to highlight your achievements while studying dance on campus and as a dance professional.

Networking, both in person and through the Internet, is how you become connected to other people in your profession. Through networking, your dance community can continuously expand and your learning can constantly grow. Taking the time to practice networking while on campus can establish a strong foundation to build on after graduation, and as such, it helps establish links between your current study of dance and future endeavors.

BUILDING YOUR BRIDGE

Throughout your time on campus, you will be prompted to personalize your dance education. This is meant to encourage expertise in your emerging dance interests and aspirations in relation to your widening and deepening awareness of dance. Your dance faculty can offer exceptional guidance through your coursework, but it is also up to you to seek and create your own opportunities to enhance your dance education through possibly pursuing individualized instruction, collaborating with your peers, and honing your practical skills and tools.

A good place to start is to identify your goals and see how they align with opportunities for individual instruction. Usually, independent studies, apprenticeships, internships, and research experiences take place toward the end of your undergraduate studies, but there is no reason why you cannot start planning now. For example, if you are intrigued by dance science and how that relates to physical therapy, you could ask your dance kinesiology professor about additional learning opportunities. You may find that your kinesiology professor has a research project you can become involved in or knows a physical therapist who would be open to working with a dance student through an internship. Maybe you are really interested in jazz dance and want to learn more about how the movement vocabulary developed from a historical perspective. There is likely a dance faculty member who could mentor an independent study in this area. For all individual instructional opportunities, you should show initiative, have a clear idea of what you are curious about while keeping an open mind, and employ your highest level of self-responsibility. These are exceptional and one-of-a-kind opportunities to accumulate practical knowledge in a specific area that you can take advantage of while studying dance on campus—if you are proactive.

Collaborating with your peers can also personalize your dance education. Remember that while on campus, every experience, whether it takes place in class or in an informal setting, has the potential to positively contribute to your dance learning. Because your classmates are your future professional peers, it makes sense to start building good working relationships. Additionally, these situations require you to challenge yourself without teacher supervision, which is what will need to happen after graduation. Students who want to make and perform dance should work together to make this happen. If you are passionate about community dance practices, maybe you could launch a small project involving your peers and a local community center to gain familiarity with this area. Student-directed projects demonstrate to your faculty and to professional organizations that you are able to seek out or create, pursue, and follow through on a project to completion. Leadership is an essential skill within the arts, which is why participating in student government and extracurricular activities is a good idea. When these attributes are applied in relation to your growing dance knowledge, your professionalism really blossoms.

Of course, at times you will need to introduce yourself to others before you can pursue opportunities, and that is why it is important to hone your practical skills and tools while studying dance on campus. It is a great idea to update your resume each semester. It helps you track your accomplishments, and it allows you to see how your dance understanding is expanding. Many students find it beneficial to attend actual auditions to build up their comfort level with the audition process. As you become involved with campus performances, conferences, or other exciting dance-related events, you can practice using social media to let others know what you are up to. Remember, it is never too early to develop an online presence. Networking happens everywhere, so you can readily start to implement those skills while studying dance on campus, pursuing off-campus

opportunities, and reaching out to new people. Keeping up-to-date with these skills and tools makes you better prepared to pursue your passions, which can then lead to a deeper understanding of dance. Following through on individual instructional opportunities, collaborating with your peers, and honing practical skills while studying dance on campus are smart ways for you to develop expertise in areas of personal interest.

SUMMARY

Achieving a broad and comprehensive view of dance is a crucial part of studying dance on campus. However, it is equally important to figure out what excites you about dance and to learn as much as possible about that area. Seeking and creating ways to do so is therefore a critical part of your evolving dance education. Recognizing the importance and roles of individualized instructional activities on your campus; understanding the value of working with your peers on student-initiated projects; familiarizing yourself with the practical tools and skills needed for professional success; and outlining a plan to connect your campus dance education to your future pursuits are ways to proactively personalize your campus dance education experience without sacrificing the breadth of knowledge you will gain through studying dance. Taking these steps makes you well informed and prepares you for success as a dance professional.

REVIEW QUESTIONS

1. Briefly describe the importance of independent studies, internships and apprenticeships, and scholarly and creative research opportunities while studying dance on campus. How do they contribute to your dance education?

2. What are the benefits of collaborating with your peers outside of class settings? How do these experiences contribute to your overall dance education? How do they best prepare you for success as a future dance professional?

3. Why are resumes, cover letters, and networking important for professional development? How do they help you succeed in and continue learning about dance after graduation?

4. Why is it important to connect your campus dance education and emerging dance interests to your evolving postgraduation goals? How does balancing a wide understanding of dance

and knowledge in specific areas best prepare you for success as a future dance professional?

GLOSSARY

apprenticeship—Refers to gaining proficiency in a specific skill or trade that is directly related to the student's career goals.

audition—An opportunity to showcase your performance abilities to an organization.

cover letter—A document that introduces you and your materials to a potential employer or organization.

independent study—A form of learning in which a teacher and student mutually agree on a topic for the student to independently investigate under the faculty member's mentorship for an agreed-upon number of credits.

internship—Can be more exploratory or broader than an apprenticeship, but it also helps students gain professional experience.

interview—A conversation between two or more people, such as you and a representative of an organization, during which the interviewer asks questions to learn more about the interviewee and his or her qualifications.

networking—Refers to building and maintaining a supportive framework among people with a common interest.

resume—A one-page (sometimes two-page) document that provides a summary of your skills, education, and relevant experiences as well as your contact information.

BIBLIOGRAPHY

Cal Alumni Association. (2013). Tips on how to network successfully. http://alumni.berkeley.edu/services/career-services/resources/articles/networking/tips-how-network-successfully.

Employment Security. (2011). Interview effectively. www.wa.gov/esd/guides/jobsearch/strategy/interview_effective.htm.

Farr, M. (2008). *The quick resume and cover letter book: Write and use an effective resume in only one day.* (4th ed.). Indianapolis: JIST.

Purdue University. (2013). Cover letter workshop: Formatting and organization. http://owl.english.purdue.edu/owl/resource/723/03.

PART *four*

Your Dance Future

Sustaining Your Engagement With Dance

After completing this chapter, you will be able to do the following:

- Comprehend the relevance of continuing professional development and self-care in relation to dance careers.
- Demonstrate the abilities needed for a successful transition to the professional realm, such as researching places to live, creating and maintaining a budget, and staying positive.
- Develop personal strategies for gaining skills needed to implement and continue increasing dance knowledge after graduation.

Your campus dance education provides you with a wide and interconnected understanding of dance that bridges your current dance understanding to your future in dance. After graduation, you will continue to learn about yourself and your art form so that you mature as a dance professional and contribute to dance in meaningful ways. Dance professionals have to balance the demands of their profession, their personal lives, and their professional development. Striking the right balance between your professional and personal life is critical to creating supportive frameworks to implement what you have mastered on campus and to continue growing as an artist.

Chapter 14 introduces various ideas and practices for starting and sustaining a career in dance. You will learn about the importance of self-care, which includes cross-training, nutrition, and stress management, and about professional development in relationship to dance careers. So that your transition from studying dance on campus to dancing after graduation can be as smooth as possible, skills needed for postgraduation life are discussed. Finally, you will develop personal strategies for gaining these abilities while on campus so that you are well prepared to fully engage in your dancing now and in the near future. Even though you are at the beginning of your campus dance education journey, it is useful to start cultivating habits and ways of thinking to advance your dance understanding after graduation.

Studying dance on campus allows you to learn about dance and take artistic risks in a supportive and structured educational environment. After college, however, you will be responsible for creating your own structures, both inside and outside of dance, to support your continued progress. Just like the dance professionals in the photograph, you will be required to focus on your career in dance while also maintaining and advancing your abilities, financial needs, and social support systems. Your campus dance education prepares you not only to enter the professional world but to keep learning about dance and yourself so that you can contribute to the dance field in meaningful ways. Learning how to balance your professional pursuits while also developing sustainable habits constructs a supportive framework for you to do so.

MEETING THE DEMANDS OF A CAREER IN DANCE

Dance professionals have a constant desire to know more about dance, and because dance is such a multifaceted discipline, there is always more to learn and experience. Additionally, many people are drawn to the physicality of this art form, and they relish

---

Engaging WITH Dance

Kyla Barkin (Dancer Performer and Choreographer)

First, it is important to recognize that dance is an art and not necessarily a balanced form of exercise. Sport-specific training, yoga, Pilates, and martial arts can be helpful. Find a discipline that balances and facilitates sound structure in the body. Avoid exercises that aggravate injuries or exacerbate imbalances.

Develop a warm-up and cool-down routine for yourself. Gear it toward the work you will be executing so that you are ready to dance at the beginning of rehearsal.

When rehearsing intensely, do gentler exercise and get plenty of rest and water, and the proper balance of calories to avoid injury and overtraining. Carbohydrates and salt are a must when dancing and sweating for extended hours. Do not complete heavy workouts before rehearsal or performances, because you will not have enough recovery time to perform at your peak level. Learn practices such as foam rolling and restorative yoga to keep soft tissue healthy.

When work is less demanding, exercise can be more rigorous or more frequent. Staying physically and mentally fit is crucial to having a strong baseline for auditions and rehearsals, and to performing with strength, flexibility, endurance, intelligence, and efficiency.

Photo by Sloane Timson. Courtesy of Kyla Barkin.

in the regularity of taking class and learning about the body and movement. After you complete your campus dance education, you will need to maintain a healthy approach to dance movement and to advancing your dance understanding. Doing so will better ensure that you are able to follow through on your dance aspirations and deepen your dance knowledge as your career progresses. Taking the time to learn about professional development opportunities, cross-training, nutrition, and stress management can help make this happen.

Professional Development

In all careers, professional development is what allows people within a given field to continuously advance their understanding of their discipline. Participating in professional development opportunities ensures that your skills are up-to-date, you are aware of current trends, and you are invested in your own learning, thereby increasing what you can share with others. Regardless of where you are in your career trajectory, taking advantage of professional development opportunities is essential to your continued growth in dance.

There are numerous ways to engage in professional development in dance while on campus and beyond. After graduation, if you are interested in performance or choreography, it is advantageous to regularly take class so that you can maintain and push your embodied understanding of dance movement and become aware of current trends in your preferred dance genre. Additionally, you will find that there are various professional workshops built around specific dance topics, such as choreography, improvisation, or somatic practices, that you can participate in both now and as an emerging professional. There are also numerous professional dance organizations that you can join, many of which offer a student membership rate. Joining a professional dance organization provides networking opportunities, online resources, and the possibility of attending regional, national, or international conferences where you can learn more about your specific discipline. You may find that you are drawn to graduate study in dance or a certification program in a related field. Regardless of what area of dance you are passionate about, it is critical that you continue learning more about dance throughout your career. Your dance education does not end on campus, but continues throughout your life in dance, and professional development opportunities facilitate your continued growth.

Cross-Training

Dance is a physically rigorous art form. Although the athletic requirements may vary from one dance genre to another, all dancers need to cultivate and balance endurance, strength, and flexibility to fully engage in the physical aspects of dance. Dance professionals who regularly participate in the physical aspects of dance, such as performers, choreographers, and educators, as well as dance students can benefit from cross-training. **Cross-training** refers to participating in a physical activity outside of your primary area to increase overall performance. In cross-training, you take advantage of the specific strengths of a selected physical activity in an attempt to strengthen imbalances that may be caused by your primary physical activity. Several dance injuries are actually caused by muscular imbalances that develop over time, so incorporating cross-training into your dance life will not only increase your endurance, strength, and flexibility, but it may prevent overuse injuries as your career progresses.

Participating in exercise can improve your dance technique, allowing you to focus more on your artistry and less on feeling fatigued or weak while dancing. When considering your cross-training options, evaluate your personal imbalances as well as skills and movement coordinations that are not addressed in, but are complimentary to, your preferred dance genres. For example, ballet dancers, who spend a lot of time outwardly rotated and are expected to perform physically demanding movements for long periods of time, may benefit from cross-country skiing because it builds cardiovascular strength while working in a parallel position. This activity balances the rotator muscles of the hip while also increasing stamina. Weight lifting would be a good choice for b-boys and b-girls because it builds strength in the whole body, which makes holding freezes much easier. Participating in yoga would assist tap dancers because it addresses the intrinsic muscles of the feet and balance. There are many options for cross-training, but remember that moderation and consistency are important. Finding a way to incorporate cross-training into your weekly routine will help you dance safely and efficiently, and this is critical to a career in dance.

Nutrition

Both studying dance and having a career in dance require a lot of energy, which is supplied through proper nutrition. To do your best, a well-balanced diet that provides you with enough calories and nutrients to support your dancing is a necessity. Fluids are also critical, because they keep you hydrated and regulate your body temperature. Although the daily life of a dance professional can be incredibly busy and at times chaotic, taking the time to fully address your nutritional requirements, whether you are an omnivore, vegetarian, or vegan, is one of the best things you can do to create a sustainable dance career.

It is generally recommended that a dancer's diet be composed of about 55 to 60 percent carbohydrate, 12 to 15 percent protein, and 20 to 30 percent fat (Clarkson 2005). Carbohydrates are vital because they are the major energy source for muscles, and dancers who do not get enough carbohydrates may feel lethargic and unfocused in classes and rehearsals. Foods such as bread, cereal, pasta, and rice are common sources of carbohydrates. Protein is used to repair muscle fibers that break down as a result of constant use; therefore, it is a fundamental nutrient for dancers. Chicken, turkey, fish, and tofu are excellent sources of protein. Fat serves many purposes in the body and digestion, including providing a structure for cell membranes, insulating the nerves, and aiding in the absorption of fat-soluble vitamins.

Along with carbohydrates, protein, and fat, dancers also need micronutrients and fluids to fully energize their bodies. Micronutrients consist of the various vitamins and minerals, such as calcium, that the body needs and can be found in fruits and vegetables. Because each type of fruit or vegetable is rich in various types of micronutrients, it is important to eat a variety of fruits and vegetables daily. Finally, the role of fluids cannot be overlooked. When you exercise or dance, your muscles produce heat, and cooling occurs as your sweat evaporates from your skin. During a very intense period of physical activity, you can lose up to 2 liters (nearly 8 1/2 cups) of fluid an hour, which is why staying hydrated is so important.

Although getting the nutrients and calories necessary to energetically engage in dance can seem challenging, it is completely doable with some planning and time management. For example, when you pack your dance bag for the day, get into the habit of including a water bottle and several snacks. Drink water during class breaks, and find time to have snacks between rehearsals, classes, and various obligations. Be sure to schedule time for meals, including breakfast and lunch, so that you are consistently refueling yourself throughout the day. Making sure that you are getting the proper nutrition will help you achieve your best in all areas of dance.

Stress Management

While a life in dance can be very exciting, at times, it can also be very stressful. Stress is a normal reaction to the increasing pressures of contemporary life. Your brain comes hardwired with an alarm system, frequently called the fight-or-flight response, to alert you of potential danger. After the threat is gone, your body should return to a relaxed state. However, if you are under nonstop stress, your alarm system rarely gets a chance to turn off, which is why stress management is beneficial. It is difficult to do your best work and to enjoy your daily activities if you always feel that you are on high alert.

At times, dance students and professionals may be inclined to equate being stressed out with working hard, but that is not necessarily true. Finding ways to manage stress allows you to spend more energy fully engaging with the things that bring you joy, such as dance. The first step in relieving stress is to decide to make a change in how you deal with stress. Identifying what triggers your stress, such as relationship problems, job demands, financial difficulties, or daily hassles, is the next step. Once you have identified what causes you stress, you can start thinking about strategies for dealing with stress. Some solutions may be simple, such as leaving your apartment 10 minutes earlier in the morning to avoid the congestion of the morning commute. If you cannot avoid a stressful scenario, you might try brainstorming ways to minimize the irritation factor of the event or asking others for assistance. While on campus, it may be helpful to visit your campus counseling center for guidance. Unfortunately, stress will never completely disappear from your life, but with some proactive steps, you can learn to manage your stress level.

Many people find that relaxation techniques are helpful for managing stress. The idea of relaxing may not seem like a top priority while you are studying dance or entering the dance field, but finding ways to relax can assist your well-being, and therefore sustain a career in dance. Most relaxation techniques, such as meditation, mindfulness, tai chi, and yoga, focus on breathing and bringing your attention to the present moment. There are also active ways to relax, such as being in nature or playing sports. Regularly practicing a relaxation technique aids in managing stress, which supports a long and engaging career in dance.

PREPARING FOR YOUR POSTGRADUATION LIFE

Just as the transition from high school to college presents new challenges, so does the transition from

Engaging WITH Dance

Whitney Tucker (Dance Performer)

I left college feeling like I could never be still. My movement practice valued the extreme, the risky, the bold. Over the last decade I have realized the rigor of stillness and sustained focus and attention. After becoming exhausted and depleting my adrenals in a variety of ways, I was forced to value what could sustain me and even restore my balance. I began to pay close attention to those who were decades ahead of me on their dance journey. I try to treat food as medicine and appreciate what my night dreams teach me. To keep things mysterious, I spend time in nature and look more closely at things I am first repelled by. I spend a fair amount of energy trying to be easier on myself and yearn for a day where I am truly relaxed. Now, I am driven by the exchange of energy we are inherently part of in this life. It took me a while to appreciate these new approaches, and I am still learning. Instead of chaos and depletion, I hope to acknowledge the vital force that I generate and aim to truly receive that of others.

© Emma Judkins

college to postgraduation life. When you graduate from college, you will encounter new freedoms and responsibilities, which can be challenging. Some students tend to think of their time in college as a "break" from the "real world" that waits for them after graduation. Although studying dance on campus does provide a stable infrastructure for exploring dance, it is to your benefit to start thinking about your life after graduation while on campus. After all, your college experiences are part of the "real world." Proactively thinking about and building a framework to continue exploring dance after graduation is an effective way to link your current experiences to your early professional life. Envisioning where you might want to live and work, learning how to create and maintain a budget, and learning to remain positive are some things you can start examining now and continue to practice beyond graduation.

Determining a Place to Live

Studying dance can take you in a variety of directions and to many different places. As your dance interests and career aspirations become clearer, certain metropolitan areas, geographic locations, and types of locales may also start to grab your attention. Careers in dance can exist just about anywhere, so you should not limit your focus to major cities, although those are certainly possibilities. If you are passionate about dance education, particularly in a

PK-12 setting, you may start looking into what states require certification, or which states have growing dance education communities. Large cities, such as New York, Los Angeles, or Las Vegas, may be a good choice if you are interested in commercial dance, working with an established dance company, or finding touring jobs. If you are headed toward graduate school, gaining admission to your ideal program may determine where you live. Many dance careers, such as teaching in a private studio, working on a project basis as a choreographer or performer, and engaging in community dance projects, can happen anywhere—if you are proactive.

As you start to contemplate how your dance interests, career aspirations, and possible places to live and work intersect, you can start to create test scenarios to participate in during your time on campus. For example, if you want to pursue commercial work, you might want to spend a few weeks one summer in Los Angeles so that you can get a sense of not only the dance scene but what it is like to live there. You should also consider your personality, temperament, and things that you enjoy outside of dance when pondering where you see yourself living in the future. For example, if you enjoy spending time in nature, you might benefit from living and working in a location where you can spend time outdoors when you are not dancing. You also want to think about your support network, which includes your relationships with family and friends. For some people, phone calls, text messages, and e-mails make

Engaging WITH Dance

Leanne Schmidt (Choreographer and Dance Educator)

Finishing a dance program and pursuing the next step is a very exciting time in your life, but be sure you are being realistic and planning for that next step.

First, contact everyone you know to tell them where you are thinking about moving. This will help you find a suitable place to live, work, show choreography, dance for people, teach dance, and so on. Network. Network. Network!

The chances of you getting to dance as your "day" job are pretty slim at first, so you'll have to think outside the box. What else do you like to do? You will want to make half your rent in a week, whatever you do! Get a job where you can make the most money in the least amount of time.

Say yes to every dance opportunity you can get your hands on! The more you get involved, the more people you will meet. The more people you meet, the more opportunities you will have. Get to class. Show work in showcases. Go to meetings about dance. Think outside of the box. Saying yes, no matter how small the opportunity is, will help you get to the next thing.

All of your hopes and dreams aren't going to happen overnight. Keep at it. If you throw the towel in too soon, you may regret it. Stay inspired. Keep your eye on the prize. Inspiration is everywhere, and oftentimes for free. Here are some things you can do: Walk. Look up. Sit in a park and people-watch. Go to a museum. Make something new out of something old. Cook your food at home. Stay social. Stay positive.

© Sam Polcer

them feel connected, whereas other people require direct interaction with their support network to thrive. Taking time to assess what you want from a location and how that relates to your career goals can help you imagine—and perhaps plan—for your life after graduation. Of course, a career in dance can take you in many directions, meaning you may end up in an unexpected location that you really love. So, as with everything else in dance, it is a good idea to have a plan, but to also keep an open mind.

Budgeting

Refining the skills to create, maintain, and update a personal budget will help you navigate your expenses both while on campus and as a professional. You will likely have times, both while studying dance on campus and in your future career, when you will need to find work outside of dance to supplement your earnings and to finance your day-to-day living expenses. Although making a budget can seem daunting, information is power, and knowing how your income and expenses relate can lead to better

financial decisions as you progress through college and into your early career.

You can create a simple budget that will give you a good idea of how your income and expenses balance in four steps. First, identify how much money you expect to take in each month. Your income may come from a paycheck, tips, or grants, so be sure to include all of them in your calculations. Next, determine how much you need to spend each month on must-have items or services, such as food, rent, utilities, insurance, gas, savings, tuition, and class fees. From there, you should also include "nice-to-have" expenses (things that are nonessential but that you would like to include), such as eating at restaurants, shopping, and entertainment costs. After you have collected all of this information, you can see how your income and expenses relate to each other so that you can plan accordingly. Creating and maintaining a budget is useful while on campus, but it is also useful in determining how much it will cost to relocate, pursue a graduate degree, or travel abroad. The more you can think of budgeting as a means of checking in with your priorities and planning for your future, the more useful a budget becomes.

Staying Positive

Without a doubt, participating in dance brings people great joy, and it is likely that you experience happiness and satisfaction on a regular basis as you learn about dance. At the same time, studying dance on campus and engaging with dance as a young professional can be overwhelming. For many dance professionals, the constant demands of and the desire to learn more about dance create a great sense of commitment to their professions. However, a career in dance can also be very stressful, especially when you make the transition from your college study of dance to your early career. Finding ways to stay optimistic and grounded allows you to stay focused on the joy that dance brings you.

Although dance may be your primary interest, you must also recognize and make room for other things that bring you joy. For example, it is necessary to spend time with family and friends, to talk about things besides dance sometimes, to go to the movies with friends, and to participate in community or religious organizations that are important to you so that your life stays balanced. There will be times, both while studying dance on campus and in your career, when you may feel discouraged about your progress.

In these times, you need to remember that although dance is a large part of your life, you have other areas of your life that are incredibly valuable and contribute to the whole of who you are. Keeping this in mind and finding ways to refresh yourself through nondance activities can help you handle some of the difficult parts of a dance career. Staying optimistic and grounded helps you stay focused on the big picture, which is a lifetime of learning about and engaging in dance, instead of on temporary or minor setbacks. These setbacks are a reality of a career in dance, and your ability to navigate and learn from them is critical for a satisfying career in dance.

DRAFTING A PLAN AND CREATING HABITS

If proactively approached, your campus dance education can connect your previous dance experiences and future career aspirations. The dance knowledge acquired through studying dance on campus will eventually be applied to your postgraduation pursuits. This means that it is advantageous to start generating habits for continued engagement with dance beyond campus. Although you may be in the starting phase of your campus dance education, it is never too early to start considering practices that will

Engaging WITH Dance

Donielle Janora (Dance Performer and Dance Educator)

There was one goal I set for myself before I moved to the Big Apple: to make ends meet and find work that connected me directly to the industry. It is extremely easy to get sucked in the vortex of waiting tables, which can provide you with instant cash, but it also takes a toll on your lifestyle and auditioning skills. That being said, you can try to find work opportunities at a studio. This could mean working for a salary or bartering for dance class, because once you leave college you need to maintain your technique. There are many dance instructor positions available at local dance studios, YMCAs, and gyms. If teaching is not for you, perhaps a flexible office job at a studio or theater could keep you in the loop. If you don't mind traveling on the weekends, you could work for a dance competition. This doesn't necessarily mean judging. Competitions also hire people to sell merchandise and hand out awards, and working at competitions is a good way to meet fellow dancers, choreographers, and studio owners with whom you will cross paths again. This dance circle is smaller than you think, and you never know how the connections you make can be the key to your future.

Dena Spellman (Spellman Sisters LLC)

Engaging WITH Dance

Kate Sedlack (Dance Educator)

Imagine yourself graduating from college. You've made it! You graduated with a degree from an excellent college or university, and you're ready to embark on your own personal professional dance journey. Now what? Making the transition from collegiate dance to the professional world can be tough. Depending on where your journey takes you, it may be filled with many talented dancers just like you who are trying to nail that same audition or book that once-in-a-lifetime job. Remember, you are on your own journey. You dance because of the feeling it gives you inside and your desire to share that joy with others. You may not book that job or you may struggle to find frequent dance work, but like choreography, you must trust the process and know that your path will unfold the way it should. I never expected once I left college I would pursue a career in dance education, but as I continued to hone my practice the universe unfolded for me, and I can honestly say my dance career is truly fulfilling and continues to bring me joy. Stay positive, enjoy taking class, find ways to hone your choreographic skill, and the universe will do the rest.

Photo courtesy of Jayson Diaz.

sustain your personal artistic growth and contribute to your overall well-being.

During your time on campus, take advantage of the resources that your college offers. Your dance curriculum will directly address professional development in many ways as well as prepare you to pursue additional on- and off-campus opportunities. Outside of your dance curriculum, your campus may have a wellness center, a variety of programs that promote healthy living, or student service organizations focused on specific aspects of health and wellness. These resources provide valuable information about cross-training, nutrition, and stress management. For example, your campus fitness center probably includes a variety of cardiovascular and strength-training equipment, group fitness classes, and low-cost personal or group training consultations for students. Each of these could lead to a cross-training routine that supplements your dance studies. Many campus wellness programs offer low-cost or complimentary nutritional counseling for students, and this would be a great way to learn about what types of foods and eating habits are best for you. You can likely learn about stress management through these resources in the form of workshops and ongoing classes. Taking the time to learn about and take advantage of each of these resources while on campus promotes healthy practices that will eventually support your professional pursuit of dance.

It is probably exciting for you to imagine what your postgraduation life will be like as you learn more about yourself and dance. To make the transition from college to your professional life as smooth as possible, it is beneficial to start thinking about where you might want to live, using a budget, and working for a balanced life while on campus. If you have an initial idea of where you would like to live after graduation, you can start by researching that area through the Internet. Discovering what dance opportunities there are, what the cost of living is, and what other things a city has to offer (such as access to nature and cultural events) can help you paint a realistic picture of your postgraduation life. It is a great idea to compare multiple locations and to frequently revisit and reconsider your plans. Knowing what opportunities are available to you and the cost of living in a specific area can help you create a budget, which gets you ready for this transition. Because budgeting will be an important part of your life after graduation, you should start creating and maintaining a budget now. Doing so gives you a complete picture of your personal finances and spending habits so that you can plan for your future. Creating time for other areas besides dance in your life, such as friends, family, and downtime, is just as valuable now as it will be in your future. Creating a supportive network, and having fun and interacting with your community in meaningful ways help you maintain a healthy perspective on your life, which is critical to a career in dance. You can start to prepare, in numerous small and large ways, for your future in dance while in college, and each of these ways will contribute to a framework for your continued exploration of dance beyond campus.

SUMMARY

You are building a bridge to your future by studying dance on campus. A large part of this bridge is built through the dance knowledge you will gain on campus. However, while in college you also need to develop aptitudes to support the implementation and continued expansion of your dance knowledge after graduation. Learning about the importance of professional development and self-care in relationship to dance careers, researching possible places to live, creating and maintaining a budget, and balancing your life help you create personal strategies for navigating the demands of a dance career after graduation. Developing these skills in tandem with consistently deepening your dance understanding makes you well prepared to continue growing, both personally and in the field of dance, beyond your campus dance education.

REVIEW QUESTIONS

1. In relation to your preferred dance genre(s) and career aspirations, why are professional development and self-care essential?

2. Discuss how considering where to live, creating and maintaining a budget, and staying positive contribute to a sustainable career in dance.

3. Why is it important to proactively develop personal strategies for implementing and continuing to increase your dance knowledge beyond your campus education?

GLOSSARY

cross-training—Participating in a physical activity outside of your primary area to increase overall performance.

BIBLIOGRAPHY

Blake, J. (2011). *Life after college: The complete guide to getting what you want*. Philadelphia: Running Press.

Clarkson, P. (2005). Nutrition fact sheet: Fueling the dancer. www.iadms.org/displaycommon. cfm?an=1&subarticlenbr=2.

Diana, J. (2012). The dos and don'ts of cross-training. www.dancespirit.com/2012/05/the-dos-and-donts-of-cross-training.

Mayo Clinic. (2011). Stress management. www. mayoclinic.com/health/stress-management/MY00435.

CHAPTER ●●●● **15**

Glimpsing Your Future in Dance

LEARNING OUTCOMES

After completing this chapter, you will be able to do the following:

- Explain how your previous dance experiences relate to your emerging dance interests and future dance aspirations.
- Articulate the range of possibilities for your future engagement with dance.
- Create tangible goals for your study of dance on campus and future engagement with dance.

Dance is a rich and multifaceted discipline, and successful dance professionals are consistently invested in their own growth as well as the advancement of the field. Regardless of their personal area of expertise within dance, successful dance professionals are driven to constantly learn more about dance and to apply that new knowledge to their work. The expertise you will develop through your campus dance education provides you with the necessary proficiencies to enter the professional realm of dance and to actively contribute to its development as a young dance professional. The range of ways that you can apply your developing dance understanding after graduation is quite expansive. As such, now is the time in your dance education to proactively think about and broadly imagine what is possible for you in dance.

Chapter 15 prompts you to consider your future engagement with dance and encourages you to connect your previous dance experiences, your emerging dance interests, and future aspirations. To start, you will examine how you are linking your past, present, and future dance interests in a proactive way that allows your dance learning to both deepen and widen. The breadth of dance opportunities available to you is discussed so that you can vividly visualize and strategically plan for your future. Finally, you will create realistic goals for your study of dance on campus and future engagement with dance, which provides a chance to reflect on how your dance understanding is evolving and preparing you for a career of learning about and engaging with dance.

Established dance professionals were once dance students, and like you, they had a wide range of previous dance experiences and dance interests. As they learned more about dance, their expanding ideas about it, eagerness to learn more, and proactive planning greatly contributed to their success. Each successful career in dance is the result of constantly learning more about dance and engaging with dance in new ways. Your campus dance education is a significant part of this journey, and the more you can view your time on campus as a way to connect your current involvement with dance to your future, the more satisfying your academic and professional pursuits will be.

YOUR DANCE JOURNEY

By studying dance, you can learn a lot not only about dance but also about yourself and the world around you. This learning will continue throughout your career in dance. As you learn more about dance both

---

Engaging WITH Dance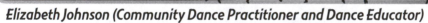

Elizabeth Johnson (Community Dance Practitioner and Dance Educator)

I always knew I wanted to be a dancer, but I had no idea how big dance could be or how my journey would evolve. Like many, I trained at a small private dance studio from an early age. I dreamed of "making it" professionally in New York someday.

I never made it to New York, and have never regretted it. I spent 13 years touring and performing with Liz Lerman's intergenerational Dance Exchange. I performed on some great stages, but also in the most unconventional of places, with people of all ages and life experiences.

Eventually, touring became lonely, and performing meant hours of tech in a cold theater. After a tough transition, I stepped down as Associate Artistic Director of the company, and I took a university position to help develop a program for training artists to work in diverse communities.

When I went to college to study dance 18 years ago, I couldn't imagine what I would be doing today. I am leading an arts-integrated HIV prevention project, dancing with a stem cell researcher, facilitating a community dance project with incarcerated women and their daughters, creating with a student who is turning 100, designing a new curriculum while teaching at a university, and I am just about to complete my graduate degree.

"Making it" means something different to me now. Despite popular opinion, a dancer's journey is long, with many rich chapters.

Photo courtesy of Megan Rowton.

on campus and beyond, your passions may become more precise or might shift from one area of dance to another, or you may find that you want to apply what you have learned through studying dance to another discipline. At this point in your dance education, it is useful to pause and consider how your dance interests, ideas about dance, and definitions of dance are evolving. This will help you see how your previous dance experiences have shaped your current comprehension of dance and give you ideas about where you might go with dance while on campus and beyond.

Your Evolving Engagement With Dance

It is likely that you selected to study dance on campus because of your passion for the art form. This dedication to dance can be the result of learning to dance in your dance studio or high school, the joy you receive through performing dances, or the excitement of dancing with others in social settings. When you started your campus dance education, you probably had specific reasons for dancing and a clear idea of your dance style, which includes the genres you are comfortable studying, your preferred ways of making dances, and your ideas about where dance can take place. You were probably familiar with a particular way of learning about dance and a personal definition of dance based on your previous dance experiences. All of this information created the foundation you have built on during your time on campus, and it has contributed to your current understanding of dance.

Now that you have been introduced to new ideas about dance, you may notice that your own ideas about dance are shifting. For example, you might be drawn to new dance genres that were once unfamiliar to you. As you are learning more about what dance teaches people, you may suddenly find yourself leaning toward a career in dance education. New ideas about how to make and perform dances may have altered your choreographic approach, and new ideas about somatic practices and dance wellness may have caused you to rethink what is best for your body. In essence, your ideas about dance are likely broadening in subtle and large ways.

Your ideas about dance expand and mature based on and because of your previous dance experiences. It is important to recognize this so you can start to see how one dance experience leads to the next, which leads to the next, and so on and so forth. As such, identifying common values between your previous dance experiences and emerging dance interests can help you imagine your future in dance.

Engaging WITH Dance

Emily Wright (Dance Educator)

I began my undergraduate studies with a general sense of curiosity about dance as an art form. I hoped that by the time I graduated, I would have all the answers and expertise I needed to pursue a performing or teaching career in dance. However, by the end of my senior year as a dance major, I realized that all I really knew was how much I didn't know, and how much more there was to learn about this exciting field that encompasses a much wider range of activities than my previous conceptions. After I graduated with a BFA in dance, I found that my curiosity for dance as an academic field of inquiry persisted.

I enrolled in an MFA program in dance and was introduced to ideas and experiences that gave me more and deeper questions. I finished my MFA with the knowledge and expertise I needed to secure an academic position in a university dance department, and with a firm understanding that my knowledge of dance would never be complete. The further along I am in this process of learning, and now teaching, dance at a university, the more layers of complexity are revealed, and the more passionate and committed I am to a continued investigation in the field of dance.

© Tim Trumble

Perhaps you really enjoyed studying ballet and are now excited about urban dance forms. Although the dance genres are stylistically different, they both value athleticism and clear musicality, and perhaps that is what you value about both genres. Making and performing dance, teaching dance, and working in community settings all value interpersonal skills, creative thinking, and sharing dance with others. Taking the time to reflect on how your previous dance experiences relate to your current dance interests can reveal what you truly value about dance and help you determine how to learn more about those values as you move forward.

Multiple Career Paths

Because dance is a multifaceted discipline, you can create numerous professional pathways within the field of dance. Therefore, it is highly beneficial to broadly interact with dance and stay open minded about what your future in dance may entail. While it is fine to have specific goals, it is beneficial to imagine multiple outcomes for achieving your goals and to stay open to new interests and opportunities that grab your attention. Essentially, during the early stages of your campus dance education, you should gather as much information about dance as possible. Doing so introduces you to a wide range of dance knowledge and life skills, which helps you appreciate the range of career options within dance, as well as the ways you can apply information learned through studying dance to other disciplines. This open-minded approach and the integrated understanding of dance better prepare you to navigate your shifting priorities within and outside of dance as you progress through your campus dance education and throughout your career.

There are many reasons for studying dance on campus. For example, some students aspire to make and perform work immediately after graduation, and then move into a teaching career. Others may not have had an express reason for studying dance at the start of their campus dance education, but they are now realizing that the anthropological, historical,

Engaging WITH Dance

Lacey Ray Althouse (Hedge Fund Manager)

When I graduated from college, I left a welcoming place for dance and entered a space where there was pressure to move on to something more common. But I didn't want to be common, and I didn't want to leave behind what I had studied in school. After a period of searching for the next thing, I moved to New York City to work for a dance organization.

I learned a lot from that job, including how to run an office, organize community programs, and eventually how to position myself for the career I wanted. I met almost everyone in the industry, and I saw in person the most amazing work by all of my favorite artists. While it may be true that there are challenges to living in a big city, working for nonprofits, and navigating life in your twenties, you can do it. As a creative person, you will find ways to be resourceful and forge your own path.

Photo by: Scott Wittrock

After working for the dance organization for 6 years, I left for a position in investment management. I now work for a hedge fund and have a huge office inside a tall building in Midtown Manhattan. Each day I work side by side colleagues who graduated from top Ivy League schools, none with dance degrees, but I don't feel out of place. In fact, my love for dance helped land me the job. Dance teaches skills you can apply to the business world, like how to be a leader, have confidence, be competitive, and do it all with grace.

My life will always be rich with dance. I see and support the work of my friends, take a wide variety of movement classes, and continue to advocate for dance by telling everyone my story and what I have learned. As you can see, there are millions of access points for participation in the field. We are lucky you are ready to dive in!